Lonergan, Social Transformation,
and Sustainable Human Development

african christian studies series (africs)

This series will make available significant works in the field of African Christian studies, taking into account the many forms of Christianity across the whole continent of Africa. African Christian studies is defined here as any scholarship that relates to themes and issues on the history, nature, identity, character, and place of African Christianity in world Christianity. It also refers to topics that address the continuing search for abundant life for Africans through multiple appeals to African religions and African Christianity in a challenging social context. The books in this series are expected to make significant contributions in historicizing trends in African Christian studies, while shifting the contemporary discourse in these areas from narrow theological concerns to a broader inter-disciplinary engagement with African religio-cultural traditions and Africa's challenging social context.

The series will cater to scholarly and educational texts in the areas of religious studies, theology, mission studies, biblical studies, philosophy, social justice, and other diverse issues current in African Christianity. We define these studies broadly and specifically as primarily focused on new voices, fresh perspectives, new approaches, and historical and cultural analyses that are emerging because of the significant place of African Christianity and African religio-cultural traditions in world Christianity. The series intends to continually fill a gap in African scholarship, especially in the areas of social analysis in African Christian studies, African philosophies, new biblical and narrative hermeneutical approaches to African theologies, and the challenges facing African women in today's Africa and within African Christianity. Other diverse themes in African Traditional Religions; African ecology; African ecclesiology; inter-cultural, inter-ethnic, and inter-religious dialogue; ecumenism; creative inculturation; African theologies of development, reconciliation, globalization, and poverty reduction will also be covered in this series.

SERIES EDITORS
Dr Stan Chu Ilo (St Michael's College, University of Toronto)
Dr Philomena Njeri Mwaura (Kenyatta University, Nairobi, Kenya)
Dr Afe Adogame (University of Edinburgh)

Lonergan, Social Transformation, and Sustainable Human Development

JOSEPH OGBONNAYA

FOREWORD BY
Robert M. Doran

☙PICKWICK *Publications* • Eugene, Oregon

LONERGAN, SOCIAL TRANSFORMATION, AND SUSTAINABLE HUMAN DEVELOPMENT

African Christian Studies Series 4

Copyright © 2013 Joseph Ogbonnaya. All rights reserved. Except for brief quotations in critical publications or reviews, no part of this book may be reproduced in any manner without prior written permission from the publisher. Write: Permissions, Wipf and Stock Publishers, 199 W. 8th Ave., Suite 3, Eugene, OR 97401.

Pickwick Publications
An Imprint of Wipf and Stock Publishers
199 W. 8th Ave., Suite 3
Eugene, OR 97401

www.wipfandstock.com

ISBN 13: 978-1-61097-881-1

Cataloging-in-Publication data:

Ogbonnaya, Joseph.

    Lonergan, social transformation, and sustainable human development / Joseph Ogbonnaya ; foreword by Robert M. Doran.

    African Christian Studies Series 4

    xxiv+ 178 p.; 23 cm—Includes bibliographical references and index.

    ISBN 13: 978-1-61097-881-1

    1. Lonergan, Bernard J. F.—Criticism and interpretation—Criticism and interpretation. 2. Sustainable development. I. Doran, Robert M., 1939–. II. Series. III. Title.

BX4705.L7133 O40 2013

Manufactured in the USA.

In loving memory of my parents,
Late Mazi Philip Ogbonnaya Kanu
and
Late Madam Felicia Erimma Nwanadiye Kanu

Content

Foreword by Robert M. Doran ix
Preface xi
Acknowledgments xiii
Introduction xv

1. Themes in Contemporary Development Discourse 1
2. Lonergan's Philosophical Anthropology 46
3. Lonergan and Social Transformation 88
4. Lonergan and Development: Points for Dialogue 128
5. General Conclusion 165

Select Bibliography 169

Foreword

I AM VERY HAPPY to have been invited to write a foreword to this fine book, *Lonergan, Social Transformation, and Sustainable Human Development*. The book joins several other recent contributions from the community of students of Bernard Lonergan pointing to the significance of Lonergan's work for the enormous challenges that face the human race in the face of globalization.[1] Recent articles in *Theological Studies* have called attention to the assistance that Lonergan's work can provide to Catholic social teaching.[2] This theme is renewed here, along with the fruitful suggestion that Lonergan can provide, in the author's words, "a theoretical bridge to bring the secular and ecclesiastical discourses together" in the discussion of development theory and globalization. That bridge takes the form of a "philosophical anthropology for development."

The problem is set forth in the introduction: development discourse tends to be concerned with vital values and the institutional structures that provide them but tend to overlook the significance of cultural values, personal integrity, and authentic religious transcendence in the establishment of human flourishing. The result is an inability to reverse processes of social decline and inequity once they have begun to take effect. Collective responsibility is overlooked, because its grounds in full human authenticity have been neglected. The first chapter aptly describes the context of contemporary discourse on the issues. Chapter 2 establishes the basics of Lonergan's thinking as these are relevant to the concerns of the book. Chapter 3 addresses Lonergan's scale of values, very kindly drawing on my

---

1. See, for example, Neil Ormerod and Shane Clifton, *Globalization and the Mission of the Church* (London, New York: T. & T. Clark, 2009) and Gaspar F. Lo Biondo, S.J., and Rita M. Rodriguez, *Development, Values and the Meaning of Globalization* (Washington: The Woodstock Theological Center at Georgetown University, 2012).

2. See Patrick D. Brown, "'Aiming Excessively High and Far': The Early Lonergan and the Challenge of Theory in Catholic Social Thought," *Theological Studies* 72 (2011) 620–44, and Neil Ormerod, Paul Oslington, and Robin Koning, S.J., "The Development of Catholic Social Teaching on Economics: Bernard Lonergan and Benedict XVI," *Theological Studies* 73 (2012) 391–421.

Foreword

efforts to elaborate the scale in ways that are pertinent to these issues. And chapter 4 puts Lonergan and his framework in direct dialogue with both contemporary secular discourse and Catholic social teaching.

Most noteworthy in this account, I believe, is the importance attached to the scale of values. I have been heartened over the last couple of years to see the way in which this theme has taken off in various related contexts. From a theological standpoint, the scale of values provides categories for a theology of social grace, transposing into a fully contemporary context the gospel message of the reign of God. Joseph Ogbonnaya's book makes clear the pertinence of the scale of values for developing the general categories of such a theology, that is, the categories that theology shares with other disciplines. Only a vast interdisciplinary effort aimed at the reorientation of economics and other social sciences will meet the challenge set by the distortions of the scale of values evident in the unfettered free-market global economy. Lonergan is supposed to have estimated that it could take 150 years for that reorientation to take place. We do not have that long, and cannot afford to wait that long. Ogbonnaya's book joins a slowly growing movement aimed at encouraging a massive non-violent reversal of priorities. I welcome its arrival on the scene.

Robert M. Doran
Marquette University

Preface

IN HIS BOOK INTERVIEW with Peter Seeward, titled *The Light of the World*, (2011) Pope Benedict XVI mentions the problematic nature of the concept of progress and freedom as having some bearing on the global catastrophe. This problem according to him arises from an understanding of progress as knowledge, where knowledge is power.

This same idea is reflected in the various secular theories of development especially their dominant expression as economic growth. In a free market economy, development reflects itself in forms of accumulation of capitals, multinational corporations, privatization etc. Neo-liberal politico-economic and social policies great as they are, emphasize only an aspect of the human good and ignores some important aspects which are equally important for human well-being. Whereas the principles of Catholic social teaching address the lacunae in contemporary theories of development, there remains a need in theology for a theoretical bridge to bring the secular and ecclesiastical discourses together.

With examples drawn from the Third World especially Africa, this book using Bernard Lonergan's philosophical anthropology dialogues with contemporary development discourse represented in the theories of development and the Catholic social teaching. It makes a case for human development respectful of the integral scale of values: vital, social, cultural, personal and religious. Because of the reality of moral impotence, it argues that sustained human development cannot be possible without the religious value of God's love.

The previous works on theology and development like Stan Chu Ilo, *The Church and Development in Africa* (2011); Gerrie ter Haar (ed.), *Religion and Development: Ways of Transforming the World* (2011); Michael W. Goheen and Erin G. Glanville (ed.), *The Gospel and Globalization* (2009); Stephen L. Martin, *Healing and Creativity in Economic Ethics* (2008); John A. Coleman and William F. Ryan, *Globalization and Catholic Social Thought* (2005), etc. did not reflect a philosophical anthropology requisite for development economics of well-being. Apart from Robert Doran's *Theology and*

Preface

the Dialectics of History (1990), *What is Systematic Theology?* (2005) which emphasises the integral scale of value and dialectic of culture, and Kenneth R. Melchin, *History, Ethics and Emergent Probability* (1987) which is a work on ethics, society and history in the work of Bernard Lonergan, there is no other work using Lonergan's philosophical anthropology and philosophy of history to dialogue Catholic social teaching and contemporary development discourse. This work is a contribution in this regard to Lonergan studies and to theology and development.

The significant contribution of this book is the points of dialogue it establishes with Lonergan's anthropology and the contemporary development discourse. This dialogue is important today because it highlights the welfare and well-being of the human person who ultimately is the originator as well as the beneficiary of development. As Lonergan says, development prescinds from the reality of human history, a cord woven with three strands: progress (the fruit of the transcendental precepts: attention, intelligence, reasonableness and responsibility), decline (the offshoot of inattention, obtuseness, unreasonableness and irresponsibility) redemption, the usually slow and long process of recovery from decline. It is necessary to point this out because development can concentrate on capital accumulation and on the social institutions that bring this about and think less or even care less about possible negative impacts on the human person. Such situations result in various forms of depersonalization and diminishing the human capacity for self-transcendence. At times it ends up perpetuating inequality and injustice in the production and distribution of the human good in the world. This book is written to draw attention to this by emphasising a philosophical anthropology for development using the framework of Bernard Lonergan.

Acknowledgments

To ALMIGHTY GOD, BE praise, honour and glory, for his guidance, protection and inspiration at all times especially during and in the course of the writing of this book.

Special thanks to Prof. John Dadosky for steering the course of this project. I am equally grateful to Prof. Robert Doran for reading through the work and writing the foreword. Thank you, Prof. Michael Vertin for your pieces of advice as I navigate the waters of Lonergan's philosophy. My sincere appreciation goes to Prof. Cyril Orji and Prof. Thomas E. Reynolds for their comments on the book. Thank you, Mrs. Thérèse Mason, Drs. Michael McGourty and Emeka Obiezu for reading through the rough drafts. Thanks to the University of St. Michael's College for granting me tuition free scholarship to complete my advanced degree studies.

I enjoyed the love and friendship of Ms. Margaret O'Neill (Peggy), John and Nancy Sidle and family, Prof. Stan Chu Ilo, as well as the support of the Igbo Catholic Community, Toronto among whom I served as the chaplain. The cordial relationship with my colleague, Fr. Emil Jude and love of the Catholic community at Sunnybrook Health Sciences Center, Toronto, were sources of strength for me. I thank Fr. Jim Hannah and the parishioners of Our Lady of Perpetual Help; Fr. Ernesto De Ciccio, and Fr. Vito Marziliano of St. Clare parish, the parishes I called home as I study and work.

Introduction

JOHN HENRY CARDINAL NEWMAN once said that "To live is to change, and to live long is to change much."[1] Human beings change, and the circumstances of their lives in various societies bring about social changes that impact on their development. Such developments then bring about further changes. And so the issues of social transformation and the problems of sustainable human development form part of the challenges facing humanity.[2] Thus various scholars in the humanities and in the social sciences as well as in the pure sciences reflect upon them.

Simeon Ilesanmi[3] for one, examines the concept of development characterized by the combination of competitive markets oriented towards the maximization of profits and objectification of the human subject. This orientation he says, transformed Africa and much of the rest of the Third World into territorial satellites of European powers, and their economies have been virtually held hostage for centuries. Thus existing side by side with the phenomenal affluence created by globalization is the increasingly desperate condition of the world's poor because of deepening poverty, helplessness and dependency. For Gilbert Rist, development co-operation between the northern and southern hemispheres, "have failed more often than not."[4] Kwame Boafo-Arthur agrees and notes, "With few exceptions, various efforts over the years to pull Africa from the brink of economic stagnation and collapse through several Western initiated and sponsored programmes and projects have failed. Neither have domestic efforts by individual governments led to any appreciable and lasting development."[5] The consequence has been reductions in the standard of living and life

---

1. Cited from Holland and Henriot, *Social Analysis*, 31.

2. This theme runs through the works of Charles Taylor, including *A Secular Age* (2007) and *Sources of the Self* (1989). See also Somerville, *Ethical Imagination* (2006) and Huntington, *Clash of Civilizations and the Remaking of World Order* (1997).

3. Ilesanmi, "Leave No Poor Behind."

4. Rist, "Is 'Development' a Panacea? How to Think Beyond Obsolete Categories."

5. Boafo-Arthur, "Tackling Africa's Developmental Dilemma," 27.

Introduction

expectancy of, for example, Africans and other peoples of the Third World. According to Ilesanmi:

> In fact, the African continent is the only developing region in the world whose human welfare indicators are worsening and the proportion of people living below poverty line is increasing (UNDP 1994, 165). Life expectancy is below sixty years in twenty-eight countries. Life expectancy is below fifty years in eighteen countries. Life expectancy in Sierra Leone is just thirty-seven years; about half of the adult populations of at least thirteen countries are illiterate. Half or more of women are illiterate in at least eighteen countries. Children under five die at rates in excess of 100 per 1,000 in at least twenty-eight countries. In Sierra Leone, the rate is 335 per 1,000 (World Bank 1999). In the words of the *1995 World Development Report*, 'the plight of African continent remains the most serious challenge for the emerging world order.' (World Bank 1995, 122).[6]

The disputations, contradictions and complexity of suggested solutions to the problems of development and social change underscore this fact of complexity of development even further. From neoliberal economic theories of development to modernization theories, to dependent and world system theories, as well as globalization and antiglobalization movements, it is clear there is no one perspective or solution to the issues of societal development and social transformation. For instance, according to Uwafiokun Idemudia, modernization and dependency theorists differ on the roles government and private sector play in growth and development. "For example while some scholars have contested the nature of the relationship between transnational corporations (TNCs) and development in developing countries, others have debated the strengths and limitations of the welfare and neo-liberal states."[7]

Neoliberal economic theories like Adam Smith's theory of self-interest and liberal capitalism opt for freedom of the market regulated by individual self-interest without any interference from the state, believing that this will result in widespread prosperity. W.W. Rostow's "Stages of Growth" theory, representative of modernization theories, outlines steps towards the realization of economic growth as lying within one of five categories: "the traditional society, the preconditions for take-off, the take-off, the drive to

---

6. Ilesanmi, "Leave No Poor Behind," 78.
7. Idemudia, "Corporate Social Responsibility and the Rentier Nigerian State," 132.

Introduction

maturity, and the age of high mass-consumption."[8] Dependency theorists tie world poverty, especially as it affects developing countries, to the colonial era starting around 1500, the period of mercantile capitalism during which the natural and human resources of Africa, South America and Asia were exploited by the wealthier countries of first Europe and then also North America.

The move to modernity, in terms of development studies, refers to three principal events in the North that transformed the world's understanding of 'development.' According to Gilbert Rist, a historian of development:

> ... Everything started with three strangely coeval events (which took place around 1776). First, the publication of the *Inquiry into the Wealth of Nations* by Adam Smith, who invented economics and discovered that the pursuit of self-interest could be conducive to collective affluence; second, the Declaration of Independence of the United States of America, which proclaimed, for the first time, that, "all men are created equal... and are endowed by their Creator with certain inalienable Rights, that among these are Life, Liberty and the pursuit of Happiness," and, finally, the perfecting of the steam engine by James Watt, i.e., the discovery of a new source of energy based on the harnessing of heat—that would rapidly succeed the wind—and watermills—and become dependent on fossil resources.... This extraordinary conjunction of apparently quite different innovations—market, individualism, and "fire engines"—that are mutually reinforcing—is a key to understanding the origin of development.[9]

The transition from modernity to economic globalization was facilitated by the imposition of the structural adjustment programme (SAP) to developing countries by international financial institutions like IMF/World Bank and the Paris Club; this included the devaluation of native currencies and the opening of their markets to outside markets under the World Trade Organization rules and treaties.

As an innovative philosopher and professor of theology, Lonergan recognized quite early in his writings the complexity of issues of social transformation. The complexity exists, Lonergan observes, because social transformation presupposes the personal integrity of persons in society as

---

8. Rostow, *Stages of Economic Growth*; Hite and Roberts, ed., *Globalization and Development Reader*, 47.

9. Rist, "Is 'Development' a Panacea? How to Think Beyond Obsolete Categories," 346.

Introduction

originating value, realizing in themselves terminal values aimed at the human good for themselves and for each other. For Lonergan, "what is good, always is concrete."[10] The various components that enter into the human good include ". . . skills, feelings, values, beliefs, cooperation, progress, and decline."[11] It also includes the equitable and recurrent distribution of goods and services to everyone, thus making it possible for everyone in the society to achieve the realization of his/her life as a work of dramatic art in a sustainable way. The realization of these issues concerning social transformation demands the promotion and implementation of the integral scale of values, vital, social, cultural, personal and religious, filling out the broad range of human societal development.[12] In order to respond to this complexity, Lonergan envisioned the necessity for a *summa sociologica*[13] and tried twice (between 1930–1944 and 1977–1983) to formulate an economic theory. According to the editors of his *Macroeconomic Dynamics: An Essay in Circulation Analysis*, his theory is ". . . (a) oriented toward the transformation of social practice; and (b) an empirical analysis of the processes and structures in the production of the material substratum of human societies and cultures."[14] Lonergan's earlier attempt at economics (1930–44), inspired by the Great Depression, inquires into how economic moral precepts could be based on or grounded in the economy itself.[15] It asks how economic moral precepts could be based on liberty as an originating value—as the principle of the human good.[16]

His second attempt at an economic theory (1977–1983) aimed at formulating laws beyond the pricing system, laws that people could apply to the personal conduct of their lives.[17] In formulating such laws, Lonergan

---

10. Lonergan, *Method in Theology*, 27.

11. Ibid.

12. See "Editors' Introduction," in Lonergan, *Macroeconomic Dynamics: An Essay in Circulation Analysis*, xxxii.

13. See Lonergan, "Panton Anakephalaiosis [Restoration of All Things]," 139–69; see also Shute, "'Let us be practical!'"

14. "Editors' Introduction," in Lonergan, *Macroeconomic Dynamics*, xxvii.

15. Lamber et al., eds., *Caring About Meaning*, 14.

16. As the Editors of his *Macroeconomic Dynamics* cited above notes, human liberty is dependent on human anthropology, that is, on human beings acting intelligently, reasonably and responsibly. See "Editors' Introduction," Lonergan, *Macroeconomic Dynamics*, xxxviii.

17. Lonergan, "An Outline of Circulation Analysis," 109–10; and "Editors' Introduction," in Lonergan, *Macroeconomic Dynamics*, xlv.

says, it is necessary and more important to attend to the reality from which the analogy of economics prescinds:

> That reality is human history, and it is a cord woven with three strands. The first is progress, which is the fruit of attention, intelligence, reasonableness, and responsibility. The second is decline, the offspring of inattention, obtuseness, unreasonableness, and irresponsibility. The third is the usually slow and long process of recovery: of removing the absurdities inflicted on the human situation by past inattention, obtuseness, unreasonableness, and irresponsibility.[18]

My interest in this book, however, is not in Lonergan's economic theory, but in attending to the reality from which the "analogy prescinds," that is, his philosophical anthropology, an anthropology intimately related to an understanding of societal development, breakdown and transformation. In the preface to *Insight*, Lonergan remarks that it is his goal to work out a philosophy based on *insight into insight*, compare it with one based on insight into oversights, and so get to the root of the problem of progress and decline.[19] Oversights refer to the various forms of the 'flight from understanding' that block insights into concrete situations. These include the three forms of bias (prejudices: dramatic, individual and group) responsible for the shorter cycle of decline and the general bias responsible for the longer cycle of decline. In "Insight Revisited" he states that the triad of progress, decline and redemption is his heuristic assumption for a theological analysis of history:

> My first approximation was the assumption that men always do what is intelligent and reasonable, and its implication was an ever increasing progress. The second approximation was the radical inverse insight that men can be biased, and so unintelligent and unreasonable in their choices and decisions. The third approximation was the redemptive process resulting from God's gift of his grace to individuals and from the manifestation of his love in Christ Jesus.[20]

This book seeks to investigate some principal aspects of Lonergan's philosophy/theology that could be helpful in understanding societal development, breakdown and transformation. It addresses such questions as

18. Lonergan, *Macroeconomic Dynamics*, 93–94.
19. Lonergan, *Insight*, 8.
20. Lonergan, "Insight Revisited," 272.

Introduction

'How does Lonergan's argument intersect with other perspectives on social development and transformation?' 'Is a dialogue between Lonergan's philosophical anthropology and contemporary development discourse beneficial to both theories of development and Lonergan studies?' 'How does this dialogue reshape an understanding of social transformation and sustainable human development?' Following from Lonergan's philosophical anthropology I argue that social transformation and sustainable human development presuppose the promotion and implementation of the integral scale of values. That is, the transformation, not only of persons obeying the transcendental precepts, but also of the meanings and values underlying a community's life and its institutional structures. And equally, that these transformations are made possible by the assistance of the religious value which includes God's grace.

Lonergan's philosophical anthropology provides a general hermeneutic for understanding social development, breakdown and transformation. As his position above indicates, by being attentive to their experiences, by understanding intelligently, by judging reasonably and by deliberating responsibly, there is "an ever increasing progress." This is true of the subject and of the community. But decline cannot be underestimated, for human beings can be affected by bias, and therein the flight from understanding takes the place of genuine inquiry.[21] The consequence is an ever increasing decline—minor and major arising from inattentiveness, unintelligibility, unreasonableness and irresponsible decisions.[22] The reality of inverse insight exposes the link between progress and decline and, hence, the unsustainability of human authenticity and development without the assistance of divine grace. Thus Lonergan makes a strong connection between anthropology and a development that is to be sustainable.[23] The editors of his *Macroeconomic Dynamics* affirms the link between anthropology and development thus:

> Lonergan's deeply Christian anthropology sets his approach to democracy apart from the secularism of both liberalism and socialism. He had no doubt that God is at work in human history bringing about a divine solution to the problem of evil. But as a theologian he also thought that this supernatural solution can

---

21. Lonergan, *Insight*, 8.
22. Ibid., 6.
23. See Lonergan, "Healing and Creating in History"; *Macroeconomic Dynamics*, lxxi.

only be fully transformative of human history with our free cooperation in the form of human *creativity*.²⁴

Contemporary development discourse and the theories of development they rely upon pay attention to some aspects of the human good but often do this to the neglect of other important aspects. It prioritizes the basic needs, the vital values of health and food, and the institutional structures that promote development as economic growth—technology and the legal and political structures aimed at protecting trade and treaties between and among nations necessary for a free market economy. However, it often stops short of addressing other values like the cultural, personal and religious values necessary for optimal human life, human flourishing, well-being and happiness. Consequently, developmental processes impact negatively on human beings culturally, resulting in various forms of depersonalization and diminishing the human capacity for self-transcendence. At times it ends up perpetuating inequality and injustice in the production and distribution of the human good in the world. For instance, it is reported that the level of world poverty is growing by leaps and bounds in an unprecedented manner. Poverty today overtakes war as the greatest cause of human misery. As the editors of *Global Ethics: Seminal Essays* observe after following an analysis of a series of UN World Development Reports:

> Many more people—some 300 million—have died from hunger and remediable diseases in peacetime in the seventeen years since the end of the Cold War than have perished from wars, civil wars, and government repression over the entire twentieth century. And poverty continues unabated, with some 830 million human beings chronically undernourished, 1100 million lacking access to safe water, and 2600 million lacking access to basic sanitation; 2000 million lacking access to essential drugs; 1000 million lacking adequate shelter and 2000 million lacking electricity; 774 million adults being illiterate, and 218 million children between five and seventeen doing wage work outside their household. Such severe deficits in the fulfillment of social and economic human rights also bring further deficits in civil and political human rights in their wake.²⁵

---

24. Lawrence, "Editors' Introduction," in Lonergan, *Macroeconomic Dynamics*, xxxviii.

25. Pogge and Horton, ed., *Global Ethics: Seminal Essays II*, xiv.

Introduction

If human development is to be sustainable, something must be done, not only to ameliorate the negative effects of development processes, but to make human beings benefit from development ultimately designed for their own good. Human well-being, Lonergan would argue, is beyond its utilitarian understanding as individual well-being that concentrates on personal advantage and achievements, seeking policies that promote self-centered choices and aims. Human well-being involves something broader than pursuit of one's individual well-being and the maximization of self-interest; it includes other objectives and values including the common good of one's community and humanity as a whole.

Lonergan's contribution to the discourse on development offers a philosophical basis for clarifying the general structures of development from the perspective of human intentional consciousness as well as the breakdowns in development due to the fourfold human bias, something unique to his thought. It also includes the implementation of a scale of values that promotes the integrity of the human spirit and of all levels of society, as opposed to promoting just the basic vital and social values. His philosophy might also remind the theorists of development of the limits of their theories when it comes to healing the social surd of sin and societal decline. His philosophy thus segues into the need for religious value which recognizes a supernatural solution—grace. This book, therefore, is an exploration of the provocative contribution of Lonergan's philosophical anthropology and the theological implications of this anthropology to contemporary discourse on development. Specifically, this includes some prominent secular theories and pertinent aspects from the social teachings of the Catholic Church. It further dialogues with contemporary discourse on sustainable human development and highlights the limitations of Lonergan's philosophical anthropology as well as suggesting areas for its further development and complementarity.

To accomplish this task, this book is divided into three parts comprising five chapters in total. Chapter 1 sets the horizon within which Lonergan's philosophical anthropology is addressed by laying out the contemporary context of the discourse on sustainable development and social transformation. It summarizes the various concerns raised in significant overviews of development debates along with some prominent interpretations of some principles of Catholic social teaching related to contemporary development discourse. Here specific mention is made of some theories of development and some moral guidelines for development as presented in some of the social teachings of the Catholic Church.

In Chapter 2, I treat Lonergan's philosophy/theology as it pertains to development and social transformation through an examination of his cognitional theory, that is, his philosophical anthropology especially as contained in the sixth and seventh chapters of *Insight*. This chapter also exposes the essential features of his philosophical anthropological insight through an examination of the dialectic of community as well as distortions in knowing, the flight from understanding arising from the various biases of the human subject and a treatment of cosmopolis as the higher viewpoint. The fact of human moral impotency which exposes the impossibility of sustainable human development by human effort alone also forms part of this chapter.

Chapter 3, dealing with social transformation, elaborates further Lonergan's theory of social development through an examination of progress, development and breakdown in *Method in Theology* as well as his development of the notion of the scale of values. This chapter also includes Robert Doran's appropriation and development of this scale of values in what he calls 'the integral scale of values' as well as its implications for sustainable human development. The integral scale of values makes the call for conversion an imperative.

Chapter 4, creating an openness for dialogue, addresses areas of convergence and divergence of Lonergan's philosophical anthropology with the contemporary discourse on development and some themes of development in Catholic social teaching. It highlights certain limitations of Lonergan's approach including the ambiguity on the language of cosmopolis and limited prognosis of globalization. Insights from this study help point to areas of Lonergan's philosophical anthropology that could benefit from contemporary development discourse. Specific mention is made of the principle of solidarity of the Catholic social teaching as complementing insights of Lonergan's philosophical anthropology. Its emphasis of mutual interdependence could heal divisions arising from distortions of spontaneous intersubjectivity in the dialectic of community especially caused by group bias. It could also be instrumental towards humanizing globalization. It could help overcome the gap between the rich and the poor. Thus, it could facilitate the just distribution of the human good to everybody and promote human flourishing, well-being and happiness. The human relationship it promotes could ideally reduce the problem of identity and subsequent

Introduction

violence bedevilling the global community on account of pursuit of varying forms of self-interest.

The general conclusion briefly summarizes the work. It also restates the major argument of the book which emphasizes the importance of integral human development through an adherence to integral scale of values as development that can be sustainable. Such development is responsible for societal development and transformation realizable through the religious value of God's grace.

1

Themes in Contemporary Development Discourse

CONTEMPORARY DEVELOPMENT DISCOURSE IS variegated and diverse. The meaning and scope of 'development' has expanded in magnitude and has been radically reformulated in various theories and discourses including dependency, world-system, Marxist, socialist, postmodernist, postcolonial, poststructural, feminist, ecological, critical modernist, etc. The world's societies have also changed dramatically in many ways (a fact evident in the explosion of discourses of 'globalization' and 'anti-globalization' or alter-globalization'), and there are many emerging new voices on the world scene discussing societal development and transformation. Knowledge production has also expanded and changed dramatically, raising new epistemological challenges and possibilities. This is the contemporary scene of development discourse divided by the secular academy and in the various notions or principles of 'development' in other areas of life as well. Thus the scale of the task of exposing the contemporary development discourse would be daunting. But this is not the task we intend to undertake here.

This chapter sets out to expose not every conversation going on in the contemporary scene of development discourse but only select themes with the aim of introducing the academic field of discourse on development that will be in conversation with Lonergan's philosophical anthropology. The chapter will be divided into two parts. The first part will discuss select theories of development. The second part will be a discussion of notions of development as contained in some principles of Catholic social teaching.

THEORIES OF DEVELOPMENT

Development means producing a better life. Development is fundamentally economic. Hence, the discipline of economics

> has to be integrally involved in the study of development. All
> theories of development have significant economic aspects,
> along with other dimensions. So, we have to know economics
> to understand development.[1]
>
> —RICHARD PEET AND ELAINE HARTWICK

In the above words Richard Peet and Elaine Hartwick lay the groundwork of their theory of development. They argue that the economic dimension plays a very important role in theories of development because all theories have significant economic dimensions. Peet and Hartwick's position is correct as far as it goes, for at least two major social revolutions—the industrial revolution and the shift to global economic production. There are other factors as equally important as economic growth. Some of these other factors could be summed up in the goal of economics as improving the living condition of people and promoting human flourishing and well-being. This is clear from the view of economists who champion human development. According to Amartya Sen, the success of economics "has to be judged ultimately in terms of what it does to the lives of human beings. The enhancement of living conditions must clearly be an essential—if not the essential—object of the entire economic exercise, and that enhancement is an integral part of the concept of development."[2] Mahbub ul Haq holds similar view by acknowledging that "today, it is widely accepted that the real purpose of development is to enlarge people's choices in all fields—economic, political, cultural. Seeking increases in income is one of the many choices people make, but it is not the only one."[3] Thus, in the United Nations for instance, we do have not only macro bodies that deal on economic planning like the World Bank, the International Monetary Fund and the regional development banks. We also have institutions that specialize on micro human development issues like the World Health Organization (WHO), United Nations International Children Emergency Fund (UNICEF), United Nations Educational Scientific and Cultural Organization (UNESCO), International Labour Organization (ILO), United Nations Population Fund (UNFPA) etc. It is very obvious "that people are

---

1. Peet and Hartwick, *Theories of Development*, 23. Emphasis mine.
2. Sen, "The Concept of Development," in Pogge and Horton, eds., *Global Ethics: Seminal Essays II*, 158.
3. Haq, *Reflections on Human Development*, xvii.

both the means and the end of economic development."[4] As will be seen below, the various theories of development approach the ends of development differently.

Adam Smith's Theory of Self-Interest

Classical economics developed following Adam Smith, whose philosophy is based on the inevitability of self-interest as the determinant of exchange and of values, as argued in his 1776 book, *An Inquiry into the Nature and Causes of the Wealth of Nations* thus:

> As every individual, therefore, endeavours as much as he can both to employ his capital in the support of domestic industry, and so to direct that industry that its produce may be of the greatest value; every individual necessarily labours to render the annual revenue of the society as great as he can. He generally, indeed, neither intends to promote public interest, nor knows how much he is promoting it. By preferring the support of domestic to that of foreign industry, he intends only his own security; and by directing that industry in such a manner as its produce may be of the greatest value, he intends only his own gain, and he is in this, as in many other cases, led by an invisible hand to promote an end which was no part of his intention. Nor is it always the worse for the society that it was no part of it. *By pursuing his own interest he frequently promotes that of the society more effectually than when he really intends to promote it.*[5]

Adam Smith contends that human beings have a natural propensity to trade, "the propensity to truck, barter, and exchange one thing for another."[6] As traders, human beings naturally pursue their self-interest, with the aim of making money, of making profit for themselves. As a result of this pursuit for self-interest, Smith argues that whoever wants to get anything from anybody should appeal to the self-interest of the person, to the others advantage to get him/her to do what one wants. For:

> It is not from the benevolence of the butcher, the brewer, or the baker, that we expect our dinner, but from their regard to their own interest. We address ourselves not to their humanity but to

---

4. Ibid., 3.
5. Smith, *Wealth of Nations*, 423. Emphasis mine.
6. Ibid., 13.

their self-love, and never talk to them of our own necessities but of their advantages.[7]

Human selfishness is thus an economic motive for the creation of wealth and production of growth. However, self-interest is tamed by virtue, a concept which to Smith meant the "exceptional powers of character and mind, the love of that which is dignified, honourable and noble in their pursuit of self-interest."[8] For although human self-interest is natural, Smith also believed that human beings' highest quest was for virtue. Consequently, self-love is mitigated by virtue. And "should that prove insufficient, selfishness (in the form of greed) should be limited by laws made by the state."[9]

Adam Smith's classical theory developed in response to the continuing social turmoil that began in the age of industrialization and state intervention to protect trade in the period of mercantilism. Adam Smith proposed letting human selfishness reign because in the pursuit of one's self-interest one simultaneously promotes an unintended goal—, "the invisible hand"[10] unintended consequence, — promoting the good of the society. For instance, in the course of promoting one's self-interest in making money, one embarks on a business venture and in the process provides jobs for other people as well. Instead of regulating the market, governments should let the invisible hands of market forces create an overall benefit for society. So within the larger scheme of *The Wealth of Nations*, Smith insisted that various countries should specialize in those areas of production where they are naturally endowed, what he termed "comparative advantage" in order to keep the machinery of the market functioning for the optimum good of all. Smith's book, therefore, lays the groundwork of economic liberalism (free markets) and assures that, in spite of its disadvantages, capitalism as economic growth and free markets would ultimately serve the greater good. According to his theory of development, economic growth depends on capital accumulation; this depends on virtue, by which Adam Smith meant the system of natural liberty, that there should be no impediments to trade.[11] Regulation in the market is to be provided, Smith argues, not by

---

7. Ibid., 14.
8. Peet and Hartwick, *Theories of Development*, 24.
9. Ibid., 31.
10. Taylor analyses this as part of social imaginary, that is, as part of the inarticulate expression of human life and history, the economy, human natural propensity to barter and trade. See, Taylor, *Secular Age*, 177.
11. Peet and Hartwick, *Theories of Development*, 32.

the state but by the free hand of the market, that is, by the competitiveness of the market which turns buyers away from traders who charge high fees for their goods as they prefer to buy from traders whose goods is cheap. As Richard Peet and Elaine Hartwick comment, under Smith's theory of self-interest:

> The web of self-regulating market was an "invisible hand" organizing the economy efficiently and yet also transforming private self-interest into public virtue. Hence, an automatic mechanism, competition in the market, led to productivity and growth without state interference. Self-interested competitive behaviour directed resources to where they could best and most efficiently be used. And all classes, Smith believed, shared in the benefits of progress.[12]

According to William T. Cavanaugh, Smith's theory of self-interest aims at creating a new heaven and a new earth where the wants of each person is satisfied through the freedom of the market:

> Through the mechanism of demand and supply, the competition of self-interested individuals will result in the production of the goods society wants, at the right prices, with sufficient employment for all at the right wages for the foreseeable future. The result is an eschatology in which abundance for all is just around the corner.[13]

The implications of Adam Smith's theory of self-interest in the development discourse will be clearer as we discuss liberal capitalism below. But suffice it to note that although it may be pervasive, as will be evident later in our treatment of other theories of development, maximization of self-interest does not sufficiently determine human behaviour. In the light of Lonergan's scale of values and Doran's later appropriation in what he calls "integral scale of values," it is very clear that Smith's theory of self-interest is limited by presuming that pursuit of particular good will inevitably result to the common good of order. And as John M. Letiche observes, development economists like Amartya Sen thinks of substantive freedom instead of maximization of self-interest as determinant of human behaviour:

> Mainstream economist theory, however, identifies rationality of human behaviour with internal consistency of choice and, further, with maximization of self-interest. But, as [Amartya] Sen notes,

---

12. Ibid., 33.
13. Cavanaugh, *Being Consumed*, 93.

> there is neither evidence for the claim that self-interest maximization provides the best approximation to actual human behaviour nor that it leads necessarily to optimum economic conditions.[14]

Sen argues against the random selection of cases of successes supposedly arising from the exercise of intelligent self-interest, saying that these are unproven and that they do not in themselves prove that rationality of human behaviour necessarily implies intelligent self-interest:

> Sometimes the alleged case for assuming self-interested action seems to be based on its expected results—arguing that this would lead to efficient outcomes. The success of some free-market economies, such as Japan, in producing efficiency has also been cited as some evidence in the direction of the self-interest theory. However, the success of a free market does not tell us anything at all about what *motivation* lies behind the action of economic agents in such an economy. Indeed, in case of Japan, there is strong empirical evidence to suggest that systematic departures from self-interested behaviour in the direction of duty, loyalty and goodwill have played a substantial part in industrial process.[15]

Thus, although self-interest may motivate human action and play an active role in rationality of human behaviour, it does not by such roles imply that maximization of self-interest alone drives human behaviour and actions.[16] People do not behave in an exclusively self-interested way.

Liberal Capitalism

Liberal capitalism refers to an economic system whereby the free market is the one essential mechanism for regulating the production and distribution of goods. Its advocates believe that liberal capitalism's free market economy will increase productivity, generate wealth and improve the well-being of members of the community. Free market economy is believed to achieve this increased production and wealth because the forces of supply and demand put in place a competitive spirit that checks the price system and maximises profit. Thus liberal capitalism emphasizes Adam Smith's 'invisible hand of the market' as a force to regulate economic activity. It conceives economics as an exact science that could easily predict human

---

14. Letiche, "Forward to Amartya Sen On Ethics and Economics," xi.
15. Sen, *On Ethics and Economics*, 18.
16. Ibid., 19.

beings' economic activity and determine human well-being. As articulated by Gregory Baum:

> The free market, the liberals argued, was the wonderful regulating device that transformed desire for gain into socially useful activity. The market liberated persons from the restraints of the past. Persons could dispense with virtue; all they needed was enlightened self-interest. While players reached for the best ideal they could get, the market mechanism, ruled simply by supply and demand, would regulate the economic activity—like a hidden hand—so that it benefited society as a whole.[17]

Underlying liberal capitalism is the pursuit of individual freedom realizable through the accumulation of capital made possible by the freedom of the market. Liberal capitalists hold a view of human beings as *economic beings* who seek to improve their material condition through competition in the market. According to Susan Braedley and Meg Luxton, "Liberalism's primary value is individual human freedom from coercion and servitude, which neoliberals believe is inevitably tied to capitalism as a system that promotes expansions of wealth and allows people the freedom to pursue wealth, and therefore to pursue their desires."[18] Advancing Adam Smith's theory of self-interest further, liberal capitalism views the market as the veritable institution whereby the interest of each individual advances the well-being of all. Consequently, liberal capitalism does not like interference either from government or other authorities in the freedom of the market. It affirms the laws of supply and demand alone for controlling economic activity. However, it is doubtful whether there has ever been unbounded liberal capitalism without any government regulation or control. According to Karl Polanyi:

> ... The idea of a self-adjusting market implied a stark utopia. Such an institution could not exist for any length of time without annihilating the human and natural substance of society; it would have physically destroyed man and transformed his surroundings into a wilderness. Inevitably, society too measures to protect itself, but whatever measures it took impaired the self-regulation of the market, disorganized industrial life, and thus endangered society in yet another way. It was this dilemma which forced the

---

17. Baum, "Liberal Capitalism," 77.
18. Braedley and Luxton, "Competing Philosophies," 7.

development of the market system into a definite groove and finally disrupted the social organization based upon it.[19]

For instance, during the Great Depression of the 1930s, Keynes writes emphasising the connection between employment, income and consumption and the economy; that one leads to the other. Therefore, in depression what the government should do is spend, create employment to enable people consume in order to kick start the economy once again.[20] Thus, governments hearkening to John Maynard Keynes' economic theory that "in a given situation of technique, resources and costs, income (both money-income and real income) depends on the volume of employment"[21] which determines the volume of consumption, intervened in the national economy. This intervention in market economy brought about Modern Welfare Capitalism or what Michael Novak describes as 'Democratic Capitalism.'[22] Also in the global economic crisis (2008) different countries injected money into their financial sector to stimulate their economies in the bid to end the recession. According to TD Waterhouse (a Canadian bank), "significant credit for the recovery is due to policy makers. Governments around the world introduced policies to boost their economies while central banks slashed interest rates and took actions to bolster their financial institutions. These rapid and coordinated actions put a floor under what could have spiralled into a much worse economic outcome."[23] For instance, the United States government's seven hundred and eighty- seven billion bailout package went to the financial sector (Wall Street), to stabilize the economy. Canada's bailout package for the auto industry amounted to over $4 Billion dollars.[24] Europe's leaders injected nearly $1 trillion bailout package, to head off Greek's default and to prevent the crisis affecting other weak economies like Portugal, Spain, Italy and Ireland.[25] Subsequently European Union announced

19. Polanyi, *Great Transformation*, 3-4.

20. Keynes, *General Theory of Employment, Interest and Money*, 24.

21. Ibid., 25.

22. Novak, *Spirit of Democratic Capitalism*, 57–58.

23. TD Waterhouse, "Trends to Shape the Year Ahead: Economic Outlook for 2010," *Wealth and Wisdom* (Winter 2010) 1.

24. Alphen and Benzie, "Bailout bill is $4B and Counting," *Toronto Star*, Dec 21 2008. Online: http://www.thestar.com/news/canada/article/556979.

25. Greece was the first country to receive a 110 billion euro EU/IMF bailout May, 2010, and Ireland was granted 80 billion euros in emergency loans in December 2010. See Reuters News, "No debt extension to 30 yrs on table—Greek finmin," Jan 31, 2011. Online: http://www.reuters.com/article/2011/01/31/idINIndia-54531120110131.

$113 billion (85 billion euros) bailout package for Ireland;[26] $110 billion (78 billion euros) for Portugal;[27] and 109bn euros Greek bailout ($155bn, £96.3bn).[28] In spite of these bailouts, the economy of the Eurozone is still wobbly and is threatening to engender another round of world economic recession.

As a theory in contemporary development discourse, liberal capitalists and their adherents (neo-liberalists) argue that allowing the forces of the market to determine economic activity is simply common sense and natural. Although it may come with some costs in the short term, its long term benefits, they argue, include promises of infinite progress for society and even for the cosmos. They believe neo-liberalism remains the best option for the globally interconnected new world order. For instance, in the midst of the financial crisis of 2008, the Group of Twenty (G20) leaders issued a declaration reaffirming the principles of neoliberalism:

> Our work will be guided by a shared belief that market principles, open trade and investment regimes, and effectively regulated financial markets foster the dynamisms, innovation, and entrepreneurship that are essential for economic growth, employment and poverty reduction... These principles ... have lifted millions out of poverty and have significantly raised the standard of living.[29]

Through such international financial institutions as the International Monetary Fund (IMF), the World Bank, Paris Club etc., the advocates of liberal capitalism spread neo-liberal ideas, such as "cutting government intervention in the economy, changing political and economic structures, and acting to stabilize macroeconomic indicators,"[30] as the engine for world development and increased standard of living throughout the world. Thus giving rise to the commercialization of society whereby the system of economics unfortunately defines the mechanisms of social order and is seen as a guarantee to world peace. Charles Taylor succinctly observes: "Conceiving

26. CNN Wire Staff, "EU leaders announce $113 billion bailout package for Ireland," http://edition.cnn.com/2010/BUSINESS/11/28/ireland.bailout/index.html

27. Huff Post Online, "Portugal Bailout: EU Approves $110 Billion Package," October 21, 2011. Online: http://www.huffingtonpost.com/2011/05/16/portugal-bailout-eu-appro_n_862597.html

28. BBC News Business, "Eurozone agrees new 109bn euros Greek bailout." Online: http://www.bbc.co.uk/news/business-14239794.

29. Braedley and Luxton, "Competing Philosophies: Neoliberalism and Challenges of Everyday Life," 5.

30. Hite and Roberts, eds., *Globalization and Development Reader*, 12.

of the economy as a system is an achievement of the eighteenth-century theory, with the Physiocrats and Adam Smith; but coming to see the most important purpose and agenda of society as economic collaboration and exchange is a drift in our social imaginary which begins in that period and continues to this day."[31]

Therefore, the problem with neo-liberal capitalism in the viewpoint of some of its critics is its dismissal of the short term costs of its policies, that is, its effects on matters of meaning and value, and hence its adverse effects on human well-being. According to J. Philip Wogaman:

> Not least of the problems with laissez-faire economics is the loss of connection between material problems and the deeper moral and spiritual values of humankind. When material things and relationships are regarded as self-sufficient, they are too easily cut adrift from the values that give direction to the human nature. The result is the trivialization of economic life, distortion of human relationships, and fragmentation of spirit. Our life as economic beings is divorced from our true humanity, and both are diminished.[32]

Hence, for its critics, liberal capitalism, in its varied forms including neo-liberal capitalism, is a fundamentalist orthodoxy, and therefore "antithetical to the spirit of both science and democracy."[33] As Lee Cormie observes:

> Neo-liberalism is infused with a spirit of blind faith in an unseen trinity of science, technology, and (allegedly) free markets, and in the capacities of elites to understand, order, and manage global changes in the interests of all people and the whole earth. It is blind to the self-interests served by these policies and their many bad fruits; it is deaf to the cries of its victims. All its claims, even its basic categories and points of reference, are suspect.[34]

We shall return to arguments for and/or against liberal capitalism in a subsequent chapter of this work. Here our concern has been an exposition of Adam Smith's theory of self-interest and liberal capitalism in contemporary discourse on development. Our exposition so far has shown that neoliberalism drew much from Adam Smith's theory of self-interest, especially in its emphasis upon free market economy. In the words of Richard Peet

---

31. Taylor, *Secular Age*, 181.
32. Wogaman, *Economics and Ethics*, xi.
33. Cormie, "Genesis of a New World," 124.
34. Ibid.

and Elaine Hartwick, "we live by Smith's ideas today—benefiting from their veracity, yet suffering . . . from their mistakes in assumptions and logic."[35]

Modernization Theory

Modernization theory emerged to further the new way of life of commercial society to other places in the world. It views human societies as developing in various stages according to their mode of economy: hunter gatherer, agricultural, etc., towards the creation of the model society centered on commerce. Modernization theorists emphasize the need for big companies, access to large amounts of capital, and modern social organization values as necessary for developing countries to catch up with the West already enjoying the benefits of commercial society centered on economics.[36] They also canvass for technology transfer[37] from the developed to the developing nations and the opening of national markets for the trans-national corporations (TNCs) to bring huge amounts of capital to developing countries in order to facilitate this development process. According to Claude Ake, "Modernization theory ... assumes that progress tends to be spatially diffused, a process by which more and more countries evolve from the state of backwardness, capitalizing on the experience of those that developed before them. The spatial distribution of progress, however skewed at any time, is not static but dynamic. By proximity and interaction, progress is diffused through space. Progress or modernity, by its very nature is apt to strain beyond its locus, overflowing into the adjacent space and transforming it. Thus uneven development is a transitional phenomenon that can be removed sooner or later by creating certain favorable conditions within the underdeveloped regions and by ensuring the appropriate interactions between them and the developed regions."[38] Prominent among the modernization theorists is W.W. Rostow and his book, *Stages of Economic Growth* (1960).

Though an economist, Rostow starts off his theory of modernization by insisting that "economic forces and motives are not unique and overriding determinant of the course of history."[39] On the contrary, economic

---

35. Peet and Hartwick, *Theories of Development*, 33.
36. See, Taylor, *Secular Age*, 218.
37. See Archibugi and Immarino, "Globalization of Technological Innovation."
38. Ake, *Democracy and Development in Africa*, 10.
39. Rostow, *Stages of Economic Growth*, and Worsely, *Three Worlds*, 17.

development requires not only appropriate economic, technological and demographic conditions, but also appropriate social institutions and value systems. This, he says, is true of all societies: "It is possible to identify all societies, in their economic dimensions, as lying within one of five categories: the traditional society, the preconditions for take-off, the take-off, the drive to maturity, and the age of high mass-consumption."[40] The stages of economic growth, he says, progress as one moves from one stage to another.

Traditional Societies: Under this umbrella, Rostow groups those societies whose political, hierarchical social structure, values and economy limit its productive capacity. They are characterized by primitive technologies and superstitious belief systems regarding the natural world. For Rostow, societies under this category historically include "the dynasties in China; the civilization of Middle East and the Mediterranean; the world of Medieval Europe."[41] Production here is quite low because the authority structure under landowners leaves little scope for social mobility. According to Rostow,

> . . . The central fact about the traditional society was that a ceiling existed on the level of attainable output per head... The area and volume of trade within them and between them fluctuated, for example, with the degree of political and social turbulence, the efficiency of central rule, the upkeep of the roads. Population—and, within limits, the level of life—rose and fell not only with the sequence of the harvests, but with the incidence of war and of plague. Varying degrees of manufacture developed; but, as in agriculture, the level of productivity was limited by the inaccessibility of modern science, its applications, and its frame of mind.[42]

Development of a Set of Preconditions for Take-Off: This refers to societies in the process of transition poised "to transform a traditional society in the ways necessary for it to exploit the fruits of modern science."[43] Rostow has in mind the pre-industrial and the early industrial periods of the late 17th and early 18th centuries in Europe when, although insights of modern science were revolutionizing agriculture, its effects had yet to blossom in 19th century western traditional societies. These preconditions

---

40. Rostow, *Stages of Economic Growth*, and Hite and Roberts, eds., *Globalization and Development Reader*, 47.
41. Ibid., 48.
42. Ibid., 47.
43. Ibid., 48.

for take-off include the idea that economic progress is not only possible but that it is a necessary condition for other purposes—"be it national dignity, private profit, the general welfare or a better life for the children."[44] This period is marked by a tension with traditional values which stunts the continuity of the process of development. Consequently, the intrusion of external societies into traditional societies is considered necessary to initiate a process by which a modern alternative to the traditional society is constructed. Thus, Rostow indirectly supports the external invasion of traditional societies in the era of colonialism, for instance, as necessitating the transition to modern society. The gains and benefits of industrialization and economic growth are felt in other areas of life as well. Traditional societies exist side by side with modern economic activity. Important at this stage throughout, Rostow says, is political order — the building of an effective central national state.

The Take-Off: This is the stage when resistance to modern life and steady growth is overcome in many societies by the influence of technological advancement. The consequence in some such countries, particularly in Britain, was an increase in investment. This came about because surplus income is ploughed back into the economy to buy new equipment. This resulted in greater productivity leading to additional income, expansion of industries and emergence of a new class of entrepreneurs. Strong political structures equally paved the way for the take-off of modern societies. According to Rostow:

> In more general case, the take-off awaited not only the build-up of social overhead capital and a surge of technological development in industry and agriculture, but also the emergence to political power of a group prepared to regard the modernization of the economy as serious, high-order political business.[45]

Drive toward Maturity: This stage of growth is characterized by sustained, even if fluctuating, progress in the economy powered by technology. Production continuously outgrows the increase in population; national income is reinvested and the economy becomes not merely local but international with more exports than imports. Rostow's words aptly describe the features of the period:

---

44. Ibid., 49.
45. Ibid.

> The make-up of the economy changes unceasingly as technique improves, new industries accelerate, older industries level off. The economy finds its place in the international economy: goods formerly imported are produced at home; new import requirements develop, and new export commodities to match them. The society makes such terms as it will with the requirements of modern efficient production, balancing off the new against the older values and institutions, or revising the latter in such ways as to support rather than to retard the growth process.[46]

The period of time Rostow gives for such maturity is 60 years, provided its growth remains steady.

The Age of High Mass Consumption: With increase in income and increased production, large numbers of people are able to consume at levels that far exceed their needs, also bringing changes in the structure of work to an urban lifestyle and to office employment. At this stage resources could be allocated to social welfare programs and to social security.

Rostow's stage theory of economic growth influenced the division of the world into developed and undeveloped and was quite influential in liberal policies towards the Third World. According to Lee Cormie:

> W. W. Rostow's *The Stages of Economic Growth* (1960) is a succinct, sophisticated, and relatively pure expression of the dominant paradigm informing social-scientific thinking about national development and political decision making in the United States in the period following World War II. The book itself was widely distributed in underdeveloped countries, and its author was very influential in the development of U.S. foreign policy in the 1960s. Moreover, in a somewhat retouched form the thinking outlined in the book still informs the developmentalist ideas of the U.S and other major Western governments and their international agencies.[47]

But in spite of the influence of Rostow's theory, it has not been accepted by all theorists of development as we shall see below.

Critique of Modernization Theory

Modernization theory has been accused of going too far in some of its assumptions. First, it is accused of being ahistorical, of not taking cognizance

46. Ibid., 50.
47. Cormie, "Sociology of National Development and Salvation History," 58.

of the various histories of other countries, regions and of structures of development.⁴⁸ Its critics argue that it is not correct in assuming that the rich variety of traditional cultures is or will only be an evolutionary process towards the modern industrial society. Rostow's modernization theory is viewed as another form of the evolutionary theory of society and the idea of necessary progress underlying modernity as a whole. Second, the theory is considered myopic in generalizing the replication of the Western model as 'development.' What Rostow termed 'modernization' was nothing but 'Americanization.' It is not right to view development as an autonomous process that is independent of variety of culture and institutional frameworks of divergent peoples. For instance, *The Report of the South Commission*, produced under the chairmanship of the former Tanzanian President Julius Nyerere which summed up the aspirations of the developing countries underlined autochthonous culture in its definition of development as:

> A process which enables human beings to realize their potential, build self-confidence, and lead lives of dignity and fulfillment. It is a process which frees people from the fear of want and exploitation. It is a movement away from political, economic, or social oppression. Through development, political independence acquires its true significance. And it is a process of growth, a movement essentially springing from within the society that is developing.⁴⁹

Unfortunately, viewing development as an autonomous process dehistoricizes development and easily leads to its objectivization ignoring its specificity. Therefore development is construed as a one-size fits all technique that produces modernization once the obstacles along its way like inefficiency, corruption, ethnicity and authoritarianism of rulers, etc., are removed. This approach puts developing countries like Africa "in a position in which everything was relevant to them and nothing was uniquely significant for understanding them. Hence the mounting anarchy of development studies and development practice in Africa. [Consequently] bits and pieces borrowed from theories and paradigms constructed for other purposes and other kinds of experience, meaningless for being incomplete and out of context, were applied in ways and for purposes that are not always clear and to realities that defy comparability."⁵⁰ Furthermore, modernization's quest to reduce the causes of poverty in traditional societies to national problems

---

48. Peet and Hartwick, *Theories of Development*, 133.
49. *Challenge to the South*, 10.
50. Ake, *Democracy and Development in Africa*, 13.

like corruption forgets such external factors as imbalances in the structures of trade that actually block development as such. According to Richard Peet, the implications of this theory are very clear:

> Development meant assuming the mental models of the West (rationalization), the institutions of the West (the market), the goals of the West (high mass consumption), and the culture of the West (the worship of commodities).[51]

The majority of the criticisms against modernization theorists come primarily from a group of scholars from the developing countries. These scholars' experience of colonialism sharpened their criticism of the Westernization of development as well as the nationalization of causes of poverty, especially as modernization theorists seemed to forget the impact of colonialism in setting the developing countries back. From these scholars comes the "dependency theory" of development.

Dependency Theory

Dependency theory is a body of social science theories predicated upon the notion that the resources of poor or underdeveloped countries flow to the rich or developed countries at the expense of the former. It emerged strongly in the 1960s in response to some theories of development, particularly in response to the modernization stages of growth theory. Dependency theorists connect world poverty—especially as it affects developing countries—to the colonial era, starting around 1500 AD, the period of mercantile capitalism when the natural and human resources of Africa, South America and Asia were exploited by the rich countries of Europe and North America. Dependency theory therefore argues that European development was based upon the *under*development of the non-European world. This underdevelopment took various forms of external destruction: violent conquests, colonial control, and theft of natural resources of non-European peoples. The consequence was the creation of two worlds: those at the center of power and the non-European world at the periphery, with the center achieving self-sustaining economic growth and the periphery lacking the basic necessities of life. For instance, the scramble and partition of Africa among different European powers in the Berlin Conference of 1884-5 was to ensure constant supply of raw materials for the industrial

---

51. Peet and Hartwick, *Theories of Development*, 132.

revolution back home without fighting one another after the abolition of slave trade which robbed Africa of the much needed human resources for its own development. It redistributed land, sometimes resorting to forced labor. It promoted agriculture but only for the production of cash crops to feed the industries back home. Ghana for example was made to farm cocoa and by 1865 started exporting that and became by 1901 the world leading producer of the commodity. Education was aimed at producing clerks and interpreters and personnel for other jobs for the optimum good of the colonial governments. Roads were constructed in order to facilitate export of commodities and importation for the interest of the home governments. The Report of the Commission for Africa, *Our Common Interest* (2005) confirms this and observes: "The railways and roads put in place in colonial times were primarily designed to transport minerals and other raw materials from the African interior to its ports for shipping to Europe. They were not designed to join one part of the continent to another or generate more links to the East."[52]

Popularized mainly by such Latin American economists as Raul Prebisch[53] and other theorists of the Economic Commission for Latin America (ECLA) and by Andre Gunder Frank (in English), dependency theory is highly critical of development economics and modernization theory. ECLA argues that the terms of trade between the 'developed' and the 'underdeveloped world' are imbalanced simply because the First World robbed the Third World of sources of raw material and the marketing of its products. They point out that, while over time the prices of manufactured products increased, the prices of raw materials depreciated. These reasons account for ECLA's emphasis on the historical pattern of relationships, in determining the terms of trade between the developed and the developing worlds.

Gunder Frank debunked the major theses of modernization theory: first, that development occurs in a succession of stages and that underdeveloped countries are still in the first stage of development. Second, that underdevelopment is the result of the socio-economic and political situations of underdeveloped countries. And third, that the development of underdeveloped countries can be achieved by economic relations with the developed countries. Frank argues: "a modest acquaintance with history shows that underdevelopment is not original or traditional and that neither

---

52. Commission for Africa, *Our Common Interest*, 21.
53. Cf. Di Marco, ed., *International Economics and Development*.

the past nor the present of the underdeveloped countries resembles in any important respect the past of the now developed countries. The now developed countries were never *under*developed, though they may have been *un*developed."[54] Furthermore, by construing the so-called underdeveloped countries as backward, modernization theory denies them their history, especially their pre-capitalist history which is often more developed than that of feudal Europe. Second, he attributes underdevelopment to the long-standing unequal relations between the developed and the underdeveloped countries.

> It is also widely believed that the contemporary underdevelopment of a country can be understood as the product or reflection solely of its own economic, political, social, and cultural characteristics or structure. Yet historical research demonstrates that contemporary underdevelopment is in large part the historical product of past and continuing economic and other relations between the satellite underdeveloped and the now developed metropolitan countries.[55]

Furthermore, because of the nature of capitalist expropriation and the appropriation of surplus value of the underdeveloped world, the only option towards the freedom of underdeveloped countries is separation and autonomy from the global capitalist system and away from the modernization influence of the urban centres.

> A related and also largely erroneous view is that the development of these underdeveloped countries and with them of their most underdeveloped domestic areas, must and will be generated or stimulated by diffusing capital, institutions, values, etc., to them from the international and national capitalist metropoles. Historical perspective based on the underdeveloped countries' past experience suggests that on the contrary in the underdeveloped countries economic development can now occur independently of most of these relations of diffusion.[56]

Dependency theorists do not, however, attribute the poverty of nations solely to external factors, for they point to the few local elites who collude with transnational corporations to rob their people by maintaining

---

54. Frank, "The Development of Underdevelopment," in Hite and Roberts, eds., *Globalization and Development Reader*, 76.

55. Ibid., 77.

56. Ibid.

unfavourable terms of trade and banking arrangements. "In other words, dependency theorists mainly saw foreign groups 'feasting' at the table of poorer nations, but elites from those poor countries, they theorized, were the ones who "set the table."[57]

Instituting the Globalization Project

The move from modernization theory to globalization was facilitated by the acceptance of the Western modernization theory of economic growth, an acceptance characterized by the accumulation of capital, huge factories and companies to replicate Western industrialization by the newly independent formerly colonial countries of the Third World. Thus many of the newly independent nations took loans and incurred huge debts from such international financial institutions as the International Monetary Fund (IMF), the World Bank, and the Paris Club. Inability to pay these loans and the need to continue development has led to the introduction of structural adjustment programs in developing countries. The aim was to reduce government expenditures so as to repay the loans from the international financial institutions and to facilitate more capital for development. This gave rise to the institutionalization of the globalization project in the neoliberal structure.

Globalization started to take the place of economic nationalism as early as 1971 when, at the meeting of the World Economic Forum, economic nationalism was declared indefensible as it inhibits the free movement of goods and services. Its place was taken by giant corporate institutions like the World Trade Organization (WTO) that seek to govern the new global project. Renator Ruggiero, the founding director of WTO, defined globalization as "…the linking together of countries at different levels of development by technology, information, and ideas, as well as by economics."[58] Thus the vision of globalization as articulated by the WTO includes the implementation of 'market rule' via the restructuring of policies and standards across the nation-state system. It also includes trade (two-thirds of which are controlled by transnational corporations) as an important vehicle of development. The World Bank sees globalization as successful participation in the world economy through liberalization, privatization of public

---

57. Ibid., 10.
58. Renato, "Reflections from Seattle"; McMichael, *Development and Social Change*, 150.

parastatals (agencies), the freeing of markets for labour, money, goods, and services.[59] The shift from economic nationalism to world market development, the imposition of structural adjustment programs and the opening up of the Second World market through Mikhail Gorbachev's *perestroika* (restructuring) in 1986, in order to join the Bretton Woods institutions, consolidated globalization.[60]

Although our emphasis has been on economic globalization, it ought to be noted that globalization is not a unified structure but a complex process that includes the multiple changes of the modern world: political, social, technological, cultural and economical. As Lee Cormie notes:

> . . . the discourses of globalization and epochal change address diverse, complex, apparently incongruent and contradictory processes. These developments reflect many forces predating the birth of neo-liberalism. They appear to be transforming virtually every aspect of global life, including the nature of the economy. They have no apparent single logical or structural imperative. There is no single center of power or kind of power. Individuals, families, communities, institutions, and movements everywhere are caught up in decision-making with epochal implications.[61]

However, neo-liberalism remains "the single most powerful unifying dimension in the dynamics of globalization."[62] Therefore, assessments of globalization often emphasize the effects of economic globalization manifested in the inequality between the rich and the poor countries in terms of trade and the consequence of dependence and increasing poverty of the poor on account of the measures employed in globalization such as global governance, liberalization, deregulation, etc. The ethical implications of this inequality are so enormous that one doubts whether 'development' is improving the life of the poorer countries. Often globalization is seen as the politics of rule whereby the First World continues to dominate the poor countries of the Third World, just as it continues to deplete the ozone layer and the exhaustible resources of nature. Development' has thus become a subtle way of promoting underdevelopment and perpetuating the hegemony of the advanced nations over the others in the periphery, and thus is just another name for domination and perpetual inequality. In the words

59. Ibid., 151.
60. Ibid., 151–52.
61. Cormie, "Genesis of a New World," 125.
62. Ibid.

of the post-developmentalist theorist, A. Escobar, "Development was—and continues to be for the most part—a top-down ethnocentric and technocratic approach, which treated people and cultures as abstract concepts, statistical figures to be moved up and down in the charts of progress."[63] But globalization is instituted today mainly through global governance.

Global governance refers to the priority given to managing the world economy as a singular entity. The IMF and the World Bank began this process of global governance by imposing structural adjustment programmes and by deregulating the global money market. The consequence of globalization is the shift in sovereignty from national governments to corporate organizations which become more powerful than their host governments, assuming more of a governing role. As McMichael succinctly observes:

> Liberalization *downgrades* the social goals of national government, while *upgrading* participation in the world economy (tariff reduction, export promotion, financial deregulation, relaxation of foreign investment rules). Together, these policies reformulated development as a global project—implemented through liberalized states incorporated into a world market constructed by transnational banks and firms, informatics, and multilateral institutions dedicated to a vision of corporate globalization.[64]

With the creation of WTO in 1995, the stage was finally set to undermine the sovereignty of nation-states, for the member states could choose to discipline a state trying to protect its trade through imposing heavy taxation on some other of its products or exports. This is true of all the aspects of WTO like "the Agreement on Agriculture (AoA), Trade-Related Investment Measures (TRIMs), Trade-Related Aspects of Intellectual Property Rights (TRIPs), and the General Agreement on Trade in Services (GATS)."[65] For instance, the AoA's deregulation of the global market for agricultural products has affected farmers of the third world since the universal reductions in trade protection, farm subsidies, and government intervention flooded the countries of the southern hemisphere with cheap farm produce from the rich countries of the north whose farmers are subsidized. Once again, "free trade" is more about consolidating a corporate food regime than truly freeing trade and making it equitable. In terms of trade and investment, AoA does not take into consideration the economic imbalance

63. Escobar, *Encountering Development*, 44.
64. McMichael, *Development and Social Change*, 158.
65. Ibid., 169.

and inability to compete colonial governments left African nations and which still continues in various forms of economic dependence. Thus as Giovanni Arrighi observes, "In the late 1970s, Sub-Saharan Africa was ... at a disadvantage in the incipient competitive struggle, not just because of its structural shortage of flexible and low-cost labour supplies, but also because of the sparsity of local entrepreneurial strata capable of mobilizing profitably whatever flexible and low-cost labour supplies existed."[66] TRIMs' attempt to reduce what GATS calls "performance requirements" demanded by host governments on foreign investments means that the foreign investors are free to do whatever they like in terms of investing and hiring staff. They are not required to invest locally, hire locally or train people in the technology they use. TRIPs aim at protecting intellectual property rights of primarily the global North, especially in its production of CDs, digital media, watches, etc. They define intellectual property rights as "rights given to persons over the creations of their minds."[67] They usually give the creator an exclusive right over the use of his/her creation for a certain period of time. But what has happened is that many of the patents are held by scientists in rich countries.[68] According to Philip McMichael:

> Patents on biological wealth give patent holders exclusive control over the use of the genetic materials. Corporations have often patented genetic material obtained from a Southern country without payment or obligation, turned it into a commodity such as medicine, and then charging a fee for use of the genetic resource in local production or high prices for the commodity—even to the country where the material originated, often for centuries.[69]

Thus TRIPs commodifies natural endowments and resources. GATS seeks to open up for corporate institutions unlimited markets for delivery of services in the areas of finance, telecommunications and transportation without restriction by the government and often without regard to the environmental hazards on the people of the host country. "In other words," Philip McMichael asserts: "GATS threatens to replace the social contract between state and citizen with a private contract between corporation and consumer. . . . In this proposal, we see the elimination of all vestiges of

---

66. Arrighi, "African Crisis," 29.
67. McMichael, *Development and Social Change*, 174.
68. Ibid., 175.
69. Ibid.

the development state and its replacement by corporate services globally."[70] For instance, eligibility for 'The African Growth and Opportunity Act,' or AGOA approved by the United States Congress in May of 2000 to assist the economies of Sub-Saharan Africa and to improve economic relations between the United States and the region considers first United States strategic interests a major factor in its decisions. According to Abdul Karim Bangura, "The major objective of the Act is to encourage African countries to make continual progress toward establishing the following aspects: market-based economies; the rule of law and political pluralism; elimination of barriers to United States trade and investment; protection of intellectual property; efforts to combat corruption; policies to reduce poverty, increasing availability of health care and educational opportunities; protection of human rights and worker rights; and elimination of certain child labor practices,"[71] Careful analysis of the implementation of the aims and objectives of AGOA by analysts indicates that the legislation "does not protect workers, human rights, or the environment; it infringes upon the sovereignty of African nations; it unfairly discriminates against other developing countries; and it would lead to exploitation by multinational corporations and foreign investors."[72] It is interesting to note that AGOA is drawn by the United States of America with little involvement of Africans in its preparation. A further list of criticisms against it indicate that it indirectly exploits Africa especially Africans of the Sub-Saharan region.[73]

However, our concern here is not so much with the effects of globalization as on investigating its institution. But as a theme in the contemporary discourse on development, economic globalization's emphasis on market economy, the importance of profit and its insistence on neo-liberal capitalist principles has adverse effects on the political, social, cultural, religious and even economic life and well-being of people. Thus, favouring globalization and reframing development as the deepening of markets negatively impacts people — vulnerable citizens unable to participate or compete in markets. Moreover, both the structural adjustment programme's reduction of government expenditures and the withdrawal of subsidies affect social reproduction in many ways. It changes the dynamics of governance for national governments as they give up part of their sovereignty to the

---

70. Ibid., 179.
71. Bangura, "Time Series Analysis," 31–32.
72. Ibid., 33.
73. See literature review on AGOA in ibid., 34–35.

transnational corporations. This is all too clear in the economic globalization of today. Lee Cormie sums up the adverse effects of globalization thus:

> For those with eyes to see and ears to hear, the signs are everywhere. Democracy is being strangled as power is transferred from governments to the executive suites of private corporations, corporate associations, institutes, think tanks, coalitions, international financial institutions, and bond-rating agencies. More and more, life is being commercialized and subjected to the single logic of private profit. Wondrous capacities for global collaboration and the advancement of knowledge and technology are being skewed in the interests of corporate power. Even in rich countries the middle class is shrinking, and everywhere gaps between rich and poor are growing… And globalization in the spirit of neo-liberalism appears even more clearly as a declaration of a global "war on the poor."[74]

In the face of such adverse effects of globalization, authentic human development is stunted.

Sustainable Development

The concept of 'sustainable development' "gained currency"[75] following the Bruntland Report (1987), titled *Our Common Future* and published by the World Commission on Environment and Development headed by Mrs. Gro Harlem Bruntland under the aegis of the United Nations in 1988.[76] According to Gilbert Rist, the term "Sustainable Development" had already been used at a United Nations Seminar in 1979 and in a study jointly sponsored in 1980 by the IUCN (International Union for the Conservation of Nature and Natural Resources): *World Conservation Strategy: Limiting Resources Conservation for Sustainable Development.*[77] The Commission, (World Commission on Environment and Development) considering the environment and development together, proposed the concept of 'Sustainable Development' thus:

---

74. Cormie, "Genesis of a New World: Globalization from Above vs. Globalization from Below," 125–26.
75. McMichael, *Development and Social Change*, 240.
76. World Commission on Environment and Development, *Our Common Future*.
77. See Rist, *History of Development*, 180.

> Humanity has the ability to make development sustainable—to ensure that it meets the needs of the present without compromising the ability of future generations to meet their own needs. The concept of sustainable development does imply limits—not absolute limits but limitations imposed by the present state of technology and social organization on environmental resources and by the ability of the biosphere to absorb the effects of human activities. But technology and social organization can be both managed and improved to make way for a new era of economic growth. The commission believes that widespread poverty is no longer inevitable. Poverty is not only an evil in itself, but sustainable development requires meeting the basic needs of all and extending to all the opportunity to fulfill their aspirations for a better life. A world in which poverty is endemic will always be prone to ecological and other catastrophes.[78]

The context of the Commission's report was the adverse effects of industrial productions [synonymous with 'development'] on the environment. They believe that natural resources are not inexhaustible and that industrialization depletes those resources in such a way that if it is not checked, future generations and human civilizations are at risk. Yet the Commission was faced with the reality of poverty and the need for continued emphasis on economic growth in order to reduce the pressure poverty puts on the environment in people's quest for survival. The Commission therefore suggested such steps as "conserving and enhancing natural resources, encouraging grassroots involvement in development, and adopting appropriate technologies (smaller scale, energy conserving)."[79] Both the admirers and the critics of the Brundtland Report acknowledge its good intentions but recognize its inability to sustain the environment in that it still emphasizes economic growth and modernization theories for development. As articulated by Rist:

> The Brundtland Report is not short on good intentions, but the positions it tries to argue are so vague that—despite a number of valuable statistical contributions—it hardly offers a new way of looking at the problem. For what is the point of denouncing the fact that 'economics and ecology can interact destructively and trip into disaster' if it is only to reaffirm that 'what is needed now is a new era of economic growth—growth that is forceful and at the

---

78. World Commission on Environment and Development, *Our Common Future*, 8.
79. McMichael, *Development and Social Change*, 240.

same time socially and environmentally sustainable?' Of course, this growth will be different from today's and less profligate with energy, but the Report has nothing to say about how to achieve it; most of the time, *it merely exposes a hope that the necessary will become possible.*[80]

However, the suggestion of the Brundtland Report for "an international conference… to review progress and promote follow-up arrangements that will be needed over time to set benchmarks and to maintain human progress with the guidelines of human needs and natural laws,"[81] was fulfilled in 1992. "More than a hundred heads of State and thousands of delegates from all over the world (including representatives of a thousand NGOs) assembled in Rio de Janeiro June 3-14 1992 to take part in the United Nations' conference on Environment and Development (UNCED), the 'Earth Summit'…"[82] Their aim was to reconcile the issues of the environment with that of 'development.' The conference produced five documents: 'The Rio Declaration,' also called the 'Earth Charter'; 'The Convention on Climate Change'; 'The Convention on Biodiversity'; 'A Declaration on the Forest'; and 'Agenda 21.' It developed further the idea of sustainable development through its declarations which cajoled nations to reduce their patterns of consumption that conflict with sustainable development. The Rio Conference was followed in 2002 by another, albeit lower profile conference, the World Summit on Sustainability in Johannesburg. Further attempts at managing the environment and sustaining planetary resources from extreme depletion due to carbon gas emission resulted in such international treaties as the Kyoto Protocol (1997) and the United Nations Framework Convention on Climate Change (UNFCCC or FCCC). Both aimed at combating global warming by reducing greenhouse gas concentrations in the atmosphere.

Further negotiations for the increased reduction of greenhouse gas emissions continue in various circles among world leaders. For instance, two years of tough and sometimes bitter negotiations brought together 192 world leaders for the Climate Change Summit in Copenhagen, Denmark in December 6-18, 2009. Yvo de Boer, the UN's top climate official, commended the summit and saw it as unprecedented: "Never in the 17 years

---

80. Rist, *History of Development*, 183.

81. World Commission on Environment and Development, *Our Common Future*, 343.

82. Rist, *History of Development*, 188.

of climate negotiations have so many different nations made so many firm pledges together.... It's simply unprecedented."[83] In order to draw attention to the importance of action on climate change, 50 newspapers in 45 countries speaking with one voice in some 20 languages in an unanimous editorial stated that "unless effective action is taken immediately to tackle climate change our planet as we know it is doomed."[84]

As one of the themes of the contemporary discourse on development, the concept of sustainable development is linked to development since it is triggered by a particular conception of development as the increase in industrial productions with the aim of increasing economic growth. 'Sustainable' here ordinarily means 'durable,' that is, the durability of the earth's resources in view of the increased tapping of its resources arising from increased industrial production and the effect of carbon emissions which can be devastating to creation and the entire environment. The environmental hazards of the oil spill at the Gulf of Mexico April 20, 2010 considered "the largest accidental oil spill in history"[85] and the ecological disaster in different parts of the world like the fifty years of oil spillage in the Niger Delta area of Nigeria[86] are examples of the effects of environmental pollution and reinforces the need for sustainability of any form of development. Thus, sustainable here also implies replenishing the resources of the planet in the midst of industrial production. The dilemma of sustainable development is the need to overcome poverty through increased industrial production, especially since the planet Earth cannot sustain or continue the rate of industrial production because it depletes the ozone layer. The president of the World Bank, Robert Zoellick, in noting the strains in multilateralism admits this in a speech on the new world economy: "Developing countries need support and finance to invest in cleaner growth paths. 1.6 billion people lack access to electricity. The challenge is to support transitions to cleaner energy without sacrificing access, productivity, and growth that can pull hundreds of millions out of poverty."[87]

83. *Toronto Star*, December 7, 2009, A6.

84. Ibid.

85. *The New York Times*, Wednesday, August 25, 2010. See http://topics.nytimes.com/top/reference/timestopics/subjects/o/oil_spills/gulf_of_mexico_2010/index.html

86. See Idemudia, "Corporate Social Responsibility," for further treatment of the effects of oil spillage on the Niger Delta peoples of Nigeria.

87. Zoellick, "End of the Third World? Modernizing Multilateralism for a Multipolar World."

Evidently the concept of sustainable development divides development economists, ecologists, social justice NGOs, and the northern and southern hemispheres. Its importance lies in the fact that development will not be possible if the earth is not sustained and if its resources are tapped in such a way that they cannot be replenished. Our interest is not with these competing conceptions of sustainable development but rather with noting its importance and the debate it has engendered in the contemporary discourse on development. One can no longer talk of development without evaluating the planet's ability to sustain, to carry through the type of increased industrial production development economic growth demands.

Notions of Development in Catholic Social Teaching

Modern Catholic social teaching, which began with *Rerum Novarum* (1891), the groundbreaking encyclical of Leo XIII, has concerned itself with societal development and transformation. Subsequent pontiffs, particularly during celebrations of the encyclical's anniversaries, have updated, revised and/or developed the insights of *Rerum Novarum* in response to the changing social, economic and political conditions of their times. Catholic social teaching on development forms part of the contemporary discourse on development.[88] In the words of John A. Coleman, "… Social Catholicism represents a serious and often distinguished tradition of investigation into the social significance of the modern nation state, economy, and the conditions of interdependence among nations which foster or impede war and human and integral development."[89] Let us then examine some of the themes on development in select principles and documents of Catholic social teaching.

---

88. This is true of Pius XI's *Quadragesimo Anno* (1931) which urges reconstruction of the social order in the context of the economic depression and economic monopoly of the 1930s. The same is true of John XXIII's *Mater et Magistra* (1961) in the context of the postwar, post-colonial welfare state; of Paul VI's *Populorum Progressio* (1967) on the issue of development in the Third World; of John Paul II's major social encyclicals: *Laborem Exercens* (1981), *Solicitudo Rei Socialis* (1981) and *Centesimus Annus* (1991) and also of Benedict XVI's *Caritas in Veritate* (2009).

89. Coleman, ed., *One Hundred Years of Catholic Social Thought*, 4–5.

Integral Human Development

Based on the theological and anthropological presupposition, which teaches that human persons have intrinsic dignity that must be respected because they are created in the image and likeness of God, Catholic social teaching calls for an integral human development. This means that development has to cater to all aspects of human life, personal, social, economic, political, and religious, and help the human person realize his/her potential as well as promote social well-being.

In his encyclical *Populorum Progressio* [On the Development of Peoples], Paul VI did not abandon the idea of wealth redistribution as one of the ways to address world poverty. Although he accepted the idea of economic growth as another way of doing this by greater productivity, he added the concept of integral development, implying that development must be holistic. As he states: "The development We speak of here cannot be restricted to economic growth alone. To be authentic, it must be well rounded; it must foster the development of each man and of the whole man."[90] The development that is integral, the Pope asserts, implies not only economic growth, but equally a growth in human values in line with the human life each person has as a vocation. This means "becoming more a person, being more, rather than having more."[91] Thus he prioritized not economic growth but, within economic growth, a growth that furthers humanity broadly understood. Quoting from the work of the French Dominican priest Louis-Joseph Lebret, *Dynamique concrète du dévelopement*,[92] Paul VI wrote: "We cannot allow economics to be separated from human realities, nor development from the civilization in which it takes place. What counts for us is man— each individual man, each human group, and humanity as a whole."[93] Thus, as one commentator on *Populorum Progressio*, Allan Figueroa Deck, states, Paul VI's concept of integral human development "adds key elements to the notion of economic development: concerns regarding culture, the family, human rights and dignity and the effect on the environment."[94]

---

90. Pope Paul VI, *Populorum Progressio*; Gremillion, *Gospel of Peace and Justice*, 387–415. See also Pope Benedict XVI's encyclical *Caritas in Veritate*, 30.

91. *Populorum Progressio*, 15.

92. Lebret, *Dynamique concrète du dévelopement*, 28.

93. *Populorum Progressio*, 14.

94. Deck, "Commentary on *Populorum Progressio*," 305.

The pope's definition of what he entitled 'authentic development'[95] as he himself goes on to explain, includes social progress as well as economic growth: "when we speak of development, we should mean social progress as well as economic growth."[96] By social progress, Paul VI understands 'personal responsibility' and communal progress, i.e., personal fulfilment in accordance with God's plan for each person as intelligent and rational beings[97] and the development of human society nationally and globally.[98]

In order to work for social progress, development must be founded on a proper range of values. The pursuit of the necessities of life must not be allowed to lead to greed, to an acquisitive tendency of unrelenting desire for more wealth or greater personal power.[99] Authentic development must guarantee higher values of love and friendship, of prayer and contemplation.[100] As Paul VI says, "This is what will guarantee man's authentic development—his transition from less than human conditions to truly human ones."[101] Thus, development as Paul VI continues to argue, gives humankind "the capacity, in the sphere of temporal realities, to improve their lot, to further their moral growth and to develop their spiritual endowments."[102] This type of development leads to truly human conditions.[103] Thus to be authentic development, the range of values must include the necessities of life, good social order, culture, personal responsibility and respect for religion.

On the other hand, economic growth made possible by the introduction of industrialization makes for human progress and is both a sign and a spur of development.[104] However, to advance authentic development, economic growth must not be divorced from the fabric of society. It must not be made to stand on its own, making the pursuit of profit, competition and private ownership supreme without due regard to its obligations to social progress.[105] Thus, Paul VI warns against what he calls "unbridled

---

95. *Populorum Progressio*, 14.
96. Ibid., 34.
97. Ibid., 15.
98. Ibid., 17.
99. Ibid., 18.
100. Ibid., 20.
101. Ibid.
102 Ibid., 34.
103. Ibid., 21.
104. Ibid., 25.
105. Ibid., 26.

liberalism" which "present[s] profit as the chief spur to economic progress, free competition as the guiding norm of economics, and private ownership of the means of production as an absolute right, having no limits nor concomitant social obligations."[106] Paul VI reiterates that economic growth and technological inventions must be for the good of human beings:

> It is not enough to increase the general fund of wealth and then distribute it more fairly. It is not enough to develop technology so that the earth may become a more suitable living place for human beings... Economics and technology are meaningless if they do not benefit man, for it is he they are to serve. Man is truly human only if he is the master of his own actions and the judge of their worth, only if he is the architect of his own progress. He must act according to his God-given nature, freely accepting its potentials and its claims upon him.[107]

We have dwelt more on Paul VI's *Populorum Progressio* because it is the social encyclical that deals most explicitly on the issue of development and because of its consonance with Lonergan's integral scale of values to be addressed later. Subsequently, many other social encyclicals written in celebration of its anniversary updated, revised and brought it forward in light of the changing social, economic and political situations of their times. For instance, John Paul II's encyclical *Solicitudo Rei Socialis* [*On Social Concern*] (1987) is a reflection on Paul VI's *Populorum Progressio*. In *Solicitudo Rei Socialis* John Paul II points to the two decades of development following the initial optimism by many that the poor countries could be lifted from poverty by financial and technological aid. He was aiming at the provision for infrastructures as recommended by Paul VI in *Populorum Progressio*. John Paul II worries that the situation of the world as regards development has deteriorated. According to him, this is evidenced in "the reality of an innumerable multitude of people—children, adults and the elderly—in other words, real and unique human persons, who are suffering under the intolerable burden of poverty."[108] Variously, he described integral development as "the development of the whole person and of every human being."[109] He warned that authentic development does not consist merely in possession of goods or the abundance of material things. On the contrary,

---

106. Ibid.
107. Ibid., 34.
108. Pope John Paul II, *Solicitudo Rei Socialis*, 13.
109. Ibid., 32.

whatever goods are available must be subordinate to the transcendent nature of human beings.[110]

John Paul II's contribution to the theme of social development was his emphasis following Paul VI on the moral character of development – the connection between authentic development and the respect for human rights. He asserts:

> When individuals and communities do not see a rigorous respect for the moral, cultural and spiritual requirements, based on the dignity of the person and on the proper identity of each community, beginning with the family and religious societies, then all the rest—availability of goods, abundance of technical resources applied to daily life, a certain level of material wellbeing, will prove unsatisfying and in the end contemptible.[111]

Moreover, to further authentic development, economic growth must not be disconnected from its social obligations:

> Development which is merely economic is incapable of setting man free; on the contrary, it will end by enslaving him further. Development that does not include the cultural, transcendent and religious dimensions of man and society, to the extent that it does not recognize the existence of such dimensions and does not endeavour to direct its goals and priorities towards the same, is even less conducive to authentic liberation. Human beings are totally free only when they are completely themselves, in the fullness of their rights and duties. The same can be said about society as a whole.[112]

Pope Benedict XVI's encyclical *Caritas in Veritate: On Integral Human Development in Charity and Truth,* building on *Populorum Progressio,*[113] emphasizes the need for love as a manifesto towards an integral human development in a globalizing age.[114] He states: "In the present social and cultural context, where there is a widespread tendency to relativize truth, practising charity in truth helps people to understand that adhering to the values of Christianity is not merely useful but essential for building a

---

110. Ibid., 29.
111. Ibid., 33.
112. Ibid., 46.
113. Benedict XVI, *Caritas in Veritate,* 8
114. He emphasized that "Development needs above all to be true and integral." Ibid., 23.

good society and for true integral human development."¹¹⁵ Thus, charity in truth, "…is the principal driving force behind the authentic development of every person and of all humanity."¹¹⁶ He sees love as an extraordinary force without which human beings would have neither social conscience nor social responsibility. Their action in society would promote only their self-interest and will result in social fragmentation.¹¹⁷ Love promotes social development by integrating economic growth with social progress. Consequently, the Pope teaches, the Church should be unrelenting in emphasizing the place of love in social development as it opens up human beings towards the reciprocity of consciences and liberties.¹¹⁸ He beautifully sums up *Populorum Progressio*'s contribution to the development discourse thus:

> Paul VI had an *articulated vision of development*. He understood the term to indicate the goal of rescuing peoples, first and foremost, from hunger, deprivation, endemic diseases and illiteracy. From the economic point of view, this meant their active participation, on equal terms, in the international economic process; from the social point of view, it meant their evolution into educated societies marked by solidarity; from the political point of view, it meant the consolidation of democratic regimes capable of ensuring freedom and peace.¹¹⁹

By this statement Pope Benedict meant a development that is not merely economic and technological but one that also promotes moral, cultural and religious well-being.

In sum, by emphasizing integral human development, Catholic social teaching envisions development that serves human well-being, development whereby economic growth is not disassociated from social progress. It is a notion of development that, while recognizing the importance of profit, sees it as serving the common good. It is a notion of development that, while acknowledging the place of the market, finance and growth arising from various processes of production, notes the importance of human relationships and values underlying the entire economic process. Therefore, it urges that authentically social relationships of friendship, fraternity and solidarity can take place within the economic activity not "outside" it

115. Ibid., 4.
116. Ibid., 1.
117. Ibid., 5.
118. Ibid., 9.
119. Ibid., 21.

or "after" it.[120] This is true also of globalization which should not be seen deterministically as merely economic process. As Benedict XVI teaches in *Caritas in Veritate*:

> The truth of globalization as a process and its fundamental ethical criterion are given by the unity of the human family and its development towards what is good. Hence a sustained commitment is needed so as to *promote a person-based and community-oriented cultural process of world-wide integration that is open to transcendence.*[121]

Integral Human development therefore invites one to privilege not the economic dimension of development above its cultural, psychological, ecological, political and religious dimensions. Integral or integrated human development is a development that considers all these dimensions as important and seeks to realize them.

The Principle of Common Good

Catholic social teaching bases its principle of the universal destination of earth's goods, its principle of solidarity and its principle of the common good on its position that the human person, the subject of the social teaching, lives his/her life fully in community. Addressing participants in the plenary assembly of the Pontifical Academy of Social Sciences (2008) on the theme: "Pursuing the common good: how solidarity and subsidiarity can work together," Benedict XVI explains how solidarity and subsidiarity can work together in the pursuit of the common good in such a way that they not only respect human dignity, but allow it to flourish:

> We can initially sketch the interconnections between these four principles by placing the dignity of the person at the intersection of two axes: one horizontal, representing 'solidarity' and 'subsidiarity', and one vertical, representing the 'common good.' This creates a field upon which we can plot the various points of Catholic social teaching that give shape to the common good.[122]

---

120. Ibid., 36.
121. Ibid., 42.
122. Vatican Information Service, "Pope Benedict XVI." Cf. http://www.catholic.org/international/international_story

Thus, by the principle of the common good, Catholic social teaching emphasizes that social orders and social institutions are to promote the good of all the members of the community. The rights and duties of each person draw from and contribute to the good of all. Against an overemphasis on individual rights, through the principle of the common good, Catholic social teaching stresses that the conditions of social life should allow social groups and their individual members access to their own fulfillment. In other words, since human beings must live in community, the social order must be such that they are enabled to fulfill themselves. Every person is responsible for the common good and ought to contribute to it according to each person's ability. The Pontifical Council for Justice and Peace states: "*The common good therefore involves all members of society, no one is exempt from cooperating, according to each one's possibilities, in attaining it and developing it.*"[123] In the same vein, "*Everyone also has the right to enjoy the conditions of social life that are brought about by the quest for the common good.*"[124]

All members of a community are to contribute to the community's well-being. All are expected to draw from the community resources for a dignified living. This is true of the rich and of the poor. Nobody is to be left wanting. Just as through the principle of subsidiarity all members of community are not to be impeded from contributing to their societal development, through the principle of solidarity members of a community are interdependent of each other in fulfilling the common good. The principle of the common good thus demands having the social systems, institutions and environments on which we all depend work in a manner that benefits all people. Pope John XXIII succinctly describes the common good as "the sum total of conditions of social living, whereby persons are enabled more fully and readily to achieve their own perfection."[125] In the same vein, *Gaudium et Spes* defines the common good as "the sum total of social conditions which allow people, either as groups or as individuals, to reach their fulfillment more fully and more easily."[126] This is true of the technological infrastructure, of the economy and of the social-cultural and political institutions of a community, state and nation. Examples of particular common

---

123. Pontifical Council for Justice and Peace, *Compendium of the Social Doctrine of the Church*, 73. Henceforth, to be known as *The Compendium*.

124. Ibid., 74.

125. Pope John XXIII, *Mater et Magistra*, 65.

126. *Gaudium et Spes*, 26.

goods or parts of the common good include an accessible and affordable public health care system, an effective system of public safety and security, peace among the nations of the world, a just legal and political system, an unpolluted natural environment and a flourishing economic system. The Pontifical Council for Justice and Peace classifies as belonging to the common good similar social conditions:

> The commitment to peace, the organization of the State's powers, a sound juridical system, the protection of the environment, and the provision of essential services to all, some of which are at the same time human rights: food, housing, work, education and access to culture, transportation, basic health care, the freedom of communication and expression, the protection of religious freedom.[127]

The principle of common good applies not only nationally but also internationally guiding the imperative of seeking the common good of humanity and of the environment upon which human life, progress and development depends. According to John Paul II, the principle of the common good guides not only the relations of people within a nation but also such international issues of relations as the problem of global governance:

> The increasing internationalization of the economy ought to be accompanied by effective international agencies which will oversee and direct the economy to the common good, something that an individual State, even if it were the most powerful on earth, would not be in a position to do. In order to achieve this result, it is necessary that in evaluating the consequences of their decisions, these agencies always give sufficient support and consideration to peoples and countries which have little weight in the international market, but which are burdened by the most acute and desperate needs, and are thus more dependent on support for their development.[128]

Benedict XVI underscores the protection of the principle of the common good in the encyclical *Caritas in Veritate* (2009), urging the establishment of a "world political authority" to oversee the economy and work for the "common good."[129] In his address to the United Nations 2008 he asserts:

---

127. *The Compendium*, 73.
128. *Centesimus Annus*, 58.
129. Donadio and Goodstein, "Pope Urges Forming New World Economic Order to Work for the 'Common Good.'"

Themes in Contemporary Development Discourse

Indeed, questions of security, development goals, reduction of local and global inequalities, protection of the environment, of resources and of the climate, require all international leaders to act jointly and to show a readiness to work in good faith, respecting the law, and promoting solidarity with the weakest regions of the planet.[130]

As a theme in contemporary development discourse, the principle of the common good anticipates societal development and transformation aiming at the good and well-being of every human being. It interprets human actions as directed towards the attainment of this human good not only for oneself but for the benefit of others as well. Social progress and economic growth for the principle of the common good can only be assessed from the purview of its promotion of human flourishing, human well-being and happiness.

Universal Destination of the Earth's Goods

In *Quadragesimo Anno* (1931), Pius XI warned against what he called "two dangerous unilateral positions." These positions result from the denial or weakening of the social function of property, on the one hand, and the function of the individual, on the other. These opposed positions lead either to individualism or collectivism.[131] This is the problem the *principle of the universal destination of earth's goods* as a notion of development confronts. There is the danger both of emphasizing the universal destination of goods to the extent that it denies the right to private property and conversely emphasizing the right to private property in such an absolute sense that the universal destination of earth's goods does not apply. For instance, Leo XIII in *Rerum Novarum*[132] emphasizes the right to personal property against socialism which, with Karl Marx, viewed private property as the source of human alienation and social disparity. Pius XI, seeking to balance Leo XIII's position, warns against either extreme of individualism or collectivism. In the light of the story of creation, Paul VI in *Populorum Progressio*, interprets the principle of the universal destination of the earth's

---

130. Benedict XVI, "Apostolic Journey to the United States of America."
131. Pope Pius XI, *Quadragesimo Anno*, 46.
132. Pope Leo XIII, *Rerum Novarum*, 4.

goods as the foundation of all other human rights "including the rights of property and free trade."[133]

Catholic social teaching bases the principle of the universal destination of the earth's goods on the doctrine of creation. Since God is the creator of all things, all the earth's goods are for human well-being. Therefore, every human being is entitled to benefit from the resources of the earth for self-fulfilment as individuals and as members of communities. As an aspect of the principle of the common good, the principle of the universal destination of the earth's goods entitles all human beings the right to the earth's resources. According to the *Compendium of the Social Doctrine of the Church*:

> This is *the foundation of the universal destination of the earth's goods*. The earth, by reason of its fruitfulness and its capacity to satisfy human needs, is God's first gift for the sustenance of human life. The human person cannot do without the material goods that correspond to his primary needs and constitute the basic conditions for his existence; these goods are absolutely indispensable if he is to feed himself, grow, communicate, associate with others, and attain the highest purposes to which he is called.[134]

The universal destination of the earth's goods is a natural right, innate in humankind by virtue of being created by God, for the resources of the earth are God's gift to humankind to realize itself. Therefore, "each person must have access to the level of well-being necessary for his full development."[135]

The universal destination of earth's goods is not aimed at supplanting the right to private property. On the contrary, private ownership of property is an exercise of the universal destination of the earth's goods. It is an exercise of human intelligence and freedom.[136] Private ownership of property as the fruit of human labour and one of the ways by which human beings make the earth their own is a human right.[137] As John Paul II beautifully clarifies:

> God gave the earth to the whole human race for the sustenance of all its members, without excluding or favouring anyone. This is *the*

---

133. *Populorum Progressio*, 22. He taught that charity to the poor is obligatory. See, *Populorum Progressio*, 23.
134. *The Compendium*, 171.
135. Ibid., 172.
136. See *Gaudium et Spes*, # 69,. *Centesimus Annus*, #30.
137. *The Compendium*, 176.

> *foundation of the universal destination of the earth's goods...* But the earth does not yield its fruits without a particular human response to God's gift, that is to say, without work. It is through work that man, using his intelligence and exercising his freedom, succeeds in dominating the earth and making it a fitting home. In this way, he makes part of the earth his own, precisely the part which he has acquired through work; this is *the origin of individual property.* Obviously, he also has the responsibility not to hinder others from having their own part of God's gift; indeed, he must cooperate with others so that together all can dominate the earth.[138]

So, the right to the ownership of private property should never become absolute but must always be subordinated to the universal destination of earthly goods.[139] As the Pastoral Constitution *Gaudium et Spes* warns: "God destined the Earth with all that it contains to the benefit of all people and nations" and therefore "these created goods must be used by all in a fair proportion."[140]

As a notion of development, the principle of the universal destination of the earth's goods will always be referred to by the Catholic social teaching in its assessment of the moral implication of development paradigms or economic theories.[141] For instance, based on the universal destination of the earth's goods, John Paul II in *Centesimus Annus* proposed a Christian ethic of society that guarantees the satisfaction of the basic needs of human beings in a society while at the same time respecting human dignity. He advocates for *"A society of free work, of enterprise and of participation.... directed against the market, but demands that the market be appropriately controlled by the forces of society and by the State, so as to guarantee that the basic needs of the whole of society are satisfied, while at the same time respecting the environment.*[142]

---

138. *Centesimus Annus,* 31.

139. John Paul II., *Laborem Exercens,* 14. Cf. http://www.vatican.va/holy_father/john_paul_ii/encyclicals/documents/hf_jp-ii_enc_14091981_laborem-exercens_en.html

140. *Gadium et Spes,* 69.

141. *The Compendium,* 175.

142. *Centesimus Annus,* 35, 37. (Citation italicized in the original).

The Principle of Solidarity

Paul VI's *Populorum Progressio* mentions the spirit of solidarity as one of the necessary conditions for development as he writes: "There can be no progress toward complete development of man without the simultaneous development of all humanity in the spirit of solidarity."[143] Solidarity is seen here as a response to the fact of human interdependence. Pope Benedict XVI equally shares this view in his encyclical *Caritas in Veritate* when he writes that solidarity should be seen "first and foremost as a sense of responsibility on the part of everyone with regard to everyone."[144] As Denis Goulet comments, solidarity within Paul VI's *Populorum Progressio* means "that perceptual and behavioural disposition that binds together the destines of all human persons, societies, and nations."[145] Thus because of the interdependence of peoples as brothers and sisters and as children of God, the wealthy nations must be concerned about the poorer ones. They must show their concern in practical ways through such acts as giving direct aid, establishing fairer trade relations, and seeing to it that no one marginalized is left behind as development advances.[146] Based on the principle of the common good that all people contribute to the good of the community, Catholic social teaching emphasizes not only the profits of solidarity but also its responsibilities. Each person should therefore participate towards the development of the human community as a whole.

John Paul II stressed the principle of solidarity in the encyclical *Solicitudo Rei Socialis* (1987) and linked it with human development by emphasizing development within the framework of solidarity and freedom without ever sacrificing either of them under any conditions.[147] Solidarity here presupposes the personhood every human being share; the recognition of the dignity of each human being as created in the image of God. Second, it demands respect for one another as persons and collaboration with each other. Such collaboration promotes a relationship of equality between individuals and society. As John Paul II writes, "the exercise of solidarity within each society is valid when its members recognize one

---

143. *Populorum Progressio*, 43.
144. *Caritas in Veritate*, 38.
145. Goulet, "Search for Authentic Development," 135.
146. *Populorum Progressio*, 44.
147. *Solicitudo Rei Socialis*, 33.

another as persons."[148] Thus, for John Paul II, at the heart of the principle of solidarity is the recognition of the basic interdependence human beings have with each other. And this recognition, he says, distinguished Paul VI's *Populorum Progressio* from the standard Western concept of development in his time and therefore revealed its originality:

> ... The originality of the Encyclical [*Populorum Progressio*] also consists in the basic insight that the very concept of development, if considered in the perspective of universal interdependence, changes notably. True development cannot consist in the simple accumulation of wealth and in the greater availability of goods and services, if this is gained at the expense of the development of the masses, and without due consideration for the social, cultural and spiritual dimensions of the human being.[149]

According to the principle of solidarity, therefore, the measure of human development is not only individual self-interest but also the welfare of others. John Paul II made clear the radical interdependence of all peoples as linked by a common destiny.

The interdependence that is key to the principle of solidarity applies not just to persons but also to nations in their relations to one another. It is a fact that the coffee produced in Kenya is consumed by a large number of people in North America. In the same way, the value system of people in Kenya is equally influenced by television programs made in North America. Furthermore, the poor nations depend on the resources of rich nations just as the rich nations depend on the resources of the poor nations. Consequently, John Paul II stretched the respect for human personhood not only in the relations among human beings individually but also including the relations between nations internationally:

> The same criterion is applied by analogy in international relationships. Interdependence must be transformed into solidarity, based upon the principle that the goods of creation are meant for all... Surmounting every type of imperialism and determination to preserve their own hegemony, the stronger and richer nations must have a sense of moral responsibility for the other nations, so that a real international system may be established which will rest on

---

148. Ibid., 39.
149. Ibid., 9.

the foundation of the equality of all peoples and on the necessary respect for their legitimate differences.[150]

As a notion of development, therefore, the principle of solidarity in response to the fact of the interdependence of peoples binds all peoples together, not only to contribute to the common good, but also to benefit from the common good for their well-being. Development is authentic and integral if it promotes communion between persons, communities and their planet. On account of the principle of solidarity, the rich are bound to help the poor while the rich and the poor alike must contribute to the common good.

The Principle of Subsidiarity

The principle of solidarity as a notion of development in Catholic social teaching is closely related to the principle of subsidiarity based on the respect to be accorded each person on account of human dignity. The interdependence of peoples, responded to by the principle of solidarity, asks that each person have the opportunity to contribute to the common good. It is not respectful of human dignity to prevent people from expressing their membership in community by preventing them from participating fruitfully at any level in the life of their community. This is the principle of subsidiarity. As enunciated by Pius XI in *Quadragesimo Anno* (1931):

> Just as it is gravely wrong to take from individuals what they can accomplish by their own initiative and industry and give it to the community, so also it is an injustice and at the same time a grave evil and disturbance of right order to assign to a greater and higher association what lesser and subordinate organizations can do. For every social activity ought of its very nature to furnish help to the members of the body social, and never destroy and absorb them.[151]

Pius XI's principle follows his conviction that "all social activity should 'prove a help (*subsidium*) to the members of the body social,' but never may destroy or absorb them."[152] Therefore, in response to the interdependence of peoples arising from their common humanity, the human person must be respected and be allowed to make his/her contribution to the common good. The principle of subsidiarity thus lays out the role of the state and

---

150. Ibid., 39.
151. Pope Pius XI, *Quadragesimo Anno*.
152. Hinze, "Commentary on Quadragesimo Anno (After Forty Years)," 161.

its relation to its members. For instance, although the state exists for the purpose of the common good, "the human being is older than the state."[153] The state's power is therefore not absolute. Society is broader than the state, and a well-functioning society must employ all its different members. The state must not take over those roles that could be performed by the human person, the family and by lesser and subordinate bodies.

The importance of the principle of subsidiarity for contemporary development discourse becomes clearer when it is viewed in relation to such systems as the welfare state that denies the human person his/her rightful creativity and freedom and claims to do everything for them. In the centenary celebration of the encyclical *Rerum Novarum* (1891), John Paul II critiqued the emergence of the so-called Welfare State and re-emphasized the need for the state to respect the principle of subsidiarity:

> A community of a higher order should not interfere in the internal life of a community of a lower order, depriving the latter of its functions, but rather should support it in case of need and help to coordinate its activity with the activities of the rest of the society, always with a view to the common good.[154]

The principle of subsidiarity demands that all societies of a higher order should adopt an attitude of help (*subsidium*) – therefore of support, promotion and development – with respect to lower-order societies. The principle protects people from abuse by higher-level social authority and calls on these same authorities to help individuals and intermediate groups to fulfill their duties. For instance, this means that voluntary organizations should do all they can to help individuals and families do what they can and should only do what individuals and families cannot do themselves. In the same way, government should intervene to help voluntary organizations and groups and do only what voluntary associations cannot accomplish on their own. This allows every person and group to participate in and contribute to the common good. It is opposed to "certain forms of centralization [like totalitarianism], bureaucratization, and welfare assistance and to the unjustified and excessive presence of the State in public mechanisms."[155] Going back to an example we gave while exposing the principle of solidarity above, by the principle of subsidiarity, Kenyans, rather than some Western company, should profit from Kenya's own coffee production. No foreign financial aid

153. *Rerum Novarum*, 6, 10.
154. Pope John Paul II, *Centesimus Annus*, 48.
155. *The Compendium*, 82.

or any other assistance should rob people of their right to contribute to their common good. Another example of the principle of subsidiarity is the conception of the family as domestic church prominent in the Dogmatic Constitution on the Church (*Lumen Gentium*) in the transmission of the Catholic belief without interference by the state. "In what could be regarded as the domestic Church, the parents, by word and example, are the first heralds of the faith with regard to their children."[156]

By way of summary, our concern in this chapter has been to lay out themes in the contemporary discourse on development with the aim of preparing the ground for a dialogue with Lonergan's philosophical anthropology. The theories of development in secular scholarship, in spite of their diversity, commonly recognize the priority of economic growth in development discourse. While liberal capitalism opts for freedom of the market and modernization theory seeks to emphasize the various stages of development in the developing parts of the world, the dependent theorists are warning against the dangers of both the freedom of the market and generalizing the Western model of development. The reality of globalization, structurally complex, raises the bar on the variegated structure of development discourse. Whatever position one takes in this discourse, development must be sustainable. The resources of the planet must be respected and renewed if development is to continue. And so in the secular realm, development discourse does not speak with one voice. There is no unified accepted position on development, which perhaps explains why we have theories rather than rules of development.

With respect to Catholic social teaching, there is a response to the variegated theories of development. The official position of the Catholic Church is continuous with various Popes building upon and updating the position of their predecessors on development. On the whole, while acknowledging the importance of economic growth, and the need to overcome poverty, Catholic social teaching emphasizes social progress, social responsibility, the priority of the human person and human well-being. The human person-in-relationship remains the goal and the beneficiary of development.

The overarching concern of Catholic social teaching is ethical. Teaching from its rich corpus of Gospel values, especially that of love, it introduces into development discourse the elements of compassion, solidarity

---

156. Dogmatic Constitution of the Church (*Lumen Gentium*) #11, in *Vatican Council II*, ed. Austin Flannery, 330. See Pope John Paul II, *Familiaris Consortio*, #21, 39, 57–62.

and the interdependence of all peoples. In other words, it teaches that the iron laws of economics must be tempered with Christian love and compassion. Responsibility, it seems to be saying, must be taken to ensure that the human person is not objectified, that no development project or theory misplaces human dignity. Solidarity of all peoples places on the rich the responsibility of caring for the poor; the poor, on the other hand, must not fold their hands—they must contribute to the common good. All peoples and nations, wealthy and poor, must equally take responsibility for the earth. Through such principles as integral human development, solidarity, the universal destination of the earth's goods, Church documents confront secular theories of development with the idea that development should be integral; it must provide for the whole person and respect creation. Whereas the principles of Catholic social teaching address the lacunae in contemporary theories of development, there remains a need in Catholic theology for a theoretical bridge to bring the secular and ecclesiastical discourses together. Hence, the foregoing insights in this chapter provide a context for a dialogue between them and Lonergan's philosophical anthropology to which we now turn.

2

Lonergan's Philosophical Anthropology

SOCIAL TRANSFORMATION, ACCORDING TO Bernard Lonergan presupposes the personal integrity of persons in society realizing themselves as originating values aimed at the human good for themselves and for others. Lonergan, following a fellow Jesuit, Heinrich Pesch, whose views formed the theoretical basis of Pope Pius XI's encyclical *Quadragesimo Anno*, thinks that "the properly economic goal is the appropriate standard of living, the betterment of the material conditions of human existence."[1] For both Lonergan and Pesch, "economic activity provides the material substratum for the cultural creations of human ingenuity and aspiration."[2] Transformation and development occur insofar as people are attentive to their experiences, understand intelligently, judge reasonably and deliberate responsibly.[3] Thus Lonergan's philosophical anthropology provides a hermeneutic for understanding his thoughts on social development, breakdown and social transformation. For instance, in the lecture, "Natural Right and Historical Mindedness," Lonergan states that the concern of development is "with human understanding where developments originate . . . and more fundamentally with the generalized empirical method that underpins both scientific and historical method to supply philosophy with a basic cognitional theory, an epistemology, and by way of corollary with a metaphysics of proportionate being."[4]

---

1. "Editors Introduction," in Lonergan, *Macroeconomic Dynamics*, xxxi.
2. Ibid.
3. Lonergan, "Insight Revisited," 272.
4. Lonergan, "Natural Right and Historical Mindedness," 590.

This chapter on Lonergan's philosophical anthropology aims at exploring Lonergan's understanding of human beings as immanently constituted by the spirit of inquiry for understanding and motivated by value to do the good. It will, as Lonergan notes, unfold the philosophic implications of understanding and the campaign against the "flight from understanding" in the treatment of the various forms of the biases that effect human and social development. It will seek to explore Lonergan's three basic questions: ". . . what precisely is it to understand, what are the dynamics of the flow of consciousness that favors insight, what are the interferences that favor oversight, what, finally, do the answers to such questions imply for the guidance of human thought and action?"[5]

It will proceed by examining how human beings come to know through the generation of insight. Next, it will explore the implication of this structure of human knowing on genuine human living by the obedience to the transcendental precepts. This chapter will also include a treatment of common sense as practical both intersubjectively and in the social order of the dialectic of community, and their relation to what Lonergan calls the "flight from understanding." It will also examine Lonergan's suggestion of *cosmopolis* as the higher viewpoint in order to integrate and likewise resolve the dialectical distortions of community. As the failure to understand is not to be treated lightly, this chapter will also include Lonergan's treatment of moral impotence and its resolution through divine grace. It is hoped that the limits of development and possible exploration will provide a sufficient framework for the intended dialogue between Lonergan and other theories of development and principles of development in the Catholic social teachings studied earlier.

Insight and the Subject

This section of our work seeks to introduce Lonergan's philosophical anthropology from the perspective of the human subject. Presupposing Lonergan's conception of human beings as intrinsically intelligent, this section will treat such questions as how human beings come to know, what goes on in the human subject in the process of knowing and in the event of distortion how intelligence is restored in the human subject.

While acknowledging "the polymorphism of human consciousness as the one and only key to philosophy,"[6] and arguing that "consciousness

---

5. Lonergan, *Insight*, 9.
6. Ibid., 452.

streams in many patterns,"[7] Lonergan equally emphasizes the unity of human consciousness.[8] Accompanying this unity and distinguishing human beings from other animals, Lonergan says, is the directed spirit of inquiry which is commonly possessed by human beings.[9] He notes that human beings unrestrictedly desire to know. This refers to the orientation human beings have to inquire intelligently and to reflect reasonably.[10] This holds true from "... the incessant What? and Why? of childhood"[11] to the 'Eureka' of scientific discovery; from the slow and gradual process of learning to the accumulation of related insights. Thus, "... the man or woman of intelligence is marked by a greater readiness in catching on, in getting the point, in seeing the issue, in grasping implications, in acquiring knowhow."[12] Although human beings have this unrestricted detached desire to know, human capacity is restricted to incremental and cumulative knowledge of being—"the objective of the pure desire to know."[13] The understanding of understanding consists in grasping human 'acts of understanding.'[14] As a constituent factor in human knowledge, "insight into insight is in some sense a knowledge of knowledge,"[15] "the apprehension of meaning of meaning."[16] To be human among other things, is to acquire knowledge, to experience, to understand, to pass judgment on the truthfulness or fail to pass such judgment on what is understood and to deliberate on the choices of action open to one in freedom. As Lonergan states in *Method in Theology*:

> As intelligent, the subject seeks insight and, as insights accumulate, he reveals them in his behavior, his speech, his grasp of situations, his mastery of theoretic domains. But as reflectively and critically conscious, he incarnates detachment and disinterestedness, gives himself over to criteria of truth and certitude, makes his sole concern the determination of what is or is not so; and now, as the self, so also the awareness of self resides in that incarnation,

7. Lonergan, "On Being Oneself," 235.
8. Lonergan, *Insight*, 538. See also Lonergan, *Method in Theology*, 17.
9. Ibid., 196.
10. Ibid., 539.
11. Ibid., 197.
12. Ibid., 196.
13. Ibid., 372.
14. Ibid., 4
15. Ibid.
16. Ibid., 5.

that self-surrender, that single-minded concern for truth. There is a still further dimension to being human, and there we emerge as persons, meet one another in a common concern for values, seek to abolish the organization of human living on the basis of competing egoisms and to replace it by an organization on the basis of man's perceptiveness and intelligence, his reasonableness, and his responsible exercise of freedom.[17]

Furthermore, to be human is to be born into a community of shared meanings and values, of cultures and religions, and of a common pool of knowledge that guides one's navigation in life.[18] From this common fund of shared meanings, human beings develop, progress, and provide for their own well-being by contributing to the common good.

Let us proceed in this attempt at understanding how human beings come to know by examining how insight is generated since, as intelligent beings, we have a natural desire to know—a desire that is not restricted.

The Generation of Insight

In the preface to *Insight* Lonergan wrote that his work is an insight into insight.[19] And in Chapter 1 of the same book, using the example of Archimedes' discovery of the answer to the riddle of King Hiero's puzzle, he lists the five features of insight:

> What we have to grasp is that insight (1) comes as a release to the tension of inquiry, (2) comes suddenly and unexpectedly, (3) is a function not of outer circumstances but of inner conditions, (4) pivots between the concrete and the abstract, and (5) passes into the habitual texture of one's mind.[20]

This means as Lonergan goes on to explain in relation to progress and development, that insights are cumulative. One insight gives rise to another as it evokes further questions that refine the original insight or generate new insights.[21] Insights, correctly arrived at, complement, correct and enhance one another, forming, as they do so, what Lonergan calls "a viewpoint."[22]

17. *Method in Theology*, 10.
18. *Insight*, 198.
19. Ibid.
20. Ibid., 28.
21. Ibid., 197.
22. Ibid., 320; 493.

Viewpoint is the habitual accumulation of insight. For instance, as Lonergan illustrated in chapter 15 of *Insight,* from the data presented by sensible presentations and imaginative representations, insights emerge and are unified and correlated in concepts, thoughts, suppositions, considerations, definitions, postulates, hypothesis, theories. These give rise to further questions. But insights do not just coalesce; since they are creative, new insights arise from the established viewpoint giving rise to what Lonergan refers to as "the higher viewpoint."[23]

A higher viewpoint is a leap in development of intelligibility. Lonergan illustrates this with Jean Piaget's theory of the cognitive development of children.[24] In the formal operational stage when children develop the ability to abstract from the concrete and are able to use language and argue, they are said to have moved to a higher viewpoint from the lower viewpoints of the concrete operational stage. Higher viewpoints make it possible for one to understand things in different contexts. Higher viewpoints manifest the cumulative process of insight and show the connection between insight and progress. Lonergan writes:

> Thus, insight into insight brings to light the cumulative process of progress. For concrete situations give rise to insights which issue into policies and courses of action. Action transforms the existing situation to give rise to further insights, better policies, more effective courses of action. It follows that if insight occurs, it keeps recurring; and at each recurrence knowledge develops, action increases its scope, and situations improve.[25]

When the fruits of a constant accumulation of higher viewpoints are integrated into society they bring about the continued progress and development of peoples. For instance, the British Enlightenment that occurred during the 17th and 18th centuries was brought about by the accumulation of viewpoints of political-economic philosophers. Their ideas gave rise to scientific revolutions which in turn gave rise to technological innovations. These technological innovations were applied in the formerly disparate

---

23. Ibid., 37–38.

24. Philips, *Origins of Intellect in Piaget's Theory.* See Lonergan, *Method in Theology,* 29. See also Lonergan, *Early Works on Theological Method,* 3–8, on Lonergan's use of Piaget that explains higher viewpoint through differentiations of operations.

25. *Insight,* 8.

textile industries of England and thus gave rise to the Industrial Revolution of the 18th and early 19th centuries.[26] Thus, as Lonergan writes:

> Growth, progress, is a matter of situations yielding insights, insights yielding policies and projects, policies and projects transforming the initial situation, and the transformed situation giving rise to further insights that correct and complement the deficiencies of previous insights. So the wheel of progress moves forward through the successive transformations of an initial situation in which are gathered coherently and cumulatively all the insights that occurred along the way.[27]

Conversely, decline is a result of unintelligent understanding and unreasonable judgments, which, when persistent and cumulative, give rise to what Lonergan calls 'the shorter and the longer cycles of decline.' The flight from understanding blocks any insight that would make for progress and the bias obstructs the complete development of intelligence.[28]

In order to distinguish progress from decline, Lonergan suggests beginning "by asking what precisely it is to understand, what are the dynamics of the flow of consciousness that favors insight, what are the interferences that favor oversight, what, finally, do the answers to such questions imply for the guidance of human thought and action."[29] And so we treat next the dynamic structure of human knowing in order to understand the dynamics of the flow of consciousness that favours correct insights. Subsequently we shall treat of biases as the interferences that prevent insight. Still later we shall consider the implications of this for human thought and action for development.

The Dynamic Structure of Human Knowing

In the eleventh chapter of *Insight* titled "Self-affirmation of the Knower," Lonergan asks the reader to make a judgment about him/herself as a knower, where this means that one is a conscious unity-identity-whole whose consciousness operates on the three levels of experience, understanding and judgment, oriented toward inquiry by the unrestricted desire to know.[30]

26. Peet and Hartwick, *Theories of Development*, 29–30.
27. Lonergan, "Healing and Creating in History," 105.
28. *Insight*, 6.
29. Ibid., 9.
30. Ibid., 343.

After a lengthy argument he asserts: "I am a knower, if I am a concrete and intelligible unity-identity-whole, characterized by acts of sensing, perceiving, imagining, inquiring, understanding, formulating, reflecting, grasping the unconditioned, and judging."[31] Such an affirmation is based on dynamic levels of conscious operation that work together towards an understanding of being and reality.

Lonergan uses Aquinas's notion of abstraction (understanding one thing separately from another) as a springboard to the structure of human knowing. He writes about the act of abstraction—"understanding one thing separately from another"[32]—and correlates this with the act of comprehension—"the simultaneous grasp of those things that are understood."[33] Now things that are understood together, he says, exhibit a structure: "they are not understood separately one from another."[34] This notion of structure is true of something known, of the structure of knowing and of the structure of objectivity. The structure of the thing known is a composite of matter and form. As a finite being it is metaphysically made up of potency, form and act. The structure of human knowing is similarly a composite of experience, understanding and judgment. Neither of them alone constitutes knowing in the strict sense. The relation between knowledge and reality (objectivity of knowing) equally exhibit a structure: empirical, normative and absolute. In the sense of a whole in relation to its parts, the structure of human knowing is dynamic.[35] Human knowing is dynamic in two ways: (1) each level is a total increment consisting of many parts. Each part makes contribution to the whole of knowing. (2) The structure is irretrievably habitual. None of the levels is comprehensive of all knowing and concrete at the same time. Each level adds an increment to our process of knowing.[36] In *Method in Theology*, Lonergan summed up the cognitional process thus:

> There is the *empirical* level on which we sense, perceive, imagine, feel, speak, move. There is an *intellectual* level on which we inquire, come to understand, express what we have understood, work out the presuppositions and implications of our expression. There is the *rational* level on which we reflect, marshal the evidence, pass

---

31. Ibid., 343–44.
32. Lonergan, "Notion of Structure," 122.
33. Ibid.
34. Ibid.
35. *Insight*, 302.
36. Ibid., 302–3.

judgment on the truth or falsity, certainty or probability, of a statement. There is the *responsible* level on which we are concerned with ourselves, our own operations, our goals, and so deliberate about possible courses of action, evaluate them, decide, and carry out our decisions.[37]

The empirical level supplies the raw materials—images – on the level of presentations (data of sense and data of consciousness) "on which we sense, perceive, imagine, feel, speak, move."[38] It is on these images that intelligence operates.[39] The empirical level involves no questions for intelligence or insights or concepts. They simply lie on the level of past and present experience, of the occurrence of acts of sensitivity. The intellectual level consists in acts of inquiry, understanding, and formulation. It asks the following questions of intelligence: 'what is it?' 'why?' and 'how often?' to determine the intelligibility of the presentations and representations of empirical consciousness. The specific contribution of the rational level (judgment) to the cognitional process consists in the grasp of the unconditioned expressed in the answers 'yes' or 'no' to the questions for intelligence. Rational consciousness results in a judgment of fact and rests epistemologically upon the self-affirmation as an immanent law operative in the cognitional process—the undeniability of the self-affirmation of the knower at the expense of performative self-contradiction.[40] The level of decision moves judgments of fact to another level, that of value and decision, or in human sciences, from theory to practice. When one makes up one's mind, having correctly judged it to be so, one decides to act. In other words, to be human is to have the natural capacity to know and to act in accordance with that knowledge. Because we experience, understand, judge and deliberate, we know not only objects but ourselves as human beings. In this way, Lonergan's philosophical anthropology equates reason with dignity or with human self-regard:

> Rationality is my very dignity, and so closely to it do I cling that I would want the best of reasons for abandoning it. Indeed I am so much one with my reasonableness that, when I lapse from its high

---

37. *Method in Theology*, 9.
38. Ibid.
39. *Insight*, 298.
40. Ibid., 353.

standards, I am compelled either to repent my folly or to rationalize it.⁴¹

Human rational self-constitution is important for an understanding of human thought and action, for promoting human progress and well-being, for correcting mistakes and for overcoming societal decline and decay, as well as, for initiating and sustaining social transformation and for setting up machineries for sustainable human development. Meanwhile, this general dynamic pattern of human consciousness is not majorly revisable since any revisions "are to be derived from the conscious and intentional operations themselves."⁴²

This dynamic structure of human knowing implies that to be normatively human is to be intrinsically constituted through acts of meaning. In "Dimension of Meaning," Lonergan asserts: "it is this addition of understanding and judgment that makes possible the larger world mediated by meaning, that gives it its structure and unity, that arranges it in an orderly whole of almost endless differences..." ⁴³ Therefore, meaning "constitutes us insofar as we are specifically men and women, specifically human beings."⁴⁴ Because we experience, understand, judge and decide, we mean what we say and do. Our actions have meanings, and we are able to represent our thoughts in symbols; we are able to create signs and give them meaning. As Lonergan writes:

> Meaning is a formal and constitutive element of human living, and to remove meaning is to remove art and symbol, literature and history, natural and human science, families, states, religions, philosophies, and theologies.⁴⁵

Meaning is constitutive of human potentiality and subjectivity as such, for unless we are able to express and create meaning, we are not able to be fully functioning human beings. Meaning is constitutive of the symbols by which we express ourselves, of our imagination, of our questions and of our answers, our policies, strategies, plans, achievements, and celebrations both sacred and secular. Lonergan writes in this regard:

---

41. Ibid., 356.
42. *Method in Theology*, 20.
43. *Collection*, CWL 4:233.
44. "Analogy of Meaning," 196.
45. Ibid., 185.

> Not only is it constitutive of what we could say, could do, could make, either on our own or with the help of others, but also, *Deo volente*, it is the ground of all that is distinctively human, the potentiality for the region or realm or field in which arise good and evil, right and wrong, truth and error, grace and sin, saving one's soul and being damned.[46]

Meaning is constitutive of human society in the sense of the transference of the common fund of human knowing and life of a community.

In *Method in Theology*, Lonergan summed up his discussion on meaning by positing the functions of meaning as cognitive, efficient, constitutive, and communicative[47] – the last two yielding the three key notions of community, existence and history. The cognitive function of meaning, by combining understanding and judgment with experience, takes human beings out of the infant's world of immediacy into the adult's world mediated by meaning. Meaning is efficient in the sense of the intention, of the end, of the product of human work as corresponding to the purposes of human beings to create and to achieve. Thus the adult world is not only mediated by meaning, it is motivated by value, by the human good intended in the acts of human beings.

We conclude by asserting that for Lonergan, the dynamic structure of human knowing recognizes a four level structure that compositely constitutes human knowledge. A faithful adherence to them gives human life meaning, keeps it genuine and promotes progress and development. John Dadosky aptly summarizes Lonergan's cognitional theory thus:

> There are four levels of *intentional* consciousness in Lonergan's cognitional theory: *experience, understanding, judgment* and *decision*. Knowing, in the strict sense, occurs to the extent that one is attentive to one's experience, intelligent in one's understanding and reasonable in one's judgment—to the extent one answers all the relevant questions to a specific inquiry through these operations. In turn a question of value arises, which one would hope, prompts a person, to make responsible decisions based on those values. To the extent that this pattern of operations is allowed to unfold properly in the subject without the distortion of human bias, then one can say with Lonergan that "Genuine objectivity is

---

46. *Insight*, 196–97.
47. *Method in Theology*, 73–81.

the fruit of authentic subjectivity. It is to be attained only by attaining authentic subjectivity."[48]

The dynamic structure of human knowing and doing is a composite of experiencing, understanding, judging, and deciding. Through fidelity to the operations of the dynamic structure described above, human beings become authentic. Insofar as they succeed there is progress, insofar as they fail, there is decline. The first place where intellectual development begins is in the human subject and this includes the body, emotions and desires. He/she is also born into a community and is enculturated into the common meaning constitutive of the community. Thus, Lonergan's philosophical anthropology emphasizes the dual dialectic of the subject and of the community. This dialectic deals with the life of the human subject in terms of the constitutive elements that combine to effect authentic living personally, psychically and spiritually. It also deals with the elements constitutive of the life of human beings in community, the structure that brings about series of schemes for the constant provision of the human good for human wellbeing. Before we turn to the dialectic of the subject and of the community let us briefly expose the ontological constitution of human development in Bernard Lonergan's thought.

Ontological Constitution of Human Development

Although Lonergan's philosophical anthropology prioritizes human intelligence, it recognizes other series of events, especially the unconscious processes that functions integrally with conscious intentionality when the censor acts constructively likewise enabling the generation of insight. This recognition of the interplay of these series of events Lonergan treats in his concept of "emergent probability."

Emergent probability describes the intrinsic intelligibility of the world process in which development occurs. This world process is characterized by recurrences of schemes of events to achieve a specific developmental end. A scheme of recurrence is characterized by divergence in the series of positive conditions that will obtain if an event is going to occur. Lonergan explains: "[T]he fundamental element in emergent probability is the conditioned series of things and schemes; that series is realized cumulatively in accord with successive schedules of probabilities."[49] For instance, using

48. Dadosky, "Healing the Psychological Subject," 77.
49. *Insight*, 290.

Lonergan's schematic illustration, a scheme consists in a series of conditionals such that "if A were to occur, B would occur. If B were to occur, C would occur. If C were to occur . . . A would occur."[50] The schemes of recurrence of events are 'emergent' subject to probabilities in that higher integrations may emerge out of previously coincidental lower manifolds. "It is 'probability' because it includes not only schemes of recurrence, to be studied by classical laws, but the coming into being, maintaining and passing away of schemes of recurrence according to probabilities, to be studied by statistical method."[51] In emergent probability, development occurs in the leaps or expansion of existing schemes to new schemes, to higher integrations.[52] So development brings the emergence of a new and higher integration; an integration that includes the prior integration while providing more understanding of the integration that existed at the former lower level.[53] Our interest here is on the implications of emergent probability for personal and societal development.

The conditioned series of schemes of recurrence of events that account for human development, Lonergan says, are organic, psychic and intellectual. For instance, from above downwards, the biological schemes organize cells, cellular schemes organize molecules, and molecular schemes organize atoms. While not all the lower things enter into the organization of higher things, all the higher things depend on the successful functioning of the lower schemes preceding them. "Chemicals will break down if the atoms fission; cells will break down if chemicals change; life breaks down if cells decompose; knowing and willing breaks down if life dies."[54] Development reaches an increasing explanatory differentiation; that is, from a generic indetermination to a highly specific perfection. Lonergan thus defines development:

> In the light of the foregoing considerations, a development may be defined as a flexible, linked sequence of dynamic and increasingly differentiated higher integrations that meet the tension of successively transformed underlying manifolds through successive applications of the principles of correspondence and emergence.[55]

50. Ibid., 143–44.
51. Tekippe, *Bernard Lonergan's Insight*, 267.
52. *Insight*, 141.
53. Flanagan, *Quest for Self-Knowledge*, 105.
54. Dunne, *Lonergan and Spirituality*, 44.
55. *Insight*, 479.

Later in his autobiographical paper "Insight Revisited," Lonergan nuanced this definition in relation to intentionality analysis: "Development is a gradual accumulation of insights that complement, qualify, correct one another. Formulation sets the development within its cultural context. Marshalling and weighing the evidence reveals judgment to be possible, probable and at times certain."[56]

By organic development, Lonergan refers to the successive changes in the stages of the organs; their successive capacities and integrations as well as their successive physical and chemical manifolds. Psychic development refers to the higher integration that takes place in the schemes which make up the nervous system laterally and vertically. That is, the increasing differentiation of the psychic events in correspondence with particular afferent and efferent nerves on the one hand, and an increasing proficiency in integrated perception and in appropriate and coordinated responses on the other hand.[57]

In his analysis of intellectual development, Lonergan discusses the circle of the development of understanding from the otherwise coincidental manifold provided by sensible presentations and imaginative representations to its unifications and correlations in concepts, thoughts, suppositions, considerations, definitions, postulates, hypotheses and theories. He also includes how through such conceptual constructions, or their deductive expansions, or their concrete implementation, insights give rise sooner or later to further questions. There is continual human development if these conditioned series of events are woven together; and where they are not, human beings become "... a mere dumping ground for unrelated, unintegrated schemes of recurrence and modes of behavior."[58]

For this reason, Lonergan lists the heuristic structures of human development to include the following. First, the unity of the individual human being at any stage of his/her development as an individual existing unity differentiated by physical, chemical, organic, psychic and intellectual schemes. Second, the realization that human beings also develop on the psychic and intellectual levels, that is, the recognition of changes and expansion in the neural, psychic and intellectual schemes - the higher integration that involves changes in the underlying manifolds. Third, the law of integration—that is, that there must be the correspondence of the

---

56. "Insight Revisited," 278.
57. *Insight*, 481.
58. Ibid., 497.

organic, the psychic and the intellectual as well as other external initiatives, and their integration, for development to be satisfied. Fourth, the law of limitation and transcendence responsible for the tension in human consciousness—the tension between neural demands for conscious representation and psychic integration, on the one hand, and the repressive or constructive censorship for dramatically patterned intentionality, on the other hand.[59] Fifth, the law of genuineness – recognition of this tension in consciousness and determination to solve and not displace it. This is true of the subject, of the community and of culture.

The relationship of these schemes of events in human development is dialectical, that is, "a concrete unfolding of linked but opposed principles of change."[60] And because they are linked but opposed principles, there is a constant tension in human consciousness. The major problem of human development, therefore, is the problem of integrating these linked but opposed principles; it is a problem of integrating the organic, psychic and intellectual schemes that constitute human development, the problem of integrating the tensions constitutive of the tension of limitation and transcendence and not displacing them. Robert Doran proposed an understanding of two senses of Lonergan's use of dialectic, namely, 'dialectic of contradictories' and 'dialectic of contraries.' In the dialectic of contradictories the two opposed principles cannot work together harmoniously. Some examples of this include the interference of bias with insight, the unrestricted desire to know with the flight from understanding, the opposition of position and counterposition, the opposition between authenticity and inauthenticity, etc. In the dialectic of contradictories we are bound to choose between the two opposed principles: of good or evil, light or darkness, love or hate, God or the devil, etc. Paul's statement "virtue is no companion for crime. Light and darkness have nothing in common… The temple of God has no common ground with idols," (2Cor. 6:14–16) etc. are instances of dialectic of contradictories. The case is different in dialectic of contraries. Two principles, though not necessarily complementary, work together. Examples include male and female, light and dark. Here the choice is not between either of the principles but of both of them in their creative tension with one another. For instance, the working together of psyche and intentionality sets up a line of pure progress for the human subject. Also, the creative tension of spontaneous intersubjectivity and practical intelligence ensures

59. Ibid., 500.
60. Ibid., 242.

constant provision of the human good for all the members of a community etc.[61]

In the human psyche and intellect, the tension revolves around the relations of consciousness to the unconscious. This involves relationship with one's neural basis, with one's psyche in the demand for images, relations with one's milieu or environment and relations with other conscious subjects. As Lonergan notes:

> Within each man there are both the attachment and interestedness of sensitivity and intersubjectivity and, on the other hand, the detachment and disinterestedness of the pure desire to know. From this conjunction of opposites there follow (1) the interference of the lower level with the unfolding of inquiry and reflection, of deliberation and decision, (2) the consequent unintelligibility of situations, and (3) the increasing irrelevance of intelligence and reasonableness to the real problem of human living.[62]

The tension is therefore within the subject and outside the subject—within the subject in the relation of the psyche to intelligence, outside the subject arising from relations with other conscious subjects, with the community and, because of relations with the social environment, with the historical milieu of the subject.[63] The tension is displaced and thus distorted when the principles are conceived in terms of 'either/or'—indicating the dominance of one of the principles over the other instead of in a 'both/and' manner of unity of consciousness. This plays itself out within the human subject in the dialectic of the subject and in the subject's relation in a group—(dialectic of community).

The Dialectic of the Dramatic Subject

In a subsection in the sixth chapter of *Insight* titled "Elements in the Dramatic Subject," Lonergan refers to "the subordination of neural process to psychic determinations"[64] as the first condition of the possibility of acting out the drama of ordinary living in the human subject. By this, he means that in human beings the neural patterns and processes demands psychic representation and conscious integration carried out by conscious inten-

---

61. Doran, *Theology and the Dialectics of History*, 71.
62. *Insight*, 749.
63. Ibid., 268.
64. Ibid., 212.

tionality. This includes the preconscious functioning of a constructive censor which prevents materials that would lead to insight and/or selects materials that give rise to insights. The relation of these demand functions, the censor, and conscious intentionality constitutes the dialectic of the subject. As Lonergan writes, "The dialectic of the subject is concerned with the entry of neural demands into consciousness."[65] It could either be constructive and integrated, giving rise to character, or repressive and disintegrated, indicating *dramatic bias*.[66] However, a repressive censorship could be transformed into a constructive censorship through what Robert Doran calls 'Psychic Conversion,' that is, "a transformation of the psychic component of the censorship over neural demands from a repressive to a constructive functioning in a person's development."[67]

The dialectic is considered to be integrated and constructive if the opposed principles of neural demands and dramatically patterned existential intentionality are in creative tension with one another.[68] It is disintegrated and restrictive if, for whatever reason, the censorship is repressive.[69] In the human subject this implies that the tension arising from the neural demand functions and the exercise of censorship by the dramatically patterned intentionality and imagination would be in a creative tension if there were no domination of either pole. This is true even when there is distortion [domination of either principle] as long as it be such that it undermines "the dominance and strengthens the opposed principle to restore an equilibrium."[70] This is to say that the opposed principles of neural demands and conscious intentionality are ultimately working together, from the same emergent orientation, with the same objective of an integrated human subjectivity—the development of good habits, a life of virtue and good character. Under such conditions relevant insights are not ignored, one does not avoid uncomfortable situations and one's life is said to be genuine and harmonious, giving rise to further insights, which in the social sphere, can lead to better policies, progress and development.

On the other hand, if there is a displacement of the creative tension of linked but opposed principles, helpful insights are ignored and further

---

65. Ibid., 243.
66. Ibid., 216.
67. Doran, *Theology and Dialectics of History*, 66.
68. Doran, *Theological Foundations II Theology and Culture*, 99.
69. Ibid., 99.
70. *Insight*, 258.

questions that would be of help in the search for direction in the movement of life are excluded with attendant consequences (what Lonergan calls 'scotosis'[71]) for the emerging personality of the human subject. The dialectic is distorted on the side of limitation when neural demands overwhelm intelligence. For instance, people who have been oppressed or abused are psychologically wounded and therefore do not dream the dreams that the questioning spirit inspires unless redeemed through the process of psychic conversion. The dialectic is distorted in the direction of transcendence when intelligence represses the neural demands to which they are meant to attend. For example, people who suffer from too much transcendence do not acknowledge their limitations and therefore want to get everything done at the same time. Such people only recognise their limitations when they burn out. When these distortions happen, there is a disorientation of intentionality that conspires with disoriented affectivity to destroy the self through a rejection of insights (not adverting to symptoms of fatigue). In the words of Robert Doran, "one's development becomes aberrant and heads in the limit to the breakdown, disintegration, collapse of the failed artist, of the person who has not found or has found and then lost, the direction that can be discovered or missed in the movement of life."[72]

The displacement of the dialectic on either side of limitation or transcendence limits one's effective freedom by incapacitating one's intellectual and volitional capacities. This is because the neural demands negatively affect the censor and thus prevent needed insights, which effect creativity and character formation. The displacement on the side of transcendence jettisons the neural demand functions for conscious integration and, because of the lack of harmony, the censor does not do the integrating. The result is a divided person; a situation Lonergan calls 'dramatic bias' which weakens humankind's effective freedom and, as he notes in chapter 18 of *Insight*, is responsible for moral impotence.

The root cause of displacement in the dialectic of the subject is the dramatic wound that makes the subject unwilling to opt for insight and love and so he/she prefers darkness to light. This lack at times arises from one's incapacity or inability to opt for psychotherapy. Therefore, the cure will be a freeing of the repressive censor. Lonergan calls this principle "universal

---

71. Ibid., 215. Further on, Lonergan describes 'scotosis' as "a weakening of the development of common sense, a differentiation of the persona and the ego, an alternation of suspicion and reassurance, of doubt and rationalization." *Insight*, 220.

72. Doran, *Theology and the Dialectics of History*, 73.

willingness,"[73] a willingness that matches the unrestricted desire to know, enabling the subject not only to opt for insight but to adopt "an effective attitude in which performance matches aspiration."[74] Universal willingness works on the human will to obey the transcendental precepts: be attentive, be intelligent, be reasonable, be responsible[75] and thus helps the human subject to live authentically. However, the integration notwithstanding, the tension remains within the human subject because the unity of consciousness remains a concrete unity of opposed principles, a unity of the duality of the sensitive psyche and the intellect. Genuineness consists in being aware of this tension of limitation and transcendence and not displacing it. The drama of human living includes living in tension. Genuine people accept this and try to persevere.

Common Sense as Object

Lonergan's distinction of the subjective field of common sense in Chapter 6 of *Insight* is complemented by his distinction of the objective field of common sense in Chapter 7. In the objective field of common sense, Lonergan concerns himself with human living in community, with the constituents of community in which the human subject lives. He treats the recurrence of schemes of events that account for the inner workings of community life, its progress and development. He recommends measures to be undertaken to restore communal integrity should it have disintegrated by the refusal of insight in various forms. Ultimately, he reminds us that on account of moral impotence, sustained human development would be impossible without the assistance of divine grace, that is, without human subjects being in a relationship of love with God and having their lives guided by such a relationship. Such a "dynamic state of love, joy and peace [with God]," Lonergan tells us, "manifests itself in acts of kindness, goodness, fidelity, gentleness and self-control (Gal. 5, 22)."[76]

Our discussion of the objective field of common sense takes us into the field of the practicality of insights generated by the human subject in community.

---

73. Ibid., 647.
74. Ibid.
75. *Method in Theology*, 20.
76. Ibid., 106.

Lonergan, Social Transformation, and Sustainable Human Development

Common Sense as Practical

Lonergan notes that not only are common sense individual and communal, it is practical and concrete. The accumulation of insights generated by human intelligence is used for getting things done, in improving the human environment, in inventing technical skills, in devising ways and means of increasing production and in the management and distribution of goods and services. It is also useful in designing ways of governing other human beings in society in such a way as to ensure a recurrent supply of goods and services for the human good. One social invention leads to further inventions which accumulate and lead to greater inventions, i.e. to a greater and more effective economy and to better policies leading to improved public administration. Lonergan sums this up:

> ... The practicality of common sense engenders and maintains enormous structures of technology, economics, politics, and culture, that not only separate man from nature but also add a series of new levels or dimensions in the network of human relationships.[77]

In other words, the dynamism of conscious intentionality should be of practical help to human beings through the accumulation of insights it generates towards ensuring the recurrence of schemes for the provision of the human good needed for greater and better living conditions. It not only regards the biography of the human subject, it includes the existence of practical affairs that foster genuine relationship for the existence of human community. It not only provides the fund of common meaning upon which a community draws rich cultural values to guide its existence, it provides schemes that recurrently feed the community, distribute the goods produced to every member of the community and establish a political order that organizes various insights in the community, leading to higher viewpoints and integrations for the common good. Therefore, ideally, human intelligence promotes progress, development and world civilization.

Lonergan lists the stages in societal development of practical common sense as follows: technology, the economy and the polity. He argues that practical common sense by its very nature generates creative insights—ideas – that recurrently make for material progress by giving rise to technological skills. "The new inventions complement the old only to suggest further improvements, to reveal fresh possibilities, and eventually to call forth in turn the succession of mechanical and technological higher viewpoints

---

77. *Insight*, 232.

that mark epochs in man's material progress."[78] Technology brings about greater productivity and more capital. For greater production and distribution of goods to consumers, technology calls forth the economy. "Thus, in correspondence with each stage in the development of practical intelligence, there is a measure and structure of capital formation, that is, of things produced and arranged not because they themselves are desired but because they expedite and accelerate the process of supplying the goods and services that are wanted by consumers."[79] Finally, the economy brings about the polity because of the need to bring people together to ensure the recurrence of schemes as well as the good of order for the production of the human good. The politician guides policies to promote the technology, and the economy towards the well-being of the community and society. Ideally, the politician makes the decisions that bring all people of common sense together to achieve the common goal of building a lasting civilization. The politician may be versed in the insights of the technician and of the entrepreneur but has the special task of being able to deal with people. He must therefore have the communication skills to convince people of common sense to work together and to jointly pursue the human good. According to Lonergan:

> As technology evokes the economy, so the economy evokes the polity. . . . Each step in the process of technological and economic development is an occasion on which minds differ, new insights have to be communicated, enthusiasm has to be roused, and a common decision must be reached. Beyond the common sense of the labourer, the technician, the entrepreneur, there is the political specialization of common sense. Its task is to provide the catalyst that brings men of common sense together. [80]

Lonergan's words indicate the functional unity in the dynamic structure of practical common sense. It is the unity aimed at the recurrent provision of the human good. Lonergan describes the structure of this functional unity in terms of the concept "emergent probability." As we saw in the subsection of this chapter on the ontological constitution of human development, "the fundamental element in emergent probability is the conditioned series of things and schemes; that series is realized cumulatively in accord

---

78. Ibid., 233.
79. Ibid.
80. Ibid., 234.

with successive schedules of probabilities."[81] The emergent probability of practical common sense revolves around human actions that, although recurrent, and although regularly functioning following a scheme, could also be irregular. Its regularity could be expressed in terms that if X occurs, Y will follow and will ultimately give rise to Z. Its irregularity implies that X might fail to occur and the scheme might be distorted. Thus there is the combination not only of classical but also of statistical laws in the schemes of practical common sense. This implies that the functional unity is not static but dynamic. Apart from the systematic process by which the schemes of recurrence function, there is also the probability of randomness in the scheme of events. In other words, the scheme not only functions, but probably could cease to function, that is, in unexpected ways. A community could decline and, from the ashes of its decline, there could emerge a new community perhaps much more vibrant than the previous one. [82] Such dynamics of the structure of practical common sense, dependent on the generation of insights as well as its use or its neglect, accounts for the differences between nations and civilizations: for the progress and development of peoples on the one hand and for their decline on the other.

> The advance of technology, the formation of capital, the development of the economy, the evolution of the state are not only intelligible but also intelligent. Because they are intelligible, they can be understood as are the workings of emergent probability in the field of physics, chemistry, and biology. But because they also are increasingly intelligent, increasingly the fruit of insight and decision, the analogy of merely natural process becomes less and less relevant. What possesses a high probability in one country or period or civilization may possess no probability in another; and the ground of the difference may lie only slightly in outward and palpable material factors and almost entirely in the set of insights that are accessible, persuasive, and potentially operative in the community.[83]

Lonergan's position indicates that a community must pay attention to the order of its generation of insights. It must be open to new insights and to the accumulation of insights into higher viewpoints towards the recurrence of schemes for the provision of the human good. Communities should also

---

81. Ibid., 290.
82. Ibid., 235.
83. Ibid., 236.

bear in mind the possible randomness of these schemes of events for the provision of the goods and services of a community and avoid situations that would give rise to any flight from understanding or suppression of any insight that should make for the progress of peoples. Since the set of insights makes all the difference, ultimately the generation of insights and the emergence of higher viewpoints depend on the human person, on his or her relationships with other persons in the community, and on the social order in which he lives and operates. As Lonergan acknowledges, though he speaks of a functional unity to be discovered, there is actually a duality to be grasped.[84] The duality in question is the duality of practical intelligence and human intersubjectivity (community). To this we now turn.

Intersubjectivity and Social Order

At issue here is the relationship between human beings and the social order set up to serve and not to dominate them. That is, the primordial basis of human communal living is "spontaneous intersubjectivity" arising from the nature of human beings as social beings on the one hand, and the order set up by human beings to promote their life and to make it more dignified on the other hand. Lonergan distinguished two levels of community: 'the primitive community' and 'the civil community,' both arising from the need to ensure the recurrence of schemes for the provision of the human good. The two communities differ in their conception of the good. Primitive communities identify the good with the object of desire, while in civil community, the good is identified with the good of order.[85] Because it could be misunderstood, it is important to emphasise here that Lonergan's use of 'primitive' to refer to community is not derogatory. He is referring to the primordial basis of human community, the original unsophisticated community bonding emergent from the social nature of human beings. Lonergan describes this using the example of family ties. Civil community is characterized by the modern sophistication of the structures of community today. When civil communities collapse, primitive communities remain as people identify with their roots. In the lecture "The Role of a Catholic University in the Modern World," Lonergan identifies what he calls in *Insight* 'Primitive community' as "intersubjective community." He describes it as the spontaneous tendency of human beings, "an elemental

---

84. Ibid., 237.
85. Ibid., 238.

feeling of belonging together." Civil community in the same lecture refers to complex structures developed from this primordial intersubjectivity. As distinct from civil community, he also distinguishes 'cultural community,' what could be called 'world-cultural community,' that transcends nations and states.[86]

However, the primordial basis of both primitive and civil communities is "spontaneous intersubjectivity."[87] It is primordial because it is not created as such. It flows from the social nature of human beings. Community originates from the nucleus of the family, the first place where "…the bond of mother and child, man and wife, father and son, reaches into a past of ancestors to give meaning and cohesion to the clan or tribe or nation. A sense of belonging together provides the dynamic premise for common enterprise, for mutual aid and succour, for the sympathy that augments joys and divides sorrows."[88] Primitive community is unlike civil community, in that its concern is with the good as the object of desire seeking immediate satisfaction; it does not set up complex structures for the provision of the human good. The reverse is the case with civil communities and our concern is with civil communities.

The good of order of a civil community seeks to provide the good for its members through the contribution of each member of the community. This is clear in Lonergan's understanding of the good of order as consisting "in an intelligible pattern of relationships that condition the fulfillment of each man's desires by his contributions to the fulfillment of the desires of others, and similarly protect each from the object of his fears in the measure he contributes to warding off the objects feared by others."[89] Providing for the good of order therefore makes it necessary for the members of a civil community to make use of their practical intelligence to generate technology, economy and politics. Technology includes such ancient mechanical arts as the spears and arrows of primitive communities and the more modern inventions of digital technology. As we noted earlier, technology calls forth the economy (capital formation), that is, "of things produced and arranged not because they themselves are desired but because they expedite and accelerate the process of supplying goods and services that are wanted

---

86. Lonergan, "Role of a Catholic University in the Modern World," 109.
87. *Insight*, 237.
88. Ibid.
89. Ibid., 238.

by consumers."⁹⁰ With the improvement of skills for the productivity of surplus goods and with the need for the distribution of the goods solved by capital formation, it becomes necessary to organize the community to ensure the recurrence of schemes for the provision of the human good. The polity as good of order, therefore, has to oversee security and the provision of other amenities necessary for the continued improvement of technology and steady capital formation. These products of practical intelligence work harmoniously with the primordial basis of civil community to form a human community enabling human beings to live more dignified lives.⁹¹

In other words, according to Lonergan the constituents of community are spontaneous intersubjectivity on the one hand and practical intelligence on the other hand. That is, the primordial intersubjectivity of human beings as social beings as belonging to a community, and the products of their practical intelligence: technology, the economy and the polity set up the good of order. The relationship of these constituents of community (the social order and a network of relationships under which people live and relate in community—locally and collectively), could be harmonious or it could be distorted. The tension between them - practical common sense and the network of relationships as spontaneous intersubjectivity constitute the 'dialectic of community.'

The Dialectic of Community

Dialectic of community refers to the two linked but opposed principles constitutive of community: 1) spontaneous intersubjectivity of individuals and 2) practical intelligence: technology, economy, and politics. It refers to the tension in community that arise as human beings negotiate these poles within a community. The principles are linked because, as we saw earlier, both spontaneous intersubjectivity and practical common sense constitute the functional unity of community. Both originate for the well-being of the human person. They are opposed because spontaneous intersubjectivity is oriented towards the good of others in community while practical intelligence, in its quest for further implementation and development ignores the impulse to spontaneous intersubjectivity.⁹²

90. Ibid., 233.
91. Ibid., 239.
92. Ibid., 243.

Thus Lonergan explains that "dialectic of community regards the history of human relationships."[93] When the tension between these linked but opposed principles constitutive of community is creative, there is the emergence and/or recurrence of schemes for the good of order. When that is the case, relationships between and among peoples in a community is cordial. People do not concentrate solely on their self-interest in social relations but contribute to practically implementing the human good. The products of practical intelligence—technology, the economy and the polity—interact creatively with spontaneous intersubjectivity. The dialectic of community, is considered integral with linked but opposed principles of community working together towards the progress and development of the members of the community.

However, as Lonergan rightly observed, the creative tension of community may not always be maintained. The relationship of spontaneous intersubjectivity and practical intelligence can be distorted on either side of the linked principles—either on the side of spontaneous intersubjectivity or on the side of practical intelligence. When the integral dialectic of community is distorted on the side of practical intelligence, spontaneous intersubjectivity suffers. For instance, Marxist social analysis' identification of basic social dialectic within practicality displaces intersubjectivity in the direction of transcendence. The setting up of state socialism to provide for each according to his/her needs according to his/her ability stifles creativity and distorts the immanent norms of intelligence equipped with sanctions which human beings do not have to invent or impose.[94] On the other hand, distortion on the side of intersubjectivity results in various forms of group bias which degenerates equally to distort practical intelligence by refusal of insights from opposing groups. Or, it can simply stifle social development as in the case of many countries in Africa due to the failure to implement broad recurrent technological, economic and political structures.

Distortion of the Dialectic of Community and Social Development

Karl Polanyi's book *The Great Transformation*[95] mirrors Lonergan's emphasis on what happens when the dialectic of community is distorted by

93. Ibid.
94. Ibid., 234.
95. Polanyi, *Great Transformation*.

prioritizing an aspect of practical intelligence over spontaneous intersubjectivity: atomization of the human person and the mechanization of humankind, "a ruthless abnegation of the social status of the human being."[96] Polanyi notes the decline of Western civilization started in the nineteenth century when it separates the economy from the social and political life of the people by instituting the market economy.[97] Whereas no human society could exist for any length of time without an economy of some sort, at no time did the economy become the determining factor of all of society's pursuits—political, intellectual, and spiritual—until the self-regulating market emerged with the industrial revolution of the nineteenth century. Polanyi warned against the tendency in the modern age, especially by classical economists who adopted Adam Smith's theory of self-interest as the propelling factor for economic life, to reduce all economic activity among the various generations of humanity to profit. Using various examples from primitive cultures where spontaneous intersubjectivity is well entrenched in reciprocity and centricity, Polanyi argued that community and social life come first and that economic life and productivity are not solely for gain but for the well-being of community.[98] Polanyi explains that ethnographic studies show that production has never been for the sole provision of one's own individual needs and desires alone. It has always been for the material well-being of the group:

> The individualistic savage collecting food and hunting on his own or for his family has never existed. Indeed, the practice of catering for the needs of one's household becomes a feature of economic life only on a more advanced level of agriculture; however, even then it has nothing in common either with the motive of gain or with the institution of markets. Its pattern is the closed group. Whether the very different entities of the family or the settlement or the manor formed the self-sufficient unit, the principle was invariably the same, namely, that of producing and storing for the satisfaction of the wants of the members of the group. The principle is as broad in its application as either reciprocity or redistribution.[99]

---

96. MacIver, foreword to Polanyi, *Great Transformation*, x.

97. Karl Polanyi expressed this in his theory of "embeddedness," remarking that ordinarily the economy is not autonomous as it must be in the dominant economic theory, but subordinated to politics, religion and social relations.

98. Polanyi, *Great Transformation*, 49.

99. Ibid., 53.

In spite of the iron laws of economics that set limits to human possibilities outside economics, and the three tenets of classical economic liberalism: "that labor should find its price on the market; that the creation of money should be subject to an automatic mechanism; that goods should be free to flow from country to country without hindrance or preference; in short, for a labor market, the gold standard, and free trade,"[100] Polanyi argues that a market economy can never subsist without social relations. As Gregory Baum surmised in his analysis of Karl Polanyi, "the consequence of the self-regulating market was above all cultural. By divorcing economic activity from its base in social relations, the free market tore apart the cultural bonds—the values and the inherited institutions—by which people constituted their identity. The new economic system created a devastating anomie which seriously damaged the humanity of workers and affected the whole of society and its relation to the natural environment."[101]

Thus, distorted dialectic of community gives rise to biases that ultimately lead to decline. More explicitly, the biases could be considered Lonergan's critique of the present development paradigms.

The Biases and Development

Since we have already treated dramatic bias arising from the psychological depths in the subject, we shall now concentrate on the three other biases that can aggravate the dialectic of community and can prevent or reverse development in a society. These biases are: individual, group and general. They affect the course of world history, progress and development. "As saint Augustine said: World history is a battle between two forms of love. Love of self—to the point of destroying the world. And love of others—to the point of renouncing oneself."[102]

Individual Bias

Lonergan chooses to call this bias the individual bias of egoism.[103] It is the preference for one's own individual good to the detriment of the good of

---

100. Ibid., 135.

101. Baum, *Karl Polanyi on Ethics & Economics*, 9.

102. Cited in Benedict XVI, *Light of the World,* translated by Miller and Walker, Kindle for PC, Location 876 of 2750.

103. *Insight*, 244.

others and the pursuit of this to the detriment of the common good. Lonergan explains: "With remarkable acumen one solves one's own problems. With startling modesty one does not venture to raise the relevant further questions, 'Can one's solution be generalized? Is it compatible with the social order that exists? Is it compatible with any social order that proximately or even remotely is possible?'"[104] Individual bias thus is the over-concentration on oneself to the neglect of the good of order of the community. Consequently, "egoism is neither mere spontaneity nor pure intelligence but an interference of spontaneity with the development of intelligence."[105] The egoist uses the disinterestedness of detached intelligent inquiry for the fulfilment of the selfish ends being pursued. For detached intelligence seeks not only to provide for particular goods but for the good of order as well. Lonergan writes:

> Egoism then is an incomplete development of intelligence. It rises above a merely inherited mentality. It has the boldness to strike out and think for itself. But it fails to pivot from the initial and preliminary motivation provided by desires and fears to the self-abnegation involved in allowing complete free play to intelligent inquiry. Its inquiry is reinforced by spontaneous desires and fears; by the same stroke it is restrained from a consideration of any broader field.[106]

The negative aspect of Adam Smith's theory of self-interest as a determinant of exchange and values examined in Chapter 1 promotes and rewards individual bias. According to Adam Smith, every person is "by nature, first and principally recommended to his own care."[107] Although human beings care for the good of others, they do not care for others more than they care for themselves.[108] Human beings contribute to societal development only in the course of pursuing their self-interest. Thomas Hobbes description of the state of the human condition as a permanent state of war of *all against all* in the thirteenth chapter of his *Leviathan* resulting from the tension between individual pursuit of self-interest and the emergent common good is also an instance of egoistic bias.[109] In the book interview titled *The*

---

104. Ibid., 245.
105. Ibid.
106. Ibid., 245–46.
107. Smith, *Theory of Moral Sentiments*, 82.
108. Ibid., 86.
109. Hobbes, *Leviathan*; Melchin, *History, Ethics and Emergent Probability*, 209–61;

Light of the World (2010) Pope Benedict mentions individual egoisms as one of the reasons people lack the will to do something to stem the tide of global warming even though they believe theoretically the findings of the scientists about the consequences on the environment and on human life. "Although they do believe it theoretically," the pontiff says, "but they tell themselves it will not affect me. In any case it will not change *my* life."[110]

However, because egoism is not spontaneous, there is a certain disquiet that abides in the egoist as s/he realises in the depth of her/his conscience of living in sin, and of waging war with the primordial human constitution of intersubjectivity and practical intelligence. This disquiet comes in the form of the proddings of practical intelligence to reconsider the love of darkness and of selfishness, to opt for the good of order, and to be open to the further insights and the demands of the detached unrestricted desire to know.[111] Egotism can therefore be overcome by the opening of self to this intersubjective responsiveness by attitudinal changes akin to conversion: psychic, intellectual, moral, and religious.

Group Bias

Group bias is a bias arising from an attachment to one's intersubjective feeling, a feeling that protecting one's group interest to the detriment of other groups is the normal course of life. It has to do with the dynamic relations of the constituents of practical common sense—technology, economy and the polity—in a social order. These constituents of the social order have various functions and ordinarily work together towards an integral dialectic of community.[112] Unfortunately, however, when the harmonious relations of these products of practical common sense to each other are distorted by non-adaptation of human spontaneity to the demands of practical intelligence, we have what Lonergan calls group bias. Group bias can easily occur among specialists as "every specialist runs the risk of turning his speciality into a bias by failing to recognize and appreciate the significance of other fields."[113]

Orji, *Ethnic and Religious Conflict in Africa*, 62–67.

110. Pope Benedict XVI, *Light of the World*, Kindle for PC, Location 710 of 2750.
111. *Insight*, 247.
112. Ibid.
113. Ibid., 252.

Group bias arising from the relations of practical intelligence, technology, the economy and the polity, distorts the social order as a whole. Relations are distorted not only by the relations of each group against other groups but with the relations within each group. Hence Lonergan in Chapter 18 of *Insight* talks of "the various types of group bias."[114] For instance, in the polity, there could be bias between the legislature and the executive or between the executive and the judiciary functions. This may result in chaos and disorder in the polity, which of course may affect developments in the economy and in technology. So the dialectic occurs within the various functions of the products of practical intelligence as well as between the various products of practical intelligence: technology, economy and the polity. Either way, the development of a social order is distorted. Either way, the functioning of a country could be paralyzed and could result in what Lonergan calls the shorter cycle of decline. As we saw in the first chapter, economic liberalism is an instance of the dominance of the economy over technology and over the polity. Global governance resulting from the loss of economic independence of the heavily indebted nations brings about the weakening of the political function in a country to such an extent that transnational corporations become the deciding body for the political structure of a country. In rich industrialized countries, technology has become the dominant aspect of social order to such an extent that the economy and the polity are subordinated to it. Resources are so devoted to increased technological inventions that the well-being of the human person in social relations is neglected.

Group bias is also seen in the spontaneous intersubjectivity where members of a particular community seek to protect the interests of its members over that of the interests of the other members in the broader community. For instance, there is group bias when people of a particular tribe within a country seek to protect the interests of their tribe to the detriment of the interests of other tribes in the country. Likewise, when people identify with their religious identity without due regard for the good of the members of other religions, group bias is present. It is also at the heart of ethnic conflicts among heterogeneous groups. For instance, the famed racial conflicts in the United States between blacks, Hispanics, Asians and whites and the then Apartheid regime in South Africa including the clashes between ethnic Kyrgyz and Uzbeks in Kyrgyzstan[115] were instances

---

114. Ibid., 651.

115. *Ottawa Citizen*. Online: http://www.ottawacitizen.com/news/Death+toll+Kyrgy

of group bias. Kyrgyzstan is a Central Asian state that emerged since the collapse of the Soviet Union. Reuters reports that clashes between southern Kyrgyzstan's main ethnic groups, Kyrgyz and Uzbeks, have killed at least 191 people since June 10, 2010. As of June 19th 2010, the death toll is estimated to be over 2,000. Another place group bias is reflected is in the tribal conflicts in Africa. The present day African countries are amalgamations of formerly independent heterogeneous city states or stateless peoples. This often makes co-existence difficult when each group accuses the others of favouritism and nepotism. The various levels of authority that have studied tribal conflicts point to tribal and religious tensions akin to Lonergan's group bias. According to Cyril Orji:

> These various levels of authority … adduced two reasons for the cause of these conflicts, one remote, and the other immediate. The remote cause, they all agreed, goes back to the historical foundations of the respective countries in question, to the colonial period when the colonial masters disregarded the ethnic mix of the African people and lumped together people of different races and ethnicities. The immediate cause, a by-product of the remote cause, provides a situation where modern African politicians and military rulers tap into the ethnic and religious differences among their people and use them for their selfish gains.[116]

For example, the amalgamation of Northern and Southern Protectorate of Nigeria in 1914, an amalgamation of people of over 250 different language groups with distinct cultural values and histories, resulted in the present day Nigeria after political independence in 1960. The ethnic tension and religious conflicts bedevilling the nation is a result of the group bias of each tribe favouring their tribe interest to that of the common good of the nation. The same is true of the present day warring Somali Republic which is a coalition of former Italian Somaliland and former British Somaliland. The animosity between the Hutu and the Tutsi of Rwanda, resulting in the genocide of 1994, is traceable to the favouritism of the French colonial powers and the inability of various tribes to live together because of tribalism, i.e. people see themselves as belonging to their tribes first before being citizens of their country. The *Report of the Commission for Africa* (2005) commissioned by the United Nations notes the prevalence of ethnic and religious conflict in Africa and remarked:

---

z+leader+says/3174772/story.html.

116. Orji, *Ethnic and Religious Conflict in Africa*, 53.

Many traditional communities of people are now divided between two, three or even four countries. Elsewhere disparate groups, some of whom were traditional enemies, are yoked together in uneasy union, many of them lacking a common language with which to speak to one another. Colonialism favoured some groups over others, creating new hierarchies. The consequences of some of these divisions are alive today as well as too readily shown in Rwanda in the relationship between the Hutu and Tutsi whose "ethnic" differences were sharpened artificially during the colonial era, with such terrible consequences in the genocide of 1994.[117]

On account of group bias, society becomes stratified and people are distinguished according to classes depending on the supposed superiority of one group over others.[118] In such situations even the brightest ideas and insights are judged not disinterestedly but only according to the group bias of their judges. Excellent ideas for the good of the social order are cast aside because those at the helm of the affairs of the social order belong to a different group and are operating under group bias. Consequently, in a social order:

> The bias of development involves a distortion. The advantage of one group commonly is disadvantageous to another, and so some part of the energies of all groups is diverted to the supererogatory activity of devising and implementing offensive and defensive mechanisms . . . Moreover, the course of development has been twisted. The social order that has been realized does not correspond to any coherently developed set of practical ideas. It represents the fraction of practical ideas that were made operative by their conjunction with power, the mutilated remnants of once excellent schemes that issued from the mill of compromise, the otiose structures that equip groups for their offensive and defensive activities.[119]

Group bias creates the conditions of its own reversal when a new idea to solve a concrete problem of a group cannot be generated by the dominant group but comes from a person or persons belonging to a different group. If the group opens up to ideas from outside its own group then the group bias is overcome by reversing itself and seeks to avoid occasions for its recurrence in the future. At the same time, however, if the dominant

---

117. Commission for Africa, *Our Common Interest*, 22.
118. *Insight*, 249.
119. Ibid.

group decides to use power to block the new idea coming from a person or persons outside their group, the social order is then headed for ruin and the longer cycle of decline as it excludes fruitful ideas and mutilates others by compromise.

General Bias

General bias restricts questions that would lead to theory. Ordinarily, "fruitful ideas are of several kinds. They may lead to technical and material improvement, to adjustments of economic arrangements, or to modifications of political structure."[120] But the general bias rules these fruitful ideas out of court because it insists only on the ideas that satisfy its needs for practicality. In *Macroeconomic Dynamics: An Essay in Circulation Analysis*, Lonergan defined general bias as "the general tendency to be content with the particular specialty, common sense, and to consider other specialties irrelevant or useless."[121] General bias therefore prevents the realization of fruitful ideas, "however appropriate and reasonable, that suppose a long view or that set up higher integrations or that involve the solution of intricate and disputed issues."[122] According to John Dadosky, "general bias resists theoretical knowledge and is content to live in the concrete world; it refuses to permit questions that might lead to theory."[123] Often human beings are prone to general bias because they prefer quick practical ideas instead of going through the rigour demanded by theoretical solutions. Lonergan asserts:

> But far more significant than these relatively superficial and overt conflicts will be the underlying opposition that general bias sets up between the decisions that intelligence and reasonableness would demand and the actual decisions, individual and common, that are made. For this opposition is both profound and unnoticed. As individuals, so societies fail to distinguish sharply and accurately between positions and counterpositions. As individuals, so societies fail to reach the universal willingness that reflects and sustains the detachment and disinterestedness of the unrestricted desire to know. More or less automatically and unconsciously, each successive batch of possible and practical courses of action is screened

120. *Insight*, 251.
121. Lonergan, *Macroeconomic Dynamics*, 94.
122. *Insight*, 253.
123. Dadosky, "Healing the Psychological Subject," 76.

Lonergan's Philosophical Anthropology

to eliminate as unpractical whatever does not seem practical to an intelligence and a willingness that not only are developed imperfectly but also suffer from bias.[124]

General bias tries to provide solutions to concrete problems without probing the causes of the problems to avoid future recurrence. The problem is complicated even more because general bias, by concentrating on practicality, considers itself as being very efficient. In *Method in Theology*, Lonergan describes general bias as "a specialization of intelligence in the particular and concrete, but usually considers itself omnicompetent."[125] Jacques Maritain's critique of practicality for disregarding theory is consonant with Lonergan's understanding of general bias:

> You are advancing in the night, bearing torches toward which mankind would be glad to turn; but you leave them enveloped in the fog of a merely experiential approach and mere practical conceptualization, with no universal ideas to communicate. For lack of an adequate ideology, your lights cannot be seen.[126]

The disregard by general bias of timely and fruitful ideas equally implies rejection of other ideas. Such discarded ideas might have innovations for progress in the social order. For, says Lonergan, general bias gives rise to three consequences. In the first place, there is the cumulative deterioration of the social situation. Second, there is the mounting irrelevance of detached and disinterested intelligence. Finally, there is the minor surrender of detached and disinterested intelligence on the level of common sense and later a major surrender on the speculative level.[127]

The longer cycle of decline sets in with this major surrender of detached and disinterested intelligence by its concentration on short term concrete solutions. One consequence is the reduction of the human subject to mechanistic thinking, an inability to distinguish between a human being and other material entities. Because the relationship between intelligence and community is distorted, common sense practicality rules the day. The measure of progress and development will be structurally economical, that is, based on profit, consumption and material well-being, on having instead of on being, on gross national product with total neglect of other aspects of

---

124. *Insight*, 651.
125. *Method in Theology*, 231.
126. Maritain, *Reflections on America*, 118.
127. *Insight*, 254–55.

the economy that cannot be quantified statistically, and of intersubjective community support, compassion, kindness and charity. Thus, according to Lonergan:

> Reality is the economic development, the military equipment, and the political dominance of the all-inclusive state. Its ends justify all means. Its means include not merely every technique of indoctrination and propaganda, every tactic of economic and diplomatic pressure, every device for breaking down the moral conscience and exploiting the secret effects of civilized man, but also the terrorism of a political police, of prisons and torture, of concentration camps, of transported or extirpated minorities, and of total war.[128]

So total and so devastating is the longer cycle of decline precipitated by general bias that the distortion of the dialectic of community it affects cannot be reversed except by a higher viewpoint.[129] The higher viewpoint will consist in the reversal of the refusal of insight that brought the longer cycle of decline in the first place. Lonergan writes:

> The refusal of insight is a fact that accounts for individual and group egoism, for the psychoneuroses, and for the ruin of nations and civilizations. The needed higher viewpoint is the discovery, the logical expansion, and the recognition of the principle that intelligence contains its own immanent norms and that these norms are equipped with sanctions which man does not have to invent or impose. Even in the sphere of practice, the last word does not lie with common sense and its panoply of technology, economy, and polity; for unless common sense can learn to overcome its bias by acknowledging and submitting to a higher principle, unless common sense can be taught to resist its perpetual temptation to adopt the easy, obvious, practical compromise, then one must expect the succession of ever less comprehensive viewpoints, and *in the limit the destruction of all that has been achieved*.[130]

In other words, general bias leads to the rejection of the function and role of the detached disinterested intelligence. Such rejection leads to nothing but an expansion of the surd of decline in a community generating the longer cycle of decline. Culture ceases its critical function of judging practical

---

128. Ibid., 257.
129. Ibid., 258.
130. Ibid., 259. Emphasis mine.

intelligence and becomes practical itself, serving the practical intelligence of which it is supposed to be critical. The consequence will be all too glaring for one not to see in its effects on the social situation:

> In the limit, culture ceases to be an independent factor that passes a detached yet effective judgment upon capital formation and technology, upon economy and polity. To justify its existence, it had to become more and more practical, more and more a factor within the technological, economic, political process, more and more a tool that served palpably useful ends.... Clearly by becoming practical, culture renounces its one essential function, and by that renunciation condemns practicality to ruin.[131]

General bias disregards the historical process: that there is progress, that there is decline and that there is the possibility of redemption. General bias generates the longer cycle of decline by rationalizing its sins and universalizing them by creating principles out of them. The reversal of general bias is a re-establishment of detached disinterested intelligence that critically judges practical intelligence and prevents it from being "shortsightedly practical and so destroying itself."[132] That is to say, the re-establishment of the critical aspect of a cultural community allows culture once more to stand outside practical intelligence, restores the spirit of inquiry and permits credible common meaning to determine the human good.

Cosmopolis as the Higher Viewpoint

Lonergan posits the notion of *cosmopolis* as an alternative to the longer cycle of decline. It is an alternative to bias-dominated society. As a higher viewpoint it is expected to free intelligence from general bias, allowing it to operate in accordance with its own immanent norms, giving free rein to the unrestricted desire to know. Lonergan asserts:

> The basic service of the higher viewpoint will be a liberation from confusion through clear distinctions. Progress is not to be confused with decline; the corrective mechanism of the minor principle of decline is not to be thought capable of meeting the issues set by the major principle.[133]

---

131. Ibid., 262.
132. Ibid., 264.
133. Ibid., 260.

Etymologically, the word cosmopolis is a combination of two Greek words: '*cosmos*,' a perceived order in the universe, and '*polis*,' this order as functionally displayed in society. Such understanding flows from the classical Greek understanding of the order of nature and the order of society and the relationship between them. The order of society was believed to proceed and to be influenced by the order of nature, that is, heaven. Hence, social and natural regularities—*cosmos* + *polis* = *cosmopolis*. As Stephen Toulmin, who sees cosmopolis as the hidden agenda of modernity, explains:

> . . . to say that a community (*koinoneia*) formed a *polis* was to recognize that its practices and organization has the overall coherence that qualified it—in both the ancient and modern senses of the term—as a "political" unit.[134]

In Toulmin's sense of the word, differing from Lonergan's meaning, as we will show below, cosmopolis means cosmopolitical order just as the Stoic philosophers understood it following Alexander the Great and the Hellenization of the world. Diogenes of Sinope, called the Cynic (c. BCE 404–327), used the Greek word *Kosmopolites* to refer to himself as "a citizen of the world." In this sense, cosmopolis means world government. Other understandings of cosmopolis follow Diogenes approach. The effort to achieve world peace following the thirty year religious conflict of Europe with the Treaty of Westphalia (1648) further extended the meaning of cosmopolis to a cosmopolitical force, a recipe for world peace by bringing the various European states together in a federation or confederation as a commonwealth in the light of their shared meanings and values.[135] Immanuel Kant opted for such world government as a cosmopolitan ideal to end the endemic wars ravaging Europe. [136] This second meaning of cosmopolis, world government, is still held today by some who canvass for a world government to oversee socio-political issues arising from conflicts in the world, especially in reference to such international organizations as the United Nations.[137] Lonergan did not clearly distinguish his meaning of cosmopolis from other meanings or state clearly what he means. Such attempt is made in a section of *Insight* where he says briefly what cosmopolis is not for him:

134. Toulmin, *Cosmopolis*, 67.

135. This position is further elaborated in Charles Onyango's treatment of the history of cosmopolis from classical Greek antiquity to the modern notion as world government. Cf. Onyango, *Lonergan's Notion of Cosmopolis*, PhD thesis, Boston College, 2005.

136. Ibid., 117.

137. Zolo, Cosmopolis, xiii.

> However, I am not saying that there should not be a United Nations or a world government; I am not saying that such political entities should not have a police force; I am saying that such political entities are not what is meant by cosmopolis.[138]

As a higher viewpoint cosmopolis is part of neither practical intelligence nor spontaneous intersubjectivity. It is conceived as a societal structure that enables the integrity of both. In his 1951 paper titled "The Role of a Catholic University in the Modern World," Lonergan identified cosmopolis as cultural community:

> Corresponding to judgments of value, there is cultural community. It transcends the frontiers of states and the epochs of history. It is cosmopolis, not as an unrealized political ideal, but as a long-standing, non-political, cultural fact. It is the field of communication and influence of artists, scientists, and philosophers. It is the bar of enlightened public opinion to which naked power can be driven to submit. It is the tribunal of history that may expose successful charlatans and may restore to honor the prophets stoned by their contemporaries.[139]

As a social structure that enables integrity of the dialectic of community, cosmopolis is the process of restoring human intelligence by promoting critical thinking in society. It aims at making society critical of itself and of the functioning of its institutions: technology, the economy and the polity. This it does through transformation of intelligence so that the good of order becomes once more ideally dynamic, possessing its own line of development, grasping ideas in concrete situations. These ideas are formulated into proposals, are accepted by explicit or tacit agreements and are executed in order to bring about further insights. As the social order is human beings coexisting and mutually contributing to the satisfaction of their desires by contributing to the good of order, cosmopolis is the transformation of intelligence to make it effective, functional and recurrent without obstacles. It is concerned with the historical process, and therefore it prioritizes ideas which ordinarily would be dismissed under general bias. Lonergan sums up the essential task of cosmopolis thus:

> It is the business of cosmopolis to prevent the formation of the screening memories by which an ascent to power hides its nastiness; it is its business to prevent the falsification of history with

138. *Insight*, 264.
139. "Role of a Catholic University in the Modern World," 109.

which the new group overstates its case; it is its business to satirize the catchwords and the claptrap and thereby to prevent the notions they express from coalescing with passions and resentments to engender obsessive nonsense for future generations; it is its business to encourage and support those that would speak the simple truth though simple truth has gone out of fashion. Unless cosmopolis undertakes this essential task, it fails in its mission. One shift of power is followed by another, and if the myths of the first survive, the myths of the second will take their stand on earlier nonsense to bring forth worse nonsense still.[140]

Moral Impotence and the Human Incapacity for Sustained Development

Regardless of human efforts to restore intelligence and to overcome the flight from understanding or to guarantee an enduring human development that persistently pursues the good and works towards bringing to effect recurrent schemes of events towards its realization, there remains the persistent problem of evil arising from the weakness of the human will to bring about the good it knows. Lonergan calls this weakness moral impotence. In Chapter 18 of *Insight* he emphasizes the imperative of not only knowing that something is to be done but of actually doing it. Such consistency between knowing and doing effects changes not only in the social environment in which human beings live but also in the way human beings carry out their daily lives. Yet often human beings do not rise up to meet this exigency. The basic question for Lonergan, therefore, in Chapter 18 of *Insight*, is how the detached and disinterested desire to know is to be extended to human living by doing what one knows is intelligent, reasonable and responsible.

Lonergan believes that human beings avoid the exigency of moral living in three ways. First, they avoid self-consciousness, that is, avoid "a moral analysis of one's deeds, one's words, one's mixed motives."[141] Second, they rationalize, that is, they justify vice to be virtue. Third, they renounce morality. Unlike the other two escapes, moral renunciation gives up hope in the struggle to bring about the good one knows into one's spontaneous living.

---

140. *Insight*, 265.
141. Ibid., 622.

> It is without the illusion generated by fleeing self-consciousness. It is without the deceit generated by rationalization. But it is content with a speculative acknowledgement of the aspiration to make one's own living intelligent and reasonable. It is ready to confess its wrongdoing, but it has given up hope of amending its ways.[142]

Lonergan attributes the inability to keep to the moral exigency demanded by the dynamics of human knowing to the insufficient development of human intelligence and to the unfortunate situation that decisions have to be made in spite of such insufficient development of intelligence. Consequently, the effectiveness of human freedom is negatively affected. This problem, described by Lonergan as the problem of liberation, is the problem of human moral impotence.

This affects the human capacity for sustained development because while in the process of acquiring the knowledge one needs for doing the right thing, for instance, one has to make decisions based on the insufficient knowledge one has. Consequently often the good is mistaken for the bad and the bad for the good.[143]

On account of the reality, the radicalness, the permanence and the immanency of the problem of moral impotence, therefore, sustainable human development will be dependent on what Lonergan described in Chapter 18 of *Insight* as "a still higher integration." According to him, this solution (1) has to take people as they are; (2) must be a solution and not a mere suppression of the problem; (3) and while maintaining the tension of limitation and transcendence, it must be able to replace the incapacity for sustained development.[144] In Chapter 7 of *Insight*, Lonergan posits cosmopolis as the viewpoint higher than the viewpoint of strict common sense bias for the restoration of human intelligence. But as we saw above, in Chapter 18 of *Insight*, he argued for "higher integrations in the realm of being"[145] which makes possible the needed higher viewpoint. While what he meant is not so clear in Chapter 18 of *Insight*, the reality of human moral impotence makes imperative a still higher integration in the realm of being. However, after raising the question of general transcendent knowledge about God that, according to him, "answers the basic questions raised by proportionate

---

142. Ibid., 623.
143. Ibid., 653
144. Ibid., 655.
145. Ibid., 656.

being,"[146] in Chapter 19 of *Insight*, Lonergan emphasizes the importance of adding a theological dimension to his analysis of progress and decline.[147]

The higher integration will consist of the absolutely supernatural solution of grace by which humankind will collaborate with God in the solution to the human problem of evil. It will consist of love, especially being in love with God, with creation and with all persons of creation on account of God and thus the meeting of evil with good. As Lonergan writes: "For it is only inasmuch as men are willing to meet evil with good, to love their enemies, to pray for those that persecute and calumniate them, that the social surd is a potential good. It follows that love of God above all and in all so embraces the order of the universe as to love all men with a self-sacrificing love."[148] He continues: "Finally such love will inform man's intellect with a hope that repudiates man's despair, especially, 'the deep hopelessness that allows man's spirit to surrender the legitimate aspirations of the unrestricted desire.'"[149] This still higher integration which "includes the higher conjugate forms of faith, hope, and charity" is the supernatural solution to the problem of evil, to the bias responsible for the longer cycle of decline.[150]

The introduction of the conjugate forms of these religious values into human intellect, will and sensitivity is transformative and leads to repentance, to sorrow, and to a conversion that regrets dramatic bias and the threefold bias of the practical subject, and that moves a person from selfishness to a self-sacrificing love of God and of one's neighbour. Under such self-sacrificing love:

> . . . rational self-consciousness deplores and regrets the scotosis of its dramatic bias and its involvement in the individual, group, and general bias of common sense; it repents its flight from self-knowledge, its rationalization of wrong, its surrender to evil; it detests its commitment to the counterpositions, its contribution to man's decline through successive adjustments of theory to ever worse practice, its share in the genesis and the propagation of the myths that confer on appearance the strength and power and passion that are due of reality.[151]

---

146. Ibid., 709.
147. Ibid., 714.
148. Ibid., 721–22.
149. Komonchak, *Foundations in Ecclesiology*, 26.
150. *Insight*, 762–63.
151. Ibid., 722.

Lonergan's position above could rightly be seen as summarizing what he set out to do in the book *Insight* as he writes: "If human historical process is such a compound of process and decline, then its redemption would be effected by faith, hope and charity. For the evils of the situation and the enmities they engender would only be perpetuated by an even-handed justice: only charity can wipe the slate clean. The determinism and pressures of every kind, resulting from the cumulative surd of unintelligent policies and actions, can be withstood only through a hope that is transcendent and so does not depend on any human prey. Finally, only within the context of higher truths accepted on faith can human intelligence and reasonableness be liberated from the charge of irrelevance to the realities produced by human waywardness."[152]

---

152. Lonergan, "Transition From a Classicist World-View," 8.

3

Lonergan and Social Transformation

IN THE PROCESS OF understanding social change, it is important to pay attention to the notion of the scale of values under which a society organizes itself. Such a range of values not only give meaning and value to the personal development of its peoples, but it also promotes actions for societal development and transformation. As we saw in chapter 2, Bernard Lonergan's theory on the constitution and goal of social order makes a case for social change. Lonergan sees "human life as basically artistic, creative."[1] For him, the issue of social progress, development and transformation involves a movement from the theoretical aspect of "the detached, disinterested, unrestricted desire to know that grasps intelligently and affirms reasonably not only the facts of the universe of being but also to its practical possibilities"[2] actuated in self-consistent knowing and doing. Within this structure, progress and decline are dependent upon the actions or inactions of human subjects seeking for ways to improve themselves and their communities. Consequently social transformation is linked to the "dialectics of history," that is, of the linked but opposed principles constitutive of human subjects as persons, as members of communities and as cultural and religious beings called to be-in-love.

As stated previously, there is progress to the extent that human beings live authentically by obeying the transcendental precepts: be attentive, be intelligent, be reasonable, be responsible and be in love. Lonergan says decline sets into a social order to the extent that people fail to be attentive,

---

1. Lonergan, "History," 235.
2. *Insight*, 622.

intelligent, reasonable and responsible. And, one can add, the failure to love, where the alternative to love - apathy and hatred can usher in decline as well. Lonergan explains "the dialectic of history," as such in the 1981–82 interviews thus:

> In so far as people are intelligent, reasonable, and responsible, there is progress. If they make mistakes they will notice them and correct them, so you have developing understanding. In so far as they are unobservant, unintelligent, unreasonable and irresponsible—any one of the four—you get the social surd, and society becomes a dump. Nothing fits together. The only thing you can do with your situation is go back to correct all the mistakes that have been made. Get things straightened out.[3]

Societal development and transformation will therefore depend upon the actions or inactions of human beings living authentically or unauthentically in accordance with the integral dialectics of the subject and of the community overcoming bias by adhering to the scale of values.

This chapter will explore further Lonergan's anthropology and its implications for societal development and transformation in the light of the scale of values he suggested for the promotion of authenticity in society. It will center on the fourth level of human intentionality concerned with conscious deliberation and action, since social change is dependent on the value choices people make. As Lonergan writes in "Philosophy and the Religious Phenomenon," the level of deliberation assumes the existential viewpoint that compels putting into action what one knows as the good. They (the levels of deliberation) "push the requirement of authenticity to the sticking point: good decisions must be complemented by good conduct and good actions; and failure in this respect is just the inner essence of hypocrisy."[4] It will explore Lonergan's notion of progress, decline and transformation in *Method in Theology*. Specific attention will be paid to the development of Lonergan's scale of values by a prominent Lonergan scholar, Robert Doran, in what he called 'the integral scale of values.' We shall also discuss the implications of Doran's appropriation of Lonergan for sustainable human development. Further, because societal development and transformation, according to Lonergan, are not possible without the conversion of the mind and heart that moves towards freeing the person and the community from the biases, the imperative of conversion—intellectual, moral, religious and

---

3. Lambert et al., *Caring About Meaning*, 87–88.
4. Lonergan, "Philosophy and the Religious Phenomenon," 130.

psychic—for sustainable human development, will also be discussed in this chapter.

Progress, Development and Decline in *Method in Theology*

A consideration of progress, development and decline in *Method in Theology* is informed by the change in Lonergan's thought between *Insight* and *Method* in regard to the notions of the good and value. This fact is underscored in "Insight Revisited," a kind of intellectual autobiography of Lonergan, thus: "In *Insight* the good was the intelligent and reasonable. In *Method* the good is a distinct notion. It is intended in questions for deliberation. . . . It is aspired to in the intentional response of feelings to values. It is known in judgments of value. . . . It is brought about by deciding and living up to one's decisions."[5] Also referring specifically to Chapter 2 of *Method in Theology* (we shall use extensively here) Frederick E. Crowe writes: . . . "Here the themes of Insight's chapter 7 are summarized and carried forward: those of technology, economics, politics, culture—and now religion is added; those also of the individual and the community, of group formation and group bias, of progress and decline."[6]

A good summary of Lonergan's position on social progress in *Method in Theology* is his assertion that "authenticity can be shown to generate progress, unauthenticity to bring about decline, while the problem of overcoming decline provides an introduction to religion."[7] As we saw above, authenticity generates progress because it generates freedom, enabling the human subject to be truly who he/she is and thus promote the actualization of his/her potentialities as a human being arising from the unrestricted desire to know and to do the good. Ideally, authenticity is free of all forms of bias—dramatic, egoistic, group, and general bias. It promotes communal solidarity because, through their obedience to the transcendental precepts, people living authentically promote genuine collaboration for the common good in such a way that the constituents of society work together under the influence of God's grace. In an integral dialectic of community, insights are not stifled, rather, the unrestricted desire to know is allowed free reign and every person is accorded due respect irrespective of language, lineage or

---

5. Lonergan, "Insight Revisited"; Crowe, "Exploration of Lonergan's New Notion of Value," 51.

6. Crowe, "Lonergan and Liberation Theology," 121.

7. *Method in Theology*, 288.

culture in a heterogeneous society. A conscious, deliberate effort is made towards recurrent provision of the human good for all members of society.

Insofar as social progress is the result of graced human authenticity, it is attainable and concrete. It is not something external to human constitution. Human beings desire the good—the particular good of the individual, the good of order of the community and life as motivated by value.[8] Societies progress genuinely by reasonable and responsible implementation of valid insights. Because human beings desire the good, one can say that for Lonergan, social progress is consonant with human nature. However, obedience to the immanent law of the human spirit—the transcendental precepts is not easy. Authenticity is not some settled quality one attains once and for all. Genuineness remains "ever precarious." As Lonergan acknowledges:

> Human authenticity is not some pure quality, some serene freedom from all oversights, all misunderstanding, all mistakes, all sins. Rather it consists in a withdrawal from unauthenticity, and the withdrawal is never a permanent achievement. It is ever precarious, ever to be achieved afresh, ever in great part a matter of uncovering still more oversights, acknowledging still further failures to understand, correcting still more mistakes, repenting more and more deeply hidden sins.[9]

Because of the precariousness of sustained authenticity, human capacity for sustainable development remains impossible without the assistance of divine grace.

Besides authenticity, there is the problem of inauthenticity resulting in societal decay and decline. Just as evil is opposed to the good, so inauthenticity is opposed to the immanent desire for the good, the true and the beautiful. Inauthenticity brings about decline just as authenticity brings about societal progress and development. A society where inattention, obtuseness, silliness and irresponsibility reign is undoubtedly headed for decline and breakdown. Societies in decline are characterized by selfishness, greed, the pursuit of group interests along with the exclusion of insights from other groups, and violence. Such societies prioritize short-term solutions and ignore long-term solutions to problems. As we saw in our treatment of the biases, societies held hostage by them are headed for the shorter (minor) and the longer (major) cycles of decline and often collapse.

8. Ibid., 302.
9. Ibid., 252.

The schemes of recurrence of events that ensure provision of the human good break down, and private or individual good takes the place of the common good. "So the good of order deteriorates."[10]

One of the effects on such societies is that development is guided by group egoism which "divides the body social not merely into those that have and those that have not but also makes the former the representatives of the cultural flower of the age to leave the latter apparent survivals from a forgotten age."[11] In the limit, such societies become a battle ground for the survival of the fittest. And it is not easy to hold back the wheel of decline. Lonergan's description aptly captures the pervasiveness of societal decline:

> Decline has a still deeper level. Not only does it compromise and distort progress. Not only do inattention, obtuseness, unreasonableness, irresponsibility produce objectively absurd situations. Not only do ideologies corrupt minds. But compromise and distortion discredit progress. Objectively absurd situations do not yield to treatment. Corrupt minds have a flair for picking the mistaken solution and insisting that it alone is intelligent, reasonable, good. Imperceptibly the corruption spreads from the harsh sphere of material advantage and power to the mass media, the stylish journals, the literary movements, the educational process, the reigning philosophies. A civilization in decline digs its own grave with a relentless consistency. It cannot be argued out of its self-destructive ways, for argument has a theoretical major premise, theoretical premises are asked to conform to matters of fact, and the facts in the situation produced by decline more and more are the absurdities that proceed from inattention, oversight, unreasonableness and irresponsibility.[12]

Moreover, Lonergan argues that the disobedience of the transcendental precepts that results in societal decline is the basic form of human alienation.[13] Human beings become alienated when they seek to justify continued disobedience to the transcendental precepts by criticizing and denying self-transcendence as ideological. Such denial itself becomes the basic form of ideology whose perpetuation, Lonergan says, only deepens societal decline. Under such circumstances, conflicting ideologies disrupt a culture and inflict on society absurdities that breed resentment, hatred,

---

10. Ibid., 54.
11. Ibid.
12. Ibid., 54–55.
13. Ibid., 55.

anger and violence.¹⁴ Decline disrupts the social order and the common meaning upon which a community functions. Instead of love, it sows the seeds of discord, hatred and division that make it difficult for people to work together for the common good. The consequences are the various forms of deviation which we have treated in the previous chapter on the biases. Lonergan names some of such evil possibilities in *Method in Theology*:

> There are the deviations occasioned by neurotic need. There are the refusals to keep on taking the plunge from settled routines to an as yet unexperienced but richer mode of living. There are the mistaken endeavors to quieten an uneasy conscience by ignoring, belittling, denying, rejecting higher values. Preference scales become distorted. Feelings soured. Bias creeps into one's outlook, rationalization into one's morals, ideology into one's thought. So one may come to hate the truly good, and love the really evil. Nor is the calamity limited to individuals. It can happen to groups, to nations, to blocks of nations, to mankind. It can take different, opposed, belligerent forms to divide mankind and to menace civilization with destruction. Such is the monster that has stood forth in our day.¹⁵

In spite of the pervasiveness of decline, as we will see later in this chapter, Lonergan was equally concerned with overcoming decline as with restoring progress and development. In the light of this, we now address his notion of development in the scale of values and the structure of the good.

Development and the Scale of Values

As we mentioned briefly in the previous chapter, in *Insight*, Chapter 18, Lonergan's notion of the good corresponds to the various levels of human consciousness. In *Method in Theology*, he did not define the good. Instead he assembles its component parts: "skills, feelings, values, beliefs, cooperation, progress, and decline."¹⁶ In a later work, "The Role of a Catholic University in the Modern World," he explains the relationship of the good with the levels of consciousness: "as human knowing rises on three levels, so also the good that men pursue contains a threefold aspect."¹⁷ First,

---

14. Ibid., 117.
15. Ibid., 39–40.
16. *Method in Theology*, 27. Cf. 108.
17. *Collection*, CWL 4, 108.

there is the good as the object of desire characterized by the satisfaction one experiences at the pleasure of obtaining the object. Lonergan calls this the 'particular good,' concerned as it is with what is good for each person as distinct from other people in society. Second, there is the 'good of order' that ensures the recurrence of schemes of events or structures for the provision of the good not only for oneself but for other people who are members of the civil community. Lonergan says ' the good of order' "consists in an intelligible pattern of relationships that conditions the fulfillment of each man's desires by his contributions to the fulfillment of the desires of others, and similarly protects each from the object of his fears in the measure he contributes to warding off the objects feared by others."[18] According to Brian Cronin, "a good of order is a system of cooperation and specialization in a group, where all contribute to the society and receive benefits from the society in a mutual complementary manner."[19] Thus the 'good of order' includes such products of practical intelligence as the polity, the economy, technology, social arrangements like marriage and the family as an institution, etc.[20] Third, there is value, that is, "the good as the possible object of rational choice."[21] Values can be true or false, terminal or originating, actual or in process, depending on whether the choice is rational or non-rational, or the objects of the possible choices and on whether the potency for transformation is realized, has the possibility of being realized or is merely under consideration.[22] When the possible choice is rational (consistent with what one knows to be true), values are true. The operations of deliberation intend terminal values; they are then the objects of possible choices. Particular goods and the true good of order are included as terminal values. Originating values are persons genuinely making responsible choices, and in so doing are modifying their habitual willingness, becoming truly virtuous persons.[23]

Thus, the invariant structure of the human good is the particular good, the good of order and values. The particular good is at the first level of the structure of human consciousness and is correlated with experience or presentations. The second level, the good of order, is correlated with understanding. It regards the social dimension of the human good, and it

18. *Insight*, 238.
19. Cronin, *Value Ethics*, 146.
20. *Insight*, 619.
21. Ibid, 624.
22. Ibid.
23. *Method in Theology*, 34.

is, according to Frederick Lawrence, "the concretely verifiable way of life as embodied in laws, technology, economy, polity, family life."[24] Value, at the third level of the structure, correlates to judgment. It comprises the cultural domain in the light of which the good of order is to be judged and evaluated. "Thus judgments of value set the good of order above private advantage, subordinate technology to economics, refer economics to social welfare, and, generally, mete out to every finite good both appreciation and criticism."[25]

Thus the structure of the human good, which Lonergan describes in Chapter 2 of *Method in Theology*, is oriented to certain concrete ends: particular goods by individuals; the good of order by groups of individuals cooperating with one another and fulfilling specific roles, and the institutions they set up to ensure constant provision of the human good for the benefit of everyone; and the level of value which reflects upon the order, development, and progress of peoples, and aims at an improved standard of living. But this can only be achieved if the balance of this structure of the human good is maintained and not distorted; if the right value guides societal life and development.

Values answer the question of the worth of things and are the fruit of human deliberation. As a transcendental notion, value promotes the subject to fullness of consciousness, directs him/her to his/her goals and provides the criteria for judging whether the goals are being reached. Values are apprehended in feelings—not in the unintentional states, urges, desires, etc.—but in the intentional feelings that regard the person, the human subject, as the originating value that appreciates the values in beauty, goodness, truth, etc. According to Lonergan, the "apprehensions of values occur in a further category of intentional response which greets either the ontic value of a person or the qualitative value of beauty, of understanding, of truth, of noble deeds, of virtuous acts, of great achievements."[26] Value then helps in self-discovery as it is the initial thrust towards moral self-transcendence. If this process of self-discovery facilitated through value is intensified and carried through, "there emerges in consciousness the significance of personal value and the meaning of personal responsibility."[27]

---

24. Lawrence, "Human Good and Christian Conversation," 91–92.
25. Lonergan, "Role of a Catholic University in the Modern World," 109.
26. Ibid., 38.
27. Ibid.

Societal development is dependent on the order of values human beings choose to recognize, live by, act upon, prioritize, include, or exclude in the conduct of their lives and actions. Lonergan distinguishes values in a preferential order or "scale of values":

> Not only do feelings respond to values. They do so in accord with some scale of preference. So we may distinguish vital, social, cultural, personal, and religious values in an ascending order. Vital values, such as health and strength, grace and vigor, normally are preferred to avoiding the work, privations, pains involved in acquiring, maintaining, restoring them. Social values, such as the good of order which conditions the vital values of the whole community, have to be preferred to the vital values of individual members of the community. Cultural values do not exist without the underpinning of vital and social values, but none the less they rank together. Not on bread alone doth man live.
>
> Over and above mere living and operating, men have to find a meaning and value in their living and operating. It is the function of culture to discover, express, validate, criticize, correct, develop, improve such meaning and value. Personal value is the person in his self-transcendence, as loving and being loved, as originator of values in himself and in his milieu, as an inspiration and invitation to others to do likewise. Religious values, finally, are at the heart of the meaning and value of man's living and man's world.[28]

By the principle of sublation, (which means the successive levels retain, preserve and go beyond and complete the previous levels),[29] the various values relate to one another, lead to one another and give rise to the other. Thus religious values guide personal values; personal values guide cultural values that equally guide social values and social values in turn guide vital values.

However, although Lonergan distinguished the scale of values that guides human self-transcendence, he did not much develop how they relate to each other. He recognizes the possibility of a shift in scales of preference on account of a conversion experience.[30] In light of this, in the functional specialty 'Dialectic,' he urges his readers to continuously scrutinize their intentional responses to values and their implicit scales of preference.[31] He

---

28. Ibid., 31–32.
29. Lonergan, "Aquinas Today," 46; "Mission and the Spirit," 29.
30. *Method in Theology*, 52.
31. Ibid., 240.

recognizes the possibility of a breakdown in the scale of values in societies headed for decline, especially the longer cycle of decline. In such societies he observes: "the body social is torn apart in many ways, and its cultural soul has been rendered incapable of reasonable convictions and responsible commitments."[32] But we do not actually know how these values lead to the unity of human life and action and how they might promote societal development and transformation. Further and deeper understanding of the relationship of these levels in the scale of values is carried out in the work of Robert M. Doran, one of Lonergan's successors and one of the editors of Lonergan's collected works. Doran's appropriation is a result of his conviction that: "The scale of values and the integral dialectics of community, culture and the subject constitute the heuristic structure of a rational society."[33] Doran appropriates Lonergan's scale of values by relating them to one another because, as he argues, the integral dialectic of community can be preserved only through integrity of cultural meanings and values.[34] We now turn to Doran's appropriation for a closer study of social transformation.

The Integral Scale of Values (Robert Doran's Appropriation).

Robert Doran's appropriation of Lonergan's scale of values spans a series of his works. As we saw earlier, Doran considers the scale of values important in his efforts at a systematic theology in the light of an understanding of history.[35] Because his appropriation has followed a continuous thread, we shall treat it as a unit without discussing each of his works separately. Doran's appropriation is in light of Lonergan's analysis of progress and decline in Chapter 7 of *Insight*.[36] Doran calls this appropriation "the integral scale of values."[37] By this he means the functioning of the scale of values towards the integral dialectics of the subject, the community and the culture. He relates the scale of values to each of the levels of consciousness, arguing that

---

32. Ibid., 244.
33. Doran, *Theology and the Dialectics of History*, 393.
34. Ibid., 415.
35. Ibid., 107. We shall consider his appropriation in three of his works: *Theology and the Dialectic of History* (1990); *Theological Foundations II: Theology and Culture* (1995); and in his *What is Systematic Theology?* (2005).
36. *Theological Foundations*, 353.
37. *Theology and the Dialectic of History*, 93.

"the scale is based on the increasing degrees of self-transcendence to which one is carried or to which a community is carried in response to values at the different levels."[38] Thus, vital values are correlated to experience, social values to understanding, cultural values to judgment, personal values to deliberation and religious values to God's gift of his love.

Further, he views the scale of values from 'above downwards,' and from 'below upwards' in the concrete life of human subjects. In this relationship of mutual conditioning Doran argues that "the higher levels condition the schemes of recurrence of the more basic levels, while problems in the effective recurrence of the more basic levels offer an occasion for, and establish the proportions to be met by, the questions that prompt the needed developments at the higher levels."[39] For example, from below upwards, vital values are conditioned by social values; social values equally require vital values to function properly. Cultural values give meaning to social order at the same time as cultural values depend on the effective functioning of the institutions of society. While the person of integrity generates the meaning that informs the culture, the common meaning of a culture forms the human person. The human person will not form meaning without the grace of God.[40] Conversely, from above downwards, religious values create the condition for personal value; personal integrity creates conditions for authentic cultural values: "cultural integrity at both levels conditions the possibility of a just social order; and a just social order conditions the possibility of the equitable distribution of vital goods."[41]

Doran is convinced that "the scale of values determines the relations among the dialectics of the subject, culture, and community."[42] As such, their integrity "is the key to the structure of society."[43] This is so because vital, social and everyday cultural values make up the infrastructure of society while the reflexive, objectifying dimension of culture makes up the superstructure of society.[44] The infrastructure of society includes sponta-

---

38. Doran, *What is Systematic Theology?* 181.
39. Doran, *Theological Foundations II*, 515.
40. Doran, *Theology and the Dialectic of History*, 95–96.
41. Ibid., 96.
42. Ibid., 93.
43. Ibid., 95.
44. Doran, *Theological Foundations II*, 515. Doran's distinction of infrastructure and superstructure of culture is important because culture is often neglected in the postmodern society as the integrator of the dialectic of community. Chapter 12 of *Theology and the Dialectics of History* elaborates this distinction and its implications.

neous intersubjectivity, technology, economic relations, politics and practical affairs of culture. The superstructure of society is the reflexive level of culture that includes scientific, scholarly, philosophical and theological objectifications and reflections on society.[45] The function of culture at the everyday infrastructural level is the integration of the social values. At the superstructural level, culture reflects critically on the everyday function of culture. Culture at its infrastructural and in its superstructural levels attends to the integrity of the community. The intellectual collaboration (Lonergan's 'cosmopolis') that is expected to carry through this integration in the event of the distortion of the dialectic of community attends primarily to the integrity of culture by examining thoroughly the cultural meaning and values operative at the infrastructural and superstructural levels of culture.[46] Doran argues that "to abandon in principle as ideological illusion the promotion of autonomous cultural, personal and religious values is to succumb to that major surrender of intelligence that is the radical reason for the long cycle of decline."[47]

Because of the importance of culture in the historical process, Doran deems it necessary to work out the relation of the three dialectics, the dialectic of the subject, the dialectic of the community and the dialectic of culture, with three of the levels of value, social, cultural, personal, from below and from above.[48] The relation of these three dialectics to one another he calls 'analogy of dialectic'.[49] As we already know, the dialectic of the subject is constituted by neural demands for psychic integration and conscious representation, on the one hand, and the censorship over these demands by dramatically patterned intelligence and imagination, on the other. The dialectic of the community is constituted by spontaneous intersubjectivity, on the one hand, and the demands of practical intelligence, on the other. The dialectic of culture, which is Doran's construction from his analysis of the search for direction in the movement of life, is constituted by the cosmological, on the one hand, and anthropological constitutive meaning, on the other.[50] Cosmological insight explains order in history from the cosmic rhythms of non-human nature while the anthropological

---

45. Doran, *Theological Foundations II*, 352–53.
46. Ibid., 353.
47. Doran, *Theology and the Dialectics of History*, 395.
48. Doran, *Theological Foundations II*, 505.
49. Ibid., 338.
50. Doran works out the dialectic of culture more elaborately in Chapters 15 and 16 of *Theology and the Dialectics of History*.

constitutive meaning interprets the paradigm of order as world-transcendent. Thus while cosmological constitutive meaning "moves from the cosmos, through society, to the individual . . . Anthropological insight moves from God through the individual, to the society."[51]

The analogy of dialectic could be a dialectic of contraries that integrally work towards progress and development. But if there is distortion caused by the dominance of either of the opposed principles, the dialectic becomes a dialectic of contradictories and suggests the presence of bias or lack of intelligence and so can head towards decline. Moreover, these dialectics are subject to the law of limitation and transcendence constituting the immanent intelligibility of genuine development by the working together of their internally constitutive principles.[52] Other characteristics of the analogy of dialectic which we have mentioned in Chapter 2 include the following: that the integrity of the dialectic does not lie in any of the constitutive principles of the dialectic but instead is the work of a third principle beyond the linked but opposed principles of the dialectic. At the higher level of the third principle, there could also be its opposite—the dialectic of contradictories. Thus the integrity of the dialectic of the subject is a function of divinely infused grace responsible for universal willingness leading the will to the good in spite of moral impotence. The integrity of the dialectic of the community is genuine cultural values—critical culture able to integrate the superstructure and the infrastructure of society to a reorientation of the common meaning of the community. The integrity of the dialectic of culture from the Christian standpoint is the soteriological differentiation of consciousness—the principle of the outer word, that is, the specifically Christian values of self-sacrificing love.[53]

The relation of the integral scale of values to the analogy of dialectic shows that the dialectic of the subject is foundational of the dialectics because, as we saw earlier, the scale of values is intimately related to the subject who participates in and contributes to the authenticity of a cultural community.[54] The dialectic of the subject is foundational also because, in the search for direction in the movement of life, it is the human subject's intentional consciousness raising and answering questions for understand-

---

51. Doran, *Theological Foundations II*, 527. See also Doran's *What is Systematic Theology?*, 188.

52. Doran, *Theological Foundations II*, 340.

53. Doran, *What is Systematic Theology?*, 173–74. Cf. *Theological Foundations II*, 340.

54. Doran, *Theological Foundations II*, 351.

ing, questions for reflection and questions for deliberation that makes this possible. It is also the human subject's openness to further knowledge and advance that promotes a social order which can better provide for the recurrence of vital values recurrently possible. Intelligent insight contributes to everyday cultural values of the infrastructure by critically reflecting upon the everyday values and structures of a community. The personal integrity of the human subject made possible by the religious values of God's love sets in motion insights for a life of integrity that adheres to the cultural values of the community and, when the need arises, effects changes in the cultural values, for the common good and not for personal gain or for egoistic purposes of self-aggrandizement. Furthermore, as we already have shown, the set of relations of the scale of values, from above downwards and from below upwards, takes place in the human subject. It is implemented by the human subject open to the generation of insights for progress and development.[55] As Lonergan rightly observes: "the rock, then, is the subject in his conscious, unobjectified attentiveness, intelligence, reasonableness, responsibility."[56] So in relation to the human subject, the scale of values is at the center not only of integral development but also is the key to the structure of society to bring about an integral dialectic of the subject and of the community.[57] All things being equal, the implementation of the integral scale of values fashions the human person obedient to the immanent norms of the human spirit and creatively contributes to progress and societal development.

When the integral scale of values is neglected, Doran says, the infrastructure of society—spontaneous intersubjectivity and practical intelligence (technology, the economy and politics), the integrity of the dialectic of community—are distorted. When that happens, the scale of values, instead of mutually conditioning each other, may lead to the neglect of some values. In place of progress, there is decline. For instance, the schemes of recurrence of events in the social order for the provision of vital values suffer breakdown. Goods and services are maldistributed. The meanings and values that inform a social order fail to inform and motivate it, and the inefficient institutions collapse. Culture either retreats to the margins of society or becomes the tool for economic interests.[58] Legal and political

---

55. Ibid., 354–55.
56. *Method in Theology*, 20.
57. Doran, *What is Systematic Theology?*, 171.
58. Doran, *Theological Foundations II*, 249.

institutions become part of the superstructure of society and take as their function the preservation of a distorted economic infrastructure, usurping more and more the initial functions of culture. Individuals can lose their personal integrity and affect the cultural values with their neurotic, individual, group and general biases:

> Problems in the effective and recurrent distribution of vital goods can be met only by a reversal of distortions in the social order; the proportions of the needed reversal are set by the scope and range of the real or potential maldistribution; the social change demands a transformation at the everyday level of culture proportionate to the dimensions of the social problem; this transformation frequently depends on reflexive theoretical and scientific developments at the superstructural level; new cultural values at both levels call for proportionate changes at the level of personal integrity; and these depend for their emergence, sustenance, and consistency on the religious development of the person.[59]

In sum, Doran's appropriation is informed by his conviction that the integral scale of values explains the process of societal development and breakdown. The three dialectical processes account for social, personal and cultural change.[60] Consequently, the integral scale of values and the analogy of dialectic have implications for sustainable human development.

Implications for Sustainable Human Development

In Chapter 1, we argued that sustainable development in contemporary development discourse, as part of the theories of development, implies fashioning development in such a way that the resources of the earth are not depleted but rather developed so that generations following us can make use of the earth's resources to continue their own development. In this section, we are using the word 'sustainable' to mean endurable, recurrent, sustained, and continuous. Sustainable human development means the continuous promotion of human development in its entirety, including self-transcendence. As we saw in Chapter 2, such sustained human development is not possible without a supernatural solution on account of moral impotence—the reality of evil that limits human attempts at self-transcendence. As our treatment of the scale of values has shown, human

---

59. Doran, *Theology and the Dialectic of History*, 96.
60. Ibid., 173.

Lonergan and Social Transformation

development can be sustained if the integral scale of values is respected. We consider further what this means for sustainable human development and as such, for social transformation. Such societal development and transformation provides alternatives to the social surd and breakdown, facilitates human authenticity and makes visible the transformative role religion can play in society.

Provides Alternatives to the Social Surd

As we saw above, according to Robert Doran, the relations among the scale of values, along with the preferential positioning of these relations, are key to the structure of society. The vital values of health are preferred to the pleasures one would derive from eating unhealthy foods or from overeating. The vitality of the community and its welfare are to be preferred to the egoistic self-preservation mentality. A cooperative health care system that provides for the health of the community, for instance, is to be preferred to private health care that serves the interests of those in the wealthy tier of society. Culture, in its everyday and superstructural levels that give meaning to the social order by making it possible for the social order to serve all people in society, must always be evaluated to ensure that it plays its critical role in society. The integrity of culture is the originating value of the human person who incarnates values and who, by opting for the common good of others, imbues cultural values with self-transcendent altruistic meanings and values. Personal value is the human person in his/her potentiality as a knowing and choosing and loving person. Personal value likewise surpasses the cultural value and any existing social order. No institution or order is to be considered more important than the individual human person. Personal integrity is dependent on the gift of God's love, for character formation and integrity of life does not come easily without the religious value of God's love. Religious value, therefore, is the supreme value—"the unrestricted and supremely transcendent value that is the orienting desire of all knowers and choosers and that therefore sets the conditions for all the different levels of valuing, or for the whole scale of values."[61]

The scale of values provides an alternative to the social surds arising from the various forms of the biases: dramatic, individual, group and general. As the key to the structure of a functioning society, the relation of mutual conditioning of the scale of values, from above downwards and

---

61. Flanagan, *Quest for Self-Knowledge*, 200.

from below upwards, overcomes various forms of egoistic tendencies at the heart of decline. As we saw in the previous section (3.4), religious values condition personal value, personal value conditions cultural values, cultural values condition social values, social values condition vital values and vice versa. Thus, the integral scale of values provides an alternative to the social surd of sin by gradually moving the human subject and society away from the exclusiveness of self-centeredness into a society that is more inclusive and open to insights for the progress and development of peoples. In place of the selfishness of egoistic bias, the scale of values offers the altruistic spirit of cooperation with others. In place of the nepotism and clannish mentality of group bias, the scale of values imbues society with an open spirit of mutual collaboration, tolerance and acceptance. In place of the flight from understanding of general bias giving rise to the longer cycle of decline, the scale of values opts for theory and practice allowing critical culture to integrate the dialectic of community and provide long term solutions. In place of the one-sidedness of a merely humanistic society bereft of the supreme value of divine transcendence, the scale of values anchors human integrity in religion based on divine love, tolerant of all, accepting all as children of one God with equal dignity, freedom and responsibility. The implementation of the integral scale of values makes it difficult for any of the constituents of society to dominate over the others. It seeks to maintain the creative tension of limitation and transcendence, resulting in genuineness in the life of the human subject, with authentic community guided by genuine common meanings and values. The integral scale of values as the key to the structure of society therefore provides an alternative to the social surd. It rescues and heals a society in decline, providing an alternative to sin and instilling lasting values which foster the progress and development of peoples.

The Facilitation of Human Authenticity

Our exposition of the integral dialectic of the subject as a process towards human authenticity and Lonergan's emphasis of this in his writings indicates the central place of the human subject in social transformation. It is the subject obeying the transcendental precepts who is a member of a civil community, who spontaneously exists with other subjects engaged in activities that form schemes of recurrence of events towards the provision of values for the members of the community. It is the human subject who

Lonergan and Social Transformation

is the originator of values in him/herself—values that give meaning to the social order and that work towards societal development and transformation. It is important to note, therefore, that any meaningful change in society must start with human subjects living authentically, trying as best they can to maintain the good of order for progress and development. Lonergan recognized this and emphasized it not only in his early work, but even more strongly in his later writings.[62] For example, in a 1968 paper, "The Subject," Lonergan observes that if the human subject "renounces authentic living and drifts into the now seductive and now harsh rhythms of his psyche and of nature, then he is alienated from himself."[63] Also, in "The Response of the Jesuit as Priest and Apostle in the Modern World" (1970), Lonergan linked human authenticity to human development. He correlated the question 'What is authenticity?' to the genuine realization of human potentiality and argued that "authentic realization is a self-transcending realization."[64] In the measure that such self-transcendence in action pervades the values of a community, in that measure they pursue what is truly good and in that measure they are authentic.

The integral scale of values facilitates obedience to the transcendental precepts which makes human authenticity possible. First, the religious value of God's love is at the heart of personal integrity. Personal value, by recognizing the human person as the originating source of values, emphasizes human dignity and moves the human person to self-actualization towards human authenticity. Culture in its infrastructural and superstructural levels gives meaning and value to human life and hence to obedience of the transcendental precepts that foster human authenticity. The social order provides the institutions—family, state, law and order, justice, basic infrastructures for fostering the necessities of life. The regular recurrence of schemes for the provision of the human good made possible by a stable and functional social order is vital and basic to human authenticity and

---

62. In many of these writings Lonergan devoted much time to the theme of human authenticity. This is true of his response to a questionnaire on Jesuit Spirituality in 1970, titled "The Response of the Jesuit as Priest and Apostle in the Modern World;" the 1974 lecture titled "Aquinas Today: Tradition and Innovation;" "Religious Experience" (1976); "Religious Knowledge" (1976); "The Ongoing Genesis of Method" (1976); "A Post-Hegelian Philosophy of Religion," (1980) etc. (in *A Third Collection*, a collection of these later writings.)

63. Lonergan, "Subject," 86.

64. Lonergan, "Response of the Jesuit as Priest and Apostle in the Modern World," 166.

hence to sustained human development. Vital values of health and strength constitute the ingredient of living without which authenticity becomes impossible.

Second, the scale of values is not only correlated with the dynamic structure of human knowing, as is made clear in Doran's appropriation of the scale of values, it is also correlated to the transcendental precepts be attentive, be intelligent, be reasonable, be responsible, be in love. As vital values correlates with the level of experience, it correlates with attentiveness. Social value correlates with being intelligent, cultural value with reasonableness, personal value with responsibility, and God's gift of his love in grace is the supreme value that makes possible the dynamic structure, the transcendental precepts and the integral scale of values. By implication, what keeps the structure of human knowing continuously dynamic also accounts for the transcendental precepts. One is authentic to the degree that one obeys the transcendental precepts. The transcendental precepts arise as the immanent norms of the human spirit propelling the human subject from experiencing to understanding, to reflection and to judgment, to decision and to love. The integral scale of values accords with the dynamic structure of human knowing. Thus it facilitates human authenticity. This is implied in the two components of human development (from below upwards—the way of achievement and from above downwards—the way of heritage)[65] developed by Lonergan in two lectures "Healing and Creating in History" (1975) and "Natural Right and Historical Mindedness." (1977).[66] These two ways agree with the various levels of consciousness: the empirical, intelligent, reasonable and responsible, or existential, level. Development from below upwards is development from experience to understanding, from understanding to judgment and from judgment to deliberation actualizing in value. Development from above downwards is the reverse of this order, from deciding value in love to judgment, from judgment to understanding and from understanding to experience. As Mark Doorley explains:

> The creative vector moves along the well-known, if infrequently visited, path of experiencing-understanding-judging. The healing vector, on the other hand, begins with a 'falling in love.' This is the love of another person, of one's family, one's nation, one's God. The creative vector moves from experience to knowledge to love; the

---

65. The way of achievement and the way of heritage are given to the two ways of human development by Crowe in *Old Things and New* (1985).

66. Both lectures are contained in *A Third Collection* (1985).

healing vector moves from a new standard of loving to knowledge to richer experience. The two vectors are dialectically linked in the developmental process.[67]

Thus, the integral scale of values as the key to the structure of society not only provides an alternative to the social surd and breakdown, it creates conditions for human, societal and cultural authenticity. Just as the individual is authentic by obeying the transcendental precepts, the social order is authentic by the recurrence of scheme of events for the constant provision of the human good. Cultural authenticity is dependent on faithful implementation of the integral scale of values as it presupposes: healthy human beings, a stable and functional social order, authentic human beings as originator of values and the supernatural value of God's love keeping the individual human person authentic.

For example, in light of societal development and transformation, fidelity to the integral scale of values makes it possible for a society to continuously provide the human good because fidelity to the transcendental precepts enhances the human freedom that enables members of community to contribute their quota to the common good. Lonergan remarks that when a society loses the faithful adherence to the scale of values, respect for the common good becomes dormant in its citizenship, leading to various forms of depersonalization:

> Wherever the demon of organization invades and tyrannizes his spirit, there are at once revealed the signs of a false and abnormal orientation of society. In some countries the modern state is becoming a gigantic administrative machine. It extends its influence over almost every phase of life. It would bring under its administration the entire gamut of political, economic, social, and intellectual life from birth to death. No wonder then, if, in this impersonal atmosphere, which tends to penetrate and pervade all human life, respect for the common good becomes dormant in the conscience of individuals, and the state loses more and more its primary character of a community of morally responsible citizens. Here may be recognized the origin and the source of that phenomenon which is submerging modern man under its tide of anguish—his "depersonalization."[68]

---

67. Doorley, "Nonviolence, Creation, Healing," 97.
68. Lonergan, "Respect for Human Dignity," 126.

Economic globalization run by the trans-national corporations merging together technology, the economy and the polity through global governance is an instance of the massive phenomenon contributing to varying forms of depersonalization.

Third, the scale of values, by moving the human subject away from too much concentration on the self, advances self-transcendence by its emphasis on the increasing realization of the human good. For instance, vital values shift attention away from harmful pleasures that would compromise health and strength. Social values shift attention away from myself and make me think, not only of my own good, but of the good of others as well. Cultural values give meaning to my life as a member of my community. Personal values move me towards higher self-actualization by enabling me to see myself as a person with dignity, with abilities and with creativity to bring about something new, not only for myself, but for others as well. Further, it makes me acknowledge and respect the personhood of others regardless of their background. The religious value of an utterly transcendent Other moves me to the height of self-transcendence where I recognize myself as the originator of values through the dynamic state of unrestricted loving. I come to know others as my brothers and sisters. I see the universe, not as inexhaustible, but as a gift from God which ought to be preserved for others who come after me.

Religion is Potentially Redemptive in Society

For Lonergan and Doran, sustainable human development is not possible without the religious value of absolute transcendent reality. Human beings, on account of moral impotence, are unable to sustain permanent authenticity or abide by the transcendental precepts. They are tempted by sin and all forms of the flight from understanding: dramatic bias, egoism, group interest, general bias that prefers short term solutions to human problems, and relying on the self instead of looking up to ultimate transcendent values. The higher principle that integrates the distorted dialectics of the subject, of community and of culture (as analyzed by Robert Doran) is the religious value of God's love. For the subject, unwillingness is transformed by the universal willingness for the good, a willingness made possible by the theological virtues of faith, hope and love. The distorted dialectic of community is integrated by cultural value when its superstructural level is imbued with the supreme value of God's transcendent love as revealed, for example, in

Lonergan and Social Transformation

the law of the cross. The higher viewpoint for the dialectic of culture is the soteriological meaning of God's outer word. Doran writes:

> ... in each case the integrity of the dialectic is a function, not of one or the other of its internally constitutive principles, but of a third principle of higher synthesis. Thus the integrity of the dialectic of the subject is a function of grace: proximately of the conjugate forms of charity, hope and faith, and of sensitive participation in them, and remotely of the communication of the very life of God that is a created change that affects, indeed effects, a topmost level of consciousness, a completion, a resting from intentional striving and psychic restlessness. Again, the integral dialectic of cosmological and anthropological constitutive meaning is a function of soteriological constitutive meaning, of the outer word of God's revelation spoken to and appropriated by cultures transformed by its message. Yet again, the integrity of the dialectic of community is a function of the integrity of the dialectic of culture itself.[69]

Religion is transformative of the human subject by healing the distortion of the dialectic of the subject through the religious value of God's love flooding the human heart. The gift of God's love sets the human subject on the path to self-transcendence and thus into a life of authenticity. According to Lonergan, the religious gift of God's love serves as an anchor upon which the human subject perseveres in seeking the good with the blessed assurance of God's abiding support and love. Under the influence of this love, the human subject endures all things, weathers through the storms of life courageously and stands fast against all odds. The human subject is thus able to gradually move to the various levels of self-transcendence, psychic, intellectual, moral and religious.[70] Concretely, our capacity for self-transcendence becomes actualized when we fall in love. This is more evident as the religious value of God's love takes over the life of the human subject. It brings about a fulfillment that satisfies our conscious intentionality. According to Lonergan, "that fulfillment is a deep-set joy that can remain despite humiliation, failure, privation, pain, betrayal, desertion. That fulfillment brings a radical peace, the peace that the world cannot give. That fulfillment bears fruit in a love of one's neighbor that strives mightily to bring about the kingdom of God on this earth."[71] In other words, the religious gift of God's love brings about changes in the horizon of the hu-

---

69. Doran, *What is Systematic Theology*, 173–74.
70. Ibid., 104–5.
71. Ibid., 105.

man subject, in his/her "desires and fears, joys and sorrows, discernment of values, decisions and deeds."[72] There is a greater readiness to seek the good not only for oneself but also for others, a greater willingness to be persuaded by others to act in accordance with the good, a greater readiness to hope and to trust the future to be in the hands of God, and a thirst and desire for communion with God as the supreme desire of the scale of values. As Lonergan reminds us:

> I have conceived being in love with God as an ultimate fulfillment of man's capacity for self-transcendence; and this view of religion is sustained when God is conceived as the supreme fulfillment of the transcendental notions, as supreme intelligence, truth, reality, righteousness, goodness.[73]

The religious value of God's love gives meaning to human life as a gift from God and influences the exercise of power for the human good. It also engenders a positive attitude towards the problem of evil as a phenomenon that can be overcome by being in love in an unrestricted manner.[74] The fulfillment of the religious value of God's love prevents, in the words of Lonergan, "the trivialization of human life in the pursuit of fun, the harshness of human life arising from the ruthless exercise of power . . . [and] despair about human welfare springing from the conviction that the universe is absurd."[75] A transformed human subject makes decisions and acts for the interest of the common good of the whole community to which he/she belongs.

However, religions that would be potentially transformative of society have to be essentially directed to the good although such directedness in individual members is precarious. As Lonergan notes, religion can easily be directed to selfishness, violence, evil, and even the demonic: "Unless religion is totally directed to what is good, to genuine love of one's neighbor and to a self-denial that is subordinated to a fuller goodness in oneself, then the cult of a God that is terrifying can slip over into the demonic, into an exultant destructiveness of oneself and of others."[76] When transformed to the demonic, as evidenced by the various forms of religious fundamentalism,

---

72. Ibid.
73. *Method in Theology*, 111.
74. See Chapter 20 of *Insight*.
75. *Method in Theology*, 105.
76. Ibid., 111.

religion becomes obstructive and destructive. For example, Lonergan refers to two approaches to religion that could potentially be destructive:

> There is bound to be formed a solid right that is determined to live in a world that no longer exists. There is bound to be formed a scattered left, captivated by now this, now that new development, exploring now this and now that new possibility. But what will count is a perhaps not numerous center, big enough to be at home in both the old and the new, painstaking enough to work out one by one the transitions to be made, strong enough to refuse half measures and insist on complete solutions even though it has to wait.[77]

As John Dadosky explains, by "the solid right" Lonergan refers to those that "simply [reject] modern secular values"; 'the scattered left' are those "who would too readily dispense with doctrines that lie at the heart of one's religion."[78] The religion that would be potentially transformative of society is a religion that takes into account the concerns of both positions "for any legitimate concerns or insights they might contribute."[79] This implies, as Lonergan insists, an awareness of "a sacralization to be resisted, a secularization to be welcomed, a secularization to be resisted and a new sacralization to be fostered."[80] Such religion must take seriously the importance of interreligious dialogue and be ready to learn from each other as well as mutually influence each other. This will be made possible by authentic human subjects operating freely both religious and secular consciousnesses. As John Dadosky suggests:

> ... Such hope lies with the human subject directed and guided by grace, with personal integrity and the ability to navigate through the various worlds of the secular and the sacred—at home with both the old and the new. The fruits of such achievement promise dramatic, social, cultural and religious transformations.[81]

In this way, religion as potentially transformative of society sets the conditions for the implementation of the integral scale of values. In the

---

77. Lonergan, "Dimensions of Meaning," in *Collection*, CWL 4:245.

78. Dadosky, "Sacralization, Secularization and Religious Fundamentalism," *Studies in Religion/Sciences Religieuses* 36 (2007): 518.

79. Ibid.

80. Lonergan, "Sacralization and Secularization," in CWL 17; Dadosky, "Sacralization, Secularization and Religious Fundamentalism," 527.

81. Ibid.

context of Christian faith, the religious value of unrestricted loving fills the human person with graces that make it easier for him/her to see it as his/her duty to contribute to the common good and to seek not only his/her own interest but to pursue the good and well-being of others as well. The religious value of transcendent love imbues the culture, the common meaning of a community, with self-transcendent meanings beyond mere material pursuits. Under the influence of authentic religious value, religion, science, philosophy, history and art of a community assume a different meaning, stretching human "transcendental subjectivity . . . towards the intelligible, the unconditioned, the good of value"[82] and similarly impacts the individual and personal life of members of the community. In the process of acculturation these new meanings are handed down to enrich the culture and civilization, not only of members of a community, but of all those who will come in contact with them. In effect, the integral scale of values can hardly be implemented in societies or discourses that disregard religion, or that prevent it from potentially being transformative of society, or that abuse it to destroy the human good in society. As Lonergan writes:

> It is not propaganda and it is not argument but religious faith that will liberate human reasonableness from its ideological prisons. It is not the promises of men but religious hope that can enable men to resist the vast pressures of social decay. If passions are to quiet down, if wrongs are to be not exacerbated, not ignored, not merely palliated, but acknowledged and removed, then human possessiveness and human pride have to be replaced by religious charity, by the charity of the suffering servant, by self-sacrificing love.[83]

In sum, authentically expressed religion is potentially transformative, not only of the individual, but also of the community. It is the condition for the integrity of the human person who gives meaning and value to culture. It emphasizes social institutions—technology, the economy, the legal and political structures—as destined to a higher purpose of the good of the human person whose authenticity lies in self-transcendence. In the event of a distortion of community, culture founded on and guided by the soteriological meaning of God's word permeates the human community with love, in order to restore primordial intersubjectivity and make human well-being the goal of practical intelligence.

82. *Method in Theology*, 103.
83. Ibid., 116.

The Imperative of Conversion

In order for the scale of values to be positively transformative of society, the human subject and the community, as well as the culture, must be converted in such a way as to embrace the integral scale of values. The fruit of conversion would be the implementation/promotion of the scale of values.

Conversion is not the explicit adoption of a religious worldview, but rather, it entails what Lonergan describes as "an about-face and new beginning."[84] People can live in accordance with the preferential scale of values and make their choices in and under the guidance of these values. This involves a process of moving away from inauthenticity to authenticity, an about-face inwards that leads outwards, a deliberate decision always to be guided by the good, and modeling one's life in accordance with the scale of values. As Lonergan emphasizes: "Conversion is a matter of moving from one set of roots to another . . . it occurs only inasmuch as a man discovers what is inauthentic in himself and turns away from it, inasmuch as he discovers what the fullness of human authenticity can be and embraces it with his whole being."[85] In other words, conversion is a "turn around"[86] a radical change from what one has been—a new beginning. This is clear in Lonergan's description of conversion in a 1968 paper, "Theology in its New Context." He states:

> For conversion occurs in the lives of individuals. It is not merely a change or even a development; rather, it is a radical transformation on which follows, on all levels of living, an interlocked series of changes and developments. What hitherto was unnoticed becomes vivid and present. What had been of no concern becomes a matter of high import. So great a change in one's apprehensions and one's values accompanies no less a change in oneself, in one's relations to other persons, and in one's relations to God.[87]

Thus conversion for Lonergan "is an individual event, a resultant change of course and direction" but it is not private.[88] "It can imply a broadening of the horizon, but principally it is that change in the subject himself [or herself]"[89] Thus the one converted understands differently and acts differ-

---

84. Ibid., 238.
85. Ibid., 271.
86. See Dadosky, "Healing the Psychological Subject" 74.
87. Lonergan, "Theology in its New Context," *A Second Collection*, 65–66.
88. Orji, *Ethnic and Religious Conflict in Africa*, 102.
89. Lonergan, *Early Works on Theological Method* 15.

ently. Conversion involves a transvaluation of values whereby one begins to belong to one's community in a new way.[90] Conversion has a way of bringing together those similarly converted to support one another in order to persevere in their new way of life. Thus conversion, Lonergan says, is not only individual but also communal. It is "an ongoing process, intensely personal and utterly intimate, concrete and dynamic."[91]

Lonergan distinguishes three distinct types of conversion: intellectual, moral and religious:

> Conversion is three-dimensional. It is intellectual inasmuch as it regards our orientation to the intelligible and the true. It is moral inasmuch as it regards our orientation to the good. It is religious inasmuch as it regards our orientation to God. The three dimensions are distinct, so that conversion can occur in one dimension without occurring in the other two, or in two dimensions without occurring in the other one. At the same time the three dimensions are solidary. Conversion in one leads to conversion in the others, and relapse from one prepares for relapse in the others.[92]

In addition to these three dimensions of conversion in Lonergan, subsequent scholars and those influenced by them have identified further dimensions of conversion, beyond Lonergan's work.[93] Most notably, Robert Doran relates Lonergan's work to the science of depth psychology. He developed *psychic conversion* to Lonergan's three dimensions of conversion. According to Doran, "psychic conversion is a transformation of the psychic component of what Freud calls 'the censor' from a repressive to a constructive agency in a person's development."[94] It is the healing of the psychic wounds; wounds that ordinarily distorts the integration of human experience.[95] Doran argues further that "Psychic conversion, enabling the self-appropriation of the psyche through interiorly differentiated consciousness, complements intellectual conversion, through which cognitional process comes to self-appropriation. It also facilitates the self-appropriation of

---

90. Lonergan, "Theology in its New Context," 66.
91. Orji, *Ethnic and Religious Conflict in Africa*, 103.
92. Lonergan, "Unity and Plurality," 247.
93. See Dadosky, "Healing the Psychological Subject," 73–91, for a short list of some of these additions to Lonergan's three-dimensional categorization of conversion.
94. Doran, *Theology and the Dialectics of History*, 59.
95. Dadosky, "Healing the Psychological Subject," 78.

moral and religious orientations, developments and conversions."[96] Bernard Tyrell, another scholar influenced by Lonergan, distinguishes "affectional conversion."[97] John Dadosky, applying Occam's razor, moves to limit further multiplication of subdivisions of conversion and argues for a fourfold notion of conversion: psychological, intellectual, moral and religious.[98] In relation to societal development and transformation we shall elaborate on these fourfold conversions, from religious to psychological.

Religious Conversion

Religious self-transcendence, which is the fulfillment of our conscious intentionality, is falling in love with God through the gift of his grace. It is this being in love with God, expressed as religious experience of ultimate reality, that Lonergan describes as religious conversion. According to him:

> Religious conversion is being grasped by ultimate concern. It is *other-worldly falling in love*. It is total and *permanent self-surrender* without conditions, qualifications, reservations. But it is such a *surrender*, not as an act, but as a *dynamic state* that is prior to and principle of subsequent acts. It is revealed in retrospect as an under-tow of existential consciousness, as a fated acceptance of a vocation to holiness, as perhaps an increasing simplicity and passivity in prayer.[99]

Religious conversion is God's gift of his love, freely given. As such it is not the product of any human knowledge and choice. It arises from experience of mystery; it evokes awe. It demands a response. Religious experience elicits a response of love, a total commitment and unconditional dedication to God, the ultimate concern who initiates the relationship by the gift of his love, and a love of other people and creation on account of the love of God. Such total and permanent self-surrender to God in faith becomes the guiding principle of all one's actions towards oneself and others, as well as one's knowledge and view of reality. Thus, according to Lonergan, "religious conversion transforms the existential subject into a subject in love,

---

96. *Theology and the Dialectics of History*, 443.
97. Tyrell, "Affectional Conversion"; Dadosky, "Healing the Psychological Subject," 73–91.
98. Dadosky, "Healing the Psychological Subject," 73–91.
99. *Method in Theology*, 240–41. Emphasis mine.

a subject held, grasped, possessed, owned through a total and so an otherworldly love."[100]

As a dynamic state of being in love in an unrestricted manner, religious conversion is interpreted differently in the context of different religions. Lonergan uses the Pauline image of God's love flooding our hearts through the Holy Spirit given to us (Roman 5:5). He identifies it with what Aquinas called operative grace by invoking the biblical image of replacing the heart of stone with a heart of flesh, "a replacement beyond the horizon of the heart of stone"; and to cooperative grace "when the heart of flesh becomes effective in good works through human freedom."[101]

> Operative grace is religious conversion. Cooperative grace is the effectiveness of conversion, the gradual movement towards a full and complete transformation of the whole of one's living and feeling, one's thoughts, words, deeds, and omissions.[102]

In the light of faith, (Lonergan calls "the eye of religious love"[103]), the scale of values is oriented to and motivated by the transcendent love of God. The scale assumes a whole new relevance potentially transformative of persons and society by providing the "basic components in the ongoing process of personal development, social organization, cultural meaning and value."[104] Lonergan states:

> Without faith the originating value is man and the terminal value is the human good man brings about. But in the light of faith, originating value is divine light and love, while terminal value is the whole universe. So the human good becomes absorbed in an all-encompassing good. Where before an account of the human good related men to one another and to nature, now human concern reaches beyond man's world to God and to God's world. Men meet not only to be together and to settle human affairs but also to worship. Human development is not only in skills and virtues but also in holiness. The power of God's love brings forth a new energy and efficacy in all goodness, and the limit of human expectation ceases to be the grave.[105]

100. Ibid., 242.
101. Ibid., 241.
102. Ibid.
103. Ibid., 119.
104. Ibid., 118.
105. Ibid., 116.

The religious value of God's love profoundly influences the conduct of one's life and action as well as setting the barometer for one's philosophical positions on reality. One's life and values flow from one's dynamic state of being in love. So from above downwards, religious love conditions one's behaviour and actions (moral conversion) and religious truth forms the basis of one's philosophical positions (intellectual conversion). Heuristically, therefore, according to Lonergan, the various forms of conversion come in this order: religious, moral and intellectual:

> First there is God's gift of his love. Next, the eye of this love reveals values in their splendor, while the strength of this love brings about their realization, and that is moral conversion. Finally, among the truths taught by the religious tradition, and in such tradition and belief are the seeds of intellectual conversion.[106]

However, this in no way means that conversion experience must follow this causal pattern as one's conversion experience could begin from a determination to change one's life following an intellectual conversion arising from what one has read, or heard, or seen and proceed from there to transform one's life, leading gradually to religious conversion. This does not preclude envisioning the conversion from below upwards—from psychic, to intellectual, moral and religious. Lonergan nuances these options thus:

> Because intellectual, moral, and religious conversions all have to do with self-transcendence, it is possible, when all three occur within a single consciousness, to conceive their relations in terms of sublation . . . Though religious conversion sublates moral, and moral conversion sublates intellectual, *one is not to infer that intellectual comes first and then moral and finally religious.*[107]

Moral Conversion

Lonergan did not dwell in great detail on moral conversion in *Method in Theology*, perhaps because moral conversion is concerned with the human action and authenticity to which he gave so much attention in many of his prior writings. However, in Chapter 2 of *Method in Theology* and in Chapter 18 of *Insight* he dwells on the fruits of moral conversion in his discussion of value and the good. Lonergan first distinguishes judgments of

---

106. Ibid., 243.
107. Ibid., 241, 243; emphasis added.

fact (truth) and judgments of value (the good) and says that "moral conversion changes the criterion of one's decisions and choices from satisfaction to values."[108] In an earlier work on theological method, Lonergan describes moral conversion as conversion "from the egocentric life, in which everything is considered from the viewpoint of desire and fear, to the rational life, in which the fundamental viewpoint is what ought to be in the order of the universe established by God."[109] Moral conversion results in the human person living according to the dictates of his/her conscience. It means living in accordance with what one knows and believes to be good; it is deliberately choosing to act in accordance with the good where the good is not only the object of desire but also includes the good of order and value as the object of possible rational choices. The good is therefore dependent not only upon the satisfaction of one's objects of desire but is rationally dependent on "the detached, disinterested, unrestricted desire to know."[110] In this sense moral conversion is moral integrity. It is, as Robert Doran writes, "a matter of *generating decisions and consequent actions that are consistent with what one knows*, that is, that are consistent with the inner words of judgments of fact and judgments of value that one has sufficient reason to hold as true."[111]

Moral conversion is avoiding the dichotomy between knowing and doing. It is deciding and acting in accordance with the good. It is overcoming the moral impotence that would ordinarily make one live a double life, either by refusing self-consciousness, by rationalizing vice to be virtue, or by moral renunciation—knowing some actions to be bad but doing them anyway. According to Walter Conn, "one straightforward way of saying what Lonergan means by moral conversion is that in it one discovers one's conscience and begins to take it seriously."[112] Moral conversion is a process of personal transformation, a degree of self-transcendence, a kind of self-creation, through which human beings—by deliberation, evaluation, decision and action—know and do, not what necessarily pleases them, but what is truly good, what is truly worthwhile.[113] Moral conversion means a sustained self-transcendent dedication to what is valuable so that it becomes

---

108. Ibid., 240.
109. *Early Works on Theological Method*, 32.
110. *Insight*, 619.
111. Doran, *What is Systematic Theology?* 106. Emphasis in the original.
112. Conn, "Desire for Authenticity: Conscience and Moral Conversion," 45.
113. *Method in Theology*, 35.

a habit. It is a persevering attitude of consistent acting in accordance with the good one knows to be worthwhile. Such a persevering habit of choosing the good is not possible without the religious value of God's grace which provides the conditions for the personal integrity at the heart of moral conversion. Moral conversion is thus part of a drive toward authenticity. It is a choice of oneself as the creator of values, the originating value of attitudes and values. It is living a life of personal integrity in accordance with the good, the worthwhile.

Moral conversion is an imperative for societal development and transformation because of its affinity with personal development and authenticity. The persevering attitude towards the good transforms the human subject to seek the good, not only for oneself, but for the good of others. It makes the human person commit to working for the recurrence of schemes for the good of order. Because it overcomes human bias, especially individual and group biases, which are responsible for the shorter cycle of decline, moral conversion promotes societal development and transformation. As we saw earlier, the personal integrity arising from moral conversion imbues culture with meanings and values that promote the common good of all.

Intellectual Conversion

By intellectual conversion Lonergan refers to the recognition that one's knowing is a compound of experience, understanding and judgment. He says it is fundamentally "the shift from prerational criteria of childhood to ultimate reliance upon rational criteria."[114] It implies a decisive break from an erroneous conception that knowing is a matter of taking a good look, a confusion that restricts knowing to the *first level* of consciousness—presentations. "It is the shift from the real as the 'reality out there now' that one can put one's paw on, to the real as *id quod est*, where *id quod est* is what is rationally affirmed."[115] In *Method in Theology*, Lonergan speaks of intellectual conversion as the decisive break with a misleading myth concerning reality, objectivity and human knowing.[116] This myth leads to faulty competing conceptions of knowing such as naïve realists, empiricists and idealists. Lonergan asserts:

---

114. *Early Works on Theological Method*, 15.
115. Ibid.
116. *Method in Theology*, 238.

> The naïve realist knows the world mediated by meaning but thinks he knows it by looking. The empiricist restricts objective knowledge to sense experience; for him, understanding and conceiving, judging and believing are merely subjective activities. The *idealist* insists that human knowing always *includes understanding as well as sense*; but he retains the empiricist's notion of reality, and so he thinks of the world mediated by meaning as not real but ideal. Only the critical realist can acknowledge the facts of human knowing and pronounce the world mediated by meaning to be the real world; and he can do so only inasmuch as he knows that the process of experiencing, understanding and judging is a process of self-transcendence.[117]

In other words, intellectual conversion deals with the problem of the objectivity of human knowing, that is, human knowledge of reality. Lonergan's position, which we saw in our second chapter, is that human knowing is structurally dynamic. As such, it is a composite of activities.[118]

Human knowing, as the incremental fruit of the unrestricted desire to know, is a compound of operations of three different kinds of objectivity: experiential, normative and absolute. Experiential objectivity consists merely in the appearance of the datum itself or data themselves. Normative objectivity requires the asking of questions for understanding and obtaining of insights. There is absolute objectivity when one has certitude (the virtually unconditioned) arising from a judgment that one's insights are correct, and that there are no other further questions.[119] While in a general sense one can be said to have empirical, normative or absolute objectivity, none of these components alone of themselves constitutes objective knowing because, as we know already from our earlier investigation in Chapter 2, human knowing itself is a structure.[120]

Intellectual conversion has implications for sustainable human development. As Lonergan says elsewhere,[121] it is the way human beings think of themselves and of others that determines the type of technical, social and cultural situations they will produce. The mechanistic thought pattern is a product of *knowing as taking a good look*, of knowing as knowledge of phenomena, of what Lonergan calls "an already out there now real." The

---

117. Ibid., 238–39. (Emphasis mine).
118. See "Philosophical Positions with Regard to Knowing," 227.
119. See, "Insight Revisited," 275.
120. Lonergan, "Cognitional Structure," *Collection*, CWL 4, 213.
121. Lonergan, "Horizon, History, Philosophy," 309.

consequences of this thought pattern have been loss of both transcendent meaning and terminal values, the substitution of vital values with the mere satisfaction of material needs, and hence the distortion of the integral scale of values.

In chapter 8 of *Insight*, Lonergan critiqued the reductionism of the modern scientific worldview evidenced in mechanistic thought patterns. 'Mechanist determinism'[122] he says, reduces human beings to bodies, mere animals, emphasizing and taking as constitutive of human beings the biological, the chemical and the physical. Any system founded on such materialist lines as mechanicist thought would treat human beings as no different as animals.[123] The raison d'être of systems like that becomes mere pursuit of self-interest. Such utilitarian philosophies as those of British ethicists Jeremy Bentham, Scottish philosophers James Mill and John Stuart Mill, influenced Adam Smith's classical economics of self-interest. As we saw in chapter 1, Adam Smith believed essentially that human beings are guided by self-interest and, when so guided, they are led also by an invisible hand to promote an end which is not their original intention.[124] However, in looking out for one's self-interest, one is also looking out for how someone else's interest might be to one's advantage. Thus, in the final analysis, 'enlightened self-interest'—the slogan of liberal democracy—is not able to surmount the biases responsible for social and cultural decline. In an indirect reference to the multinational corporations and to Adam Smith's theory of self-interest, Lonergan asserts:

> What was desirable in individual entrepreneurs at the beginning of the nineteenth century, can be disastrous in the conduct of multinational corporations towards the end of the twentieth. If intelligent self-interest has a defensible meaning, it can also be a cloak for bias—for the individual bias of the individual that grabs what he can get away with; for the far more insidious bias of the group insensitive to the rights of outsiders and unaware that its own function has diminished or disappeared; for the general bias

---

122. This is Lonergan's preferred use especially in his criticism of mechanistic and organistic worldview. Cf. *Insight*, 280, 504–5.

123. For instance, Rodney Brooks, a thinker influenced by mechanist thought, argued in his book *Flesh and Machines: How Robots Will Change Us* (2002) that humans are not special in any relevant sense from animals and, therefore, there is only a difference in degree, not a difference in kind. Cf. Somerville, *Ethical Imagination: Journeys of the Human Spirit*, 162.

124. Smith, *Wealth of Nations*; Niebuhr, "Children of Light and the Children of Darkness," 156.

> of mankind, at best ready to heed the dictates of common sense, but impatient and even contemptuous of criticism that rests on a theoretical source . . .[125]

Mechanistic determinism casts for itself the iron laws of classical economics and poses itself as the only alternative to capital accumulation. As Lonergan recalls in a series of interviews, fidelity to such necessary and ironclad laws led British policy-makers not to violate the market laws of supply and demand in order to relieve the Irish famine.[126]

Intellectual conversion is necessary to redirect the principal focus of sustainable human development. Through intellectual conversion, one respects the human person as integrally constituted by both nature and spirit. Consequently, the human person possesses an intrinsic dignity which must be respected whatever his/her status, level of education, possessions, etc. Therefore, in order to be sustainable, all developments must bear the human person in mind. This calls for a liberation from the blunder of "confusing the criteria for knowledge of the world of immediacy with the criteria for knowledge of the world mediated by meaning."[127] This is important because "if knowing is like looking then the existence of the Other becomes meaningless in a pluralistic society. One sees only a tribe, a person, an ethnic group and not a human person with equal rights and dignity."[128]

Intellectual conversion is also important for societal development and transformation in pointing out the importance of appropriation of one's own rational self-consciousness for sustainable human development. It shows that development begins with human understanding, with the self-appropriation of oneself as a knower. It distinguishes the various forms of intervention in terms of financial aid from development which, to be sustainable, passes through the arduous process of self-discovery and self-appropriation; it includes a conversion from the myth of knowing to a knowing attuned to the immanent norms of the human spirit, a knowing generating insights for progress and reversing the various cycles of decline occasioned by the various forms of bias.

---

125. Lonergan, "Prolegomena to the Study of the Emerging Religious Consciousness of Our Time," 62.

126. This historical fact infuriated Lonergan and accordingly led him into economics. He was intent on discovering how one can get economic moral precepts that are based on the economy itself. Cf. Lambert et al., eds., *Caring About Meaning*, 30–31.

127. Lonergan, "Unity and Plurality," 247–48.

128. Orji, *Ethnic and Religious Conflict in Africa*, 121.

Psychic Conversion

By the term "psyche" Doran understands "only the complex flow of empirical consciousness, whether sublated by successively higher levels or not."[129] Reference here is to the feelings ('the affect-ladden images'[130] like the dream) that accompany the intentional operations of human consciousness. For there is a duality to human consciousness, the spirit (intentional consciousness) and the psyche, that is, the sensitive psyche—the neural demands for conscious representation moving towards vertical finality of participating "in the life of the spirit."[131]

In "Philosophy and Religious Phenomenon," Lonergan writes of a level preceding the level of experience in the structure of human knowing. This level, the psyche, is characterized "by a symbolic operator that coordinates neural potentialities and needs with higher goals through its control over the emergence of images and affects."[132] The activities in question take place not on the conscious level of the detached and disinterested intellectual pattern of experience, but in the dramatic pattern of experience "in which images are tinged with affects."[133] Thus, as Doran explains, "the core intelligibility of psychic conversion has to do with the censorship that regulates the transition from the neural to the psychic . . ."[134]

Potentially the psyche could nourish the spirit by a "continuous influx of energy"[135] or block it by draining its energy flow (i.e., images that generate insight). Thus the relationship of spirit and psyche could be either orderly or disorderly. Psychic disorder refers to the complexes of psychic energy that interfere with, block, or prevent the sustained performance of the operations of human intentionality. Psychic disassociation arises, for instance, in those rare cases of split personality or double consciousness when there is a collision between the psychic function and physiological compulsions that disintegrates the unity of consciousness. Psychic order is the opposite of this blockage. By psychic order the complexes promote the sustained performance of the operations of human intentionality. The

---

129. Doran, *Theology and the Dialectics of History*, 46.

130. Doran, *What is Systematic Theology?* 110.

131. Doran, *Theology and the Dialectics of History*, 47.

132. Lonergan, "Philosophy and the Religious Phenomenon," 400; Doran, *What is Systematic Theology?* 113.

133. *Insight*, 225, See also Doran, *What is Systematic Theology?* 114.

134. Ibid., 115.

135. Doran, *Subject and Psyche*, 220.

order and the disorder result because the psyche as the "middle ground between the organism (Jung's 'instinct') and the spirit"[136] participates in the tension of the law of limitation and transcendence. The tension could be creative (integrated) or distorted (disintegrated). Doran writes:

> Affective integrity is an abiding in the creative tension of matter and spirit... Affective integrity is a habitual abiding in a tension of opposites, an aesthetic detachment that allows there to emerge the inevitability of form, an equilibrium that is no mere homeostasis, but rather the calm assurance and serenity of the woman or man who knows that faithful perseverance in the spirit of inquiry operating from below, sustained by the gift of divine and human love working from above, is the source from which there can authentically be constituted the first and only edition of oneself.[137]

Doran is saying that "the emergence of the capacity to disengage the symbolic constitution of the feelings in which the primordial apprehension of values occurs"[138] is a form of conversion, called psychic conversion, to be added to Lonergan's three forms of conversion. In his earliest formulation of psychic conversion Doran asserts:

> Psychic conversion may be understood as the gaining of the capacity of intentional consciousness to integrate this flexible psychic system and even to effect a cumulative harmony with instinct and spirit, in such a way that 'all systems are working' and working more or less in harmony. It is a self-appropriation of the psychic system on the part of the existential subject, an appropriation based on the dialectic of the symbol and its more than purely personalistic intentionality.[139]

The events constitutive of psychic conversion aim at genuine harmony between instinct and spirit towards authentic individuation of the human subject. There is psychic vitality if the creative tension of both is maintained. But if the events are displaced on either side of limitation or transcendence, psychic vitality is restored through a conversion of the psyche. The psychic integrity is displaced on the side of limitation when the censor is repressed,

---

136. Doran, *Theology and the Dialectics of History*, 55.
137. Ibid.
138. Doran, *Subject and Psyche*, 219.
139. Ibid., 224.

Lonergan and Social Transformation

leading in the limit to depression. When it is displaced on the side of transcendence, it may lead to schizophrenia or mania.[140]

Psychic conversion addresses the healing of dramatic of bias. For instance, a man abused in childhood may become paranoid of men or women in authority. A woman who grew up with an alcoholic father who abused her mother may after marriage suffer from rages because of the fear of being abused or seeing herself in her mother's condition. A child abused by a pedophile clergyman whom he trusted may have problem of trust as an adult. Psychic conversion therefore, is according to Doran, "the transformation of what Lonergan (following Freud but with a somewhat different meaning) calls the censor, from a repressive to a constructive intrasubjective agency in personal development."[141]

Psychic conversion affects the first level of consciousness of the dramatic subject and is the foundation of the transformation of the human subject.[142] Psychic conversion transforms by restoring "the natural orientation of incarnate spirit."[143] It is an appropriation of the empirical level of consciousness "that consists in the sensitive flow of sensations, memories, images, conations, emotions, associations, spontaneous intersubjective responses, bodily movements, and received meanings and values."[144] By the transformation of the censor[145] from repressive to constructive function, it removes obstacles that inhibit insight by admitting into consciousness sensitive and imaginal materials that provide data for insight. Thus, it promotes insight, rational judgment and responsible decision. In this way, Doran asserts: "psychic conversion is integrally related to the religious, moral, and intellectual conversions specified by Lonergan as qualifying authentic human subjectivity."[146]

The relation of psychic conversion to societal development and transformation relates to what Doran hesitates to call "social conversion."[147] He argues that paying attention to the 'lower openness' of one's life where one

---

140. Doran, *Theological Foundations*, 47–48.

141. Ibid., 43.

142. Dadosky, "Healing the Psychological Subject," 78.

143. Doran, *What is Systematic Theology?* 110.

144. Ibid., 111.

145. Lonergan explains the censor as "the rule or law of interrelations between successive levels of integration." See *Insight*, 482.

146. Doran, *Subject and Psyche*, 217.

147. Doran, *What Is Systematic Theology?* 123.

has little or no control disposes one to identify with those people whose participation in the dialectic of history make them victims of the structures of sin in the world. Empathy can emerge from reckoning with our own psychic darkness. It places one in solidarity with "those most in need, those left unattended to in the normal course of events in society where the social surd is a fact..."[148]

To Doran's position above, I will add that psychic conversion is important for societal development and transformation because it aids human authenticity. A depressed or schizophrenic individual finds it difficult to fully contribute to societal development or transformation. Leaders with dramatic biases can wreak havoc to the development of a country or a continent as the case may be. For instance, military leaders who ruled most of Africa for decades destroyed not only their social fabric intensifying ethnic and religious tensions but also ruined their economies, looting state treasuries and taking massive loans from international financial institutions that still holds back the pace of development of the continent. Ghana's economy almost collapsed during this period leading most of them into self-imposed exile. Nigeria's social values were destroyed leading to the present day scams and fraudulent activities that harm her image internationally.[149]

Psychic conversion, by transforming the repressed censor to a constructive censor, promotes insights that make for societal development. Authentic individuals faithful to the transcendental precepts are needed for the progress and development of peoples. Psychic conversion promotes social progress and development in this regard. Joseph Flanagan emphasizes the importance of psychic conversion for societal development and transformation using an example from Freud's preoccupation with sexual feeling and feelings of self-preservation:

> If you do not successfully integrate these neurophysiological changes into your higher conscious, psychic, and intellectual schemes, but suppress them instead, the result may be a variety of abnormal patterns of behaviors. Such abnormalities may remain within the field of your own inner consciousness, resulting in a split between the outer persona you disclose to others in playing

---

148. Ibid., 124.

149. See Ake, *Democracy and Development in Africa* (1996); Mazrui, *African Condition* (1980); Mazrui, *Africans* (1986) for further explanation of the harm leaders with dramatic biases can do to the development of their people.

social roles and the inner ego that behaves in quite different ways on the private stage of your own awareness.[150]

---

150. Flanagan, *Quest for Self-Knowledge*, 81–82.

4

Lonergan and Development: Points for Dialogue

THUS FAR IN OUR attempt to bring Lonergan's anthropology in dialogue with themes in contemporary development discourse, we have examined certain themes in the "economic oriented" theories of development, on one hand, and the principles of development in Catholic social teaching on the other. We analyzed Lonergan's philosophical anthropology and drew upon some of its implications for sustainable development in light of Robert Doran's appropriation of Lonergan's scale of values. In this chapter, we embark on bringing Lonergan's philosophical anthropology into dialogue with the themes in contemporary development discourse we have examined. The aim here is to discover, by correlating their areas of convergence and divergence, how contemporary development discourse and Lonergan's anthropology could enrich one another as well as noting some of the limitations and challenges of such a dialogue.

Convergence and Divergence of Lonergan's Philosophical Anthropology with Themes in Contemporary Development Discourse.

The major area where Lonergan's philosophical anthropology and secular theories of development converge is at their prioritization of the human good, that is, their commitment to increasing the standard of living of people and making it possible for people to actualize themselves by making available the ways and means of bringing this about. The human good includes individual self-interest, the common good and value. It includes the production and distribution of goods and services, the economy, the polity and the social order. It involves a whole web of human relationships and the whole community with its institutional structures that ensure the recurrence of schemes to continuously provide the good human beings need for dignified living. The convergence here, as we shall subsequently see, also forms areas of divergence as well. Both agree in some aspects of the human good, but they equally differ in certain aspects and in their emphasis on the human good as well.

The Prioritization of the Human Good

Obviously, the theories of development we discussed in Chapter 1 and Lonergan's philosophical anthropology prioritize the human good as foremost for enhancing the quality of life of human beings. The point is their respective notions of the good, as implicit or explicit, are different.

Liberal capitalism's pursuit of increased production and increased consumption is, as it claims, for the most part aimed at satisfying human hunger and basic survival needs—what Lonergan would call vital values. As we noted in Chapter 1, the advocates of liberal capitalism believe that a free market economy alone will increase productivity, generate wealth and improve the well-being of members of community. They see in the 'free market economy' an institution whereby the self-interest of each individual advances the well-being of all. Through a higher rate of turnover facilitated by increased consumption, the industries and corporations generate profits which are reinvested back into the economy with the aim of improving overall human living conditions. Through the transnational corporations with their large capitalization and structures, liberal capitalism, modernization theory, etc. aim at gradually passing through the various stages of growth suggested by W.W. Rostow. The products of practical intelligence are used optimally to insure increased output, profit and growth. The state is not supposed to intervene in the market mechanism. However, it is expected to insure stability in the markets by making sure that citizens abide by the rules of law and that peoples and nations keep to the terms of agreement in business so as to guarantee a conducive environment for trade. Modern technologies are invoked to quicken the process of production. Sustainable energy, water resources and other forms of infrastructure are established for service industries and other mechanisms for increased output in production. The recurrent production and distribution of goods and services are the work of the economy. The end point of democratic capitalism, the political structure of liberal capitalism, is an increase in the Gross

National Product of the economy of a country, and therefore, an increased standard of living for people.

That the theories of development prioritize the human good is also underscored by the lofty aims of liberal capitalism, modernization theorists, corporate organizations and the various conferences aimed at checking global warming by the reduction of fossil fuel emissions into the environment. The authors of the report from the international forum on globalization acknowledge this commitment to the human good through promotion of free-market enterprise as the goal of the various theories of development. They state:

> Corporate globalists inhabit a world of power and privilege. They see progress at hand everywhere, because from their vantage point the drive to privatize public assets and free the market from governmental interference spreads freedom and prosperity around the world, improving the lives of people everywhere and creating the financial and material wealth necessary to end poverty and protect the environment. They see themselves as champions of an inexorable and beneficial historical processes toward erasing the economic and political borders that hinder corporate expansion, eliminating the tyranny of inefficient and meddlesome public bureaucracies, and unleashing the enormous innovation and wealth-creating power of competition and private enterprise. Corporate globalists undertake to accelerate these trends as a great mission. They seek public policies and international agreements that provide greater safeguards for investors and private property while removing restraints to the free movement of goods, money, and corporations in search of economic opportunity wherever it may be found. They embrace global corporations as the greatest and most efficient human institutions, powerful engines of innovation and wealth creation that are peeling away the barriers to human progress and accomplishment everywhere.[1]

This is true not only of global corporations but of neo-liberalists, including modernization theorists and of other proponents of sustainable development. These theories defend international financial institutions like the World Bank, the International Monetary Fund and the World Trade Organization. They see them as essential institutions for global governance to rewrite the rules of commerce and to ensure economic growth. The passionate defence of these financial agencies by these theories of development

---

1. Cavanagh and Mander, eds., *Alternatives to Economic Globalization*, 21–22.

as institutions that improve living standards is another indication of their dedication to the human good. For instance, as Richard Jolly et al. writes, "... meeting basic needs or basic human needs became the dominant development priority, capturing the attention of donors and winning the support of World Bank president Robert McNamara and others in positions of international leadership."[2]

In order to do this, that is, to promote the human good, liberal capitalism continuously seeks out sources for raw materials at minimal costs, ready markets for distribution of increased products and a steady supply of cheap labour in order to cut the cost of production, thus ensuring increased profit and maximized opportunities for economic growth and a better standard of living—at least for the host country of the multinational corporations.[3] Amartya Sen, a renowned economist who views development as the process of expanding the real freedom of people, agrees that development prioritizes the human good as seen in the removal of oppressive circumstances. He writes:

> Development requires the removal of major sources of unfreedom: poverty as well as tyranny, poor economic opportunities as well as systematic social deprivation, neglect of public facilities as well as intolerance or overactivity of repressive states.[4]

Lonergan's position is consonant with Amartya Sen's because for him [Lonergan], "liberty as an originating value is the principle of the human good."[5] This liberty is realized when human beings devise courses of action in accordance with answers to the questions for judgments of value and deliberation in order to act in accordance with what they consider worthwhile. Development thus works towards human [effective] freedom whereby human beings are enabled to be attentive, to be intelligent, to be reasonable and to be responsible without being coerced to do so by external factors or extenuating circumstances like poverty.

Lonergan's philosophical anthropology locates the source of the human good in the authentic subject striving to be attentive, intelligent, reasonable, responsible and living in love. In the authentic subject insight is generated through experience, understanding, judgment and decision.

2. Jolly et al., *UN Ideas That Changed the World*, 187.

3. However, as we saw in Chapter 1, the argument of its critics is that increased profit and not human good is the absolute for liberal capitalism.

4. Sen, *Development as Freedom*, 3.

5. Lawrence, "Editors' Introduction," in Lonergan, *Macroeconomic Dynamics*, xxxviii.

Such insights accumulate into viewpoints; viewpoints accumulate into higher viewpoints and bring about progress and development of peoples to the extent that those viewpoints are judged to be true and valuable. In the practical field of common sense, the tension between spontaneous intersubjectivity and practical intelligence that constitute the dialectic of community, buttress the good of order that insures the recurrence of schemes for the provision of the human good. The ultimate goal is to live a meaningful life that promotes human dignity, freedom and creativity. But alongside this, the various biases prevent understanding and freedom thus bringing about individual and collective decline. This comes out clearly in the products of practical intelligence Lonergan constructed in chapter 7 of *Insight* and in the first part of *Method in Theology*. According to him, technology is subordinate to the economy and the economy is subordinate to the political order. In this order, the politician is charged with the responsibility of organizing other aspects of practical intelligence under the guidance of normative scale of values and in response to the need of the community.

The ways the values within the preferential scale are related to each other have been treated in Chapter 3 of this work. The point I wish to emphasize here is that for Lonergan, the products of practical intelligence aim at providing a recurrence of schemes for the constant provision of the human good. Lonergan thus agrees with the noble goals of free-enterprise economy for promoting economic innovation and growth, of forging equal opportunities in the market and of improving the living conditions.

However, the notion of the human good is different for both the theories of development I addressed in Chapter 1 and Lonergan's philosophical anthropology. Liberal capitalism emphasizes the human good as the result of individuals hoping to maximize the varying circumstances of the market for their own interest. Modernization theory represented in W. W. Rostow's stages of growth lays out ways and means for the realization of development as economic growth, that is, how to maximize human self-interest to bring about the greatest good for the greatest number of people. The concept of sustainable development struggles with how to maximize the use of the various natural resources to enhance economic growth without depleting the resources so that it remains readily available for future generations to continue developing economically. The measure of progress and development for the theories of development is structurally economical, that is, based on profit, on consumption and on material well-being. This is often measured in terms of Gross Domestic Product (the totality of a country's economic output per year including foreign investments) and Gross National Product (the value of all the goods and services produced in an economy). Amartya Sen and other economists who insist on the non-separation of development economics from human well-being as the goal of economics argue that the distinction between development and growth instantiated in GNP often leaves out the question of the distribution of that GNP among the population. Thus capability deprivation is often assessed in terms of income deprivation to the neglect of other related variables like healthcare, unemployment, lack of education and social exclusion. GDP in terms of this assessment may not sufficiently be an accurate representation of the situation in the living standard of people whether in developed or in developing countries. For instance, although African Americans may be making more income than Africans in sub-Saharan Africa, they may have lower life expectancy resulting from other variables of their circumstance like proneness to violence. Consequently, it is possible that while the GNP of a country grows its distribution could become unequal and make the lives of the poor population more destitute. Finally, while GNP might measure " . . . the amount of the *means* of well-being a people may have, it does not tell us what the people involved are succeeding in getting out of these means, giving their ends."[6]

The limitation of measuring development as economic growth and the inadequacy of assessing its success through the Gross National Product (GNP) have pitted defenders and critics of the free-market enterprise against one another as to the positive and adverse effects of globalization for reducing poverty. Martin Ravallion summarized some of the debates and concluded that globalization has to redress the antecedent inequalities of opportunity within developing countries as they open up to external trade; this is crucial to realizing the poverty-reducing potential of globalization.[7] For the same reason, there have been protests by anti-globalization/anti-free-trade groups wherever the Group of Eight nations (G8) and the expanded Group of Twenty (G20) world economies or World Trade Organization meet. These protests are seen by the proponents of neo-liberalism as misdirected and as coming from people who do not understand the dynamics of the market. However, according to Amartya Sen, the real concern of the so-called 'anti-globalization' protesters is surely not globalization per

---

6. Sen, "The Concept of Development," in Pogge and Horton, eds., *Global Ethics*, 162–63.

7. Ravallion, "Debate on Globalization, Poverty and Inequality."

se; rather, their concerns seem to stem in large part from the continuing deprivations and rising disparities in levels of living that they see globally.[8] For instance, the cost of hosting the 2010 G8 and the G20 meeting in Ontario, Canada is put at $1.1B paid by the tax payers for a 72 hour meeting of the world leaders.[9]

Moreover, when dependency theorists criticize modernization theorists, they are decrying the attendant neglect of cultural, personal and religious values arising from some of the methods adopted for the promotion of the human good by modernization theorists. Even when it is recognized that development is not merely economic growth, not much is done to integrate these dimensions of human life into development discourse. For example, as early as 1961, during the first so-called development decade, it was clear that development is not merely economic growth. As Richard Jolly et al. observe:

> The forward to the *Proposals for Action* for that decade stated that "development concerns not only man's material needs but also the improvement of the social conditions of his life and his broad aspirations. Development is not just economic growth, it is growth plus change." Notwithstanding these brave words, the UN failed to develop an *integrated intellectual framework* for catalyzing a new system-wide approach to economic and social development.[10]

Unlike the theories of development, the structure of the human good in Chapter 2 of Lonergan's *Method in Theology* and Doran's appropriation might provide this potential 'integrated intellectual framework.' These aims at social and economic ends by overcoming self-interest through the actualization of the preferential scale of values: vital, social, cultural, personal and religious. The human good is not just pursuing one's happiness and pleasure but the realization of the common good, ensuring the recurrence of schemes for the whole range of values not only for oneself, but for the good of the other members of one's community or nation as well. Human well-being comes about through transcending individual and group interests and opting for terminal values that are not merely apparently good but of real value, those that facilitate overall well-being and promote human

---

8. Sen, "Globalization, Inequality and Global Protest," *Development*, 45, 2 (2002): 11–16.

9. See "Summit costs hit $1.1B." Online: http://www.cbc.ca/canada/toronto/story/2010/05/26/g8-g20-security-summit-toews.html.

10. Jolly et al., *UN Ideas That Changed the World*, 187. Emphasis added.

Lonergan and Development: Points for Dialogue

self-transcendence. The human good is therefore aimed beyond merely material or economic ends (vital values). In other words, as human and social transformation goes hand in hand, the human good is not measured by profit and increased production or by an abundance of material prosperity alone. Rather, it has to consider the entire range of values which promote human well-being as oriented to self-transcendence. As Lonergan remarks, beyond our material needs satisfied by the vital values:

> There is a still further dimension to being human, and there we emerge as persons, meet one another in a common concern for values, seek to abolish the organization of human living on the basis of competing egoisms and to replace it by an organization on the basis of man's perceptiveness and intelligence, his reasonableness, and his responsible freedom.[11]

Contrary to the liberal and socialist economic ideologies, Lonergan's philosophical anthropology prioritizes human freedom through the implementation of the integral scale of values into the social order. Since neither of the constituents of community is to dominate the other if there is to be an integral dialectic of community, an overemphasis on technology, on the market or on the polity, in the long run distorts the integral scale of values at the heart of both free enterprise and liberal democracy. Lonergan's philosophical anthropology, with its preferential scale of values, avoids the extremes of liberalism and socialism by critiquing the liberal meaning of freedom as doing as one pleases, on the one hand, and the socialist view of freedom (under the influence of group bias) in the form of social totalitarianism, on the other.

Thus we reiterate that although themes in contemporary development discourse and Lonergan's philosophical anthropology prioritize the human good, they differ in what constitutes the human good as well as in the means of realizing it. For Lonergan, the human good is not just the satisfaction of one's basic needs but the gradual process towards human self-transcendence through the implementation of the scale of values. Its goal is to promote full human living, and it inheres on the dignity of human beings as mediators of meaning and motivated by value. While economics is important in realizing the human good, development is not merely economic growth but must include the fuller range of the scale of values. Insofar as social transformation and sustainable human development are the goals connected to the human good for Lonergan, they [transformation

11. Lonergan, *Method in Theology*, 10.

and development] presuppose human authenticity—obedience to the transcendental precepts: be attentive, be intelligent, be reasonable, be responsible and be in love. Human authenticity considers the human good in the warp and weft of human history, bearing in mind the human moral impotence which precipitates decline and the slow and possibly difficult process of recovery from the ashes of decline through the religious value of God's grace.

Lonergan's philosophical anthropology can contribute the notions of authenticity, self-transcendence and the scale of values to the secular theories of development. Human constitutive meaning is characterized by the self-transcendent quality of going beyond the self by holding unto some reality beyond us, that is, "something that is independent of ourselves, somehow have reached beyond, transcended ourselves."[12] Besides questions for intelligence (What? Why? How? What for?) and questions for reflection (Is that so?), there are questions for deliberation, (Is it worthwhile?); the question of value, which is existential, on which the subject deliberates, decides and acts, thinking not only of the effects of one's action on oneself, but on the effects of one's actions on others as well. Thus there are the questions for the moral conscience. Although one's intention can be selfish, limiting the process of deliberation to oneself, to "what is most to one's advantage, what best serves one's interests, what on the whole yields a maximum of pleasure and a minimum of pain,"[13] human freedom is not limited to that. Lonergan's philosophical anthropology potentially offers the theories of development the fuller dimension of human self-constitution more in tune with the horizon of the dynamic structure of human knowing—the transcendent dimension, concerned with the integral scale of values, realized not only for oneself but promoted in others as well.[14] It addresses one of the basic problems of liberal capitalism, one known all too well in the recent financial crises and as, in the words of Philip Wogaman, "the loss of connection between material problems and the deeper moral and spiritual values of humankind."[15] Finally, Lonergan's thought, especially his notion of egoistic bias, may serve to address the distortions of Adam Smith's theory

---

12. Lonergan, "Self-transcendence: Intellectual, Moral, Religious," 317.
13. Ibid., 318.
14. Ibid.
15. Wogaman, *Economics and Ethics*, xi.

of self-interest that prioritizes self-interest as primary and the good of the society as secondary or as an indirect offshoot to self-interest.[16]

Convergence/Divergence with Principles of Catholic Social Teaching on Development

Our exposition of Catholic social teaching in the second section of Chapter 1 concentrates on the notions of development in the principles of the social teachings of the Catholic Church. In this section of our work, we seek to investigate areas of convergence and divergence of these principles with Lonergan's anthropology. Our aim is to see how the principles of the Catholic social teaching will contribute to Lonergan studies. We are also interested in seeing what Lonergan will bring to the discussion. Considering that Lonergan wrote as a Catholic theologian hoping to contribute to the program *vetera novis augere et perficere* (to add to and perfect the old by means of the new)[17] of Pope Leo XIII in the encyclical *Aeterni Patris*, one anticipates a complementarity between Lonergan's thought and Catholic social teaching. In actual fact, the relationship of Lonergan's philosophical anthropology and Catholic social teaching could be further viewed in terms of the relationship between the functional specialties of doctrine and systematics. One could see that Lonergan is providing the explanation in general categories of what appears in special categories in the social teachings of the Catholic Church. Thus in spite of their areas of convergence, there are areas of divergence between them as well. To both of these aspects we now turn.

The Importance of the Human Person in Societal Development

The Catholic Church believes that "the origin of social life is found in the human person."[18] Based on its theological anthropological assumption that human beings are created in the image and likeness of God (Gen. 1:27), Catholic social teaching emphasizes the importance of the human per-

---

16. Adam Smith, in his *Wealth of Nations*, argues that "by pursuing his own interest [the human being] frequently promotes that of the society more effectually than when [he/she] really intends to promote it" (423).

17. Translation of the editors of the Collected Works of Lonergan (CWL) 3: *Insight*, 773.

18. *The Compendium*, 49.

son in societal development. The Church thus demands the provision of resources necessary for optimum human development and human participation in their development. As we saw in Chapter 1, through the principle of the universal destination of earth's goods, Catholic social teaching holds that the resources of the earth are provided by God for every human being. Consequently, every human being is entitled to benefit from the resources of the earth for self-fulfillment as individuals and as members of community. Also, by the principle of subsidiarity, Catholic social teaching maintains that every member of any community must be allowed to participate in their societal development. This principle implies that it is an affront to human dignity for a government or any agency to prevent people from doing what they can for their sustainable development. As created in the image and likeness of God, human beings are also creative and, through the resources of the earth, they can transform their own lives and their society. Work gives human beings entitlement to the resources of the earth as private property. But private property is not an end in itself. *Gaudium et Spes*, the Pastoral Constitution of the Church in the Modern World of the Second Vatican Council, teaches that "the social order and its development must invariably work to the benefit of the human person, since the order of things is to be subordinate to the order of persons, and not the other way around."[19] Paul VI in *Populorum Progressio* emphasizes the universal destination of the earth's goods and notes the right of people to help themselves to the earth's resources in order to defend human dignity.[20] In justifying the involvement of the Church in social and economic issues, John Paul II insists that "at stake is the dignity of the human person whose defense and promotion have been entrusted to us by the Creator . . . "[21] In *Centesimus Annus* (1991) he adds: " . . . the main thread and, in a certain sense, the guiding principle . . . of all of the Church's social doctrine is a *correct view of the human person* and of his unique value . . . "[22]

Lonergan's philosophical anthropology presupposing the human creatureliness in the image and likeness of God provides the general categories for upholding the dignity of the human person by concentrating

---

19. "The Pastoral Constitution of the Church in the Modern World: Vatican II, *Gaudium et Spes*," #26; See also #29: "the equal dignity of persons demands that a more humane and just condition of life be brought about."

20. *Populorum Progressio*, 23.

21. *Solicitudo Rei Socialis*, 47.

22. *Centesimus Annus*, 11.

on human beings as self-transcending through obedience to the transcendental precepts. As we said in Chapter 2, in our treatment of the subjective field of common sense, to be authentically human is to experience, to understand, to pass correct judgments on the truthfulness and falsehood of what is understood and to deliberate on the choices of action open to one in freedom. Furthermore, to be human is to be born into a community of shared meanings and values, of culture and religion and of a common pool of knowledge that guides one throughout life. The implication of the dynamic structure of human knowing is the dignity of the human person. Any form of development and societal transformation must take note of this and respect the human person who is the beneficiary of development. In other words, for Lonergan as well as for Catholic social teaching, the dignity of the human person is at the heart of societal development.

The difference between Catholic social teaching and Lonergan's philosophical anthropology on the role/dignity of the human person in societal development is thus one of emphasis, of Lonergan providing the general categories of what the Catholic social teaching specifies in special categories. For Lonergan, the authenticity of the human person, by obedience to the transcendental precepts, brings about progress and societal development. On the other hand, for Catholic social teachings, societal development must respect the inherent dignity of the human person and, by the principle of subsidiarity, must allow the human person contribute to societal development. Lonergan's philosophical anthropology upholds societal development as arising from the human subject and from the products of practical intelligence developed through human insights, technological, economical and political.[23] For him, societal development hinges on the human person as intelligent playing his/her role towards the constant provision of the human good.

Because it is consonant with basic assumptions of Catholic social teaching, Lonergan's philosophical anthropology could offer an intellectual framework for construing the place of the human person in societal development. For example, a person is created in the image and likeness of God, and human beings are rational, intelligent, creative and responsible. Because they are so, through the principle of subsidiarity no system or social order or institution is to take away from them their due responsibility in improving their social order. In light of Lonergan's aim of responding to the program *vetera novis augere et perficere*, one could see Lonergan's

23. *Insight*, 232.

philosophical anthropology grounding some of the theological assumptions of Catholic social teaching in a new and perhaps more comprehensible manner that may even foster appreciation outside the Catholic faith.

His philosophical contributions could also bring about further appreciation of historical consciousness which is making inroads into the Catholic social teaching.[24] Historical consciousness is the appreciation of the place of history, of the various contexts of peoples like their cultural differences and varying historical circumstances. It contrasts with the earlier Neo-Scholastic argument for one culture as normative and the expectation that other cultures should strive to emulate the one cultural norm. According to Lonergan, historical consciousness effects a shift from concern with the ideal, the norm, the law, the rule the 'what ought to be', from the universal to the particular, from man as substance to man as subject. "Moreover, historical consciousness effects the transition from an ideal order, what the family, the state, the law, education, the economy should be, to what de facto is, the good of order that de facto concretely functions here and now in this society."[25]

The advance of the historical argument is exemplified in John Paul II's statements in *Solicitudo Rei Socialis* recognizing notable changes in the world events which have to be attended to by the Church's social doctrine. He affirms that the Church "reads events as they unfold in the course of history;"[26] that "the Church's teaching in the social sphere . . . is ever new because it is subject to the necessary and opportune adaptations suggested by the changes in historical conditions and by the unceasing flow of the events which are the setting of the life of people and society."[27] John Paul II's affirmations are reminiscent of John XXIII's *Pacem in Terris* (Peace on Earth) "reading the signs of the times"[28] aimed at discerning gospel values underlying social and political transformations of humanity. It also recalls Paul VI's call in the 1971 encyclical *Octogesima Adveniens* (Call to Action) to each local Church to adjudicate situations proper to their country in the

24. See Curran, *Catholic Social Teaching 1891–Present*, 53–100.
25. Lonergan, *Early Works on Theological Method 1*, 73.
26. Pope John Paul II, *Solicitudo Rei Socialis*, 1.
27. Ibid., 3.
28. In *Pacem in Terris* #126–29, Pope John XXIII mentioned "signs of the times." In #39–43 he specified these signs of the times as "the characteristics of the present day." See also DeBerri et al., *Catholic Social Teaching* (2003); Cf. "Catholic Social Teaching—Theological Context: Reading the Signs of the Times." Online: http://famvin.org/en/archive/catholic-social-teaching-theological-context-reading-the-signs-of-the-times.

light of "the daring and creative innovations that the present state of the world requires."[29]

Consolidating historical consciousness will benefit the theological and anthropological presuppositions of Catholic social teaching by introducing a clearer articulation of the reality of sin, of evil potentially immanent in human thought and action. As we have shown in Chapter 2, Lonergan's work conceives the historical process not just in terms of human intentions leading to progress and development in all fields of action, in cultural achievements, building social institutions for the human good, civilization and religion but also in terms of their limitations, decline and decay.[30] Thus, human action is an aggregate of three elements: "according to nature, contrary to nature and above nature, that is, nature, sin, grace."[31] This equally means (as he expresses them in other places): progress, sin and grace,[32] progress, decline and redemption:[33] healing and creating in history.[34] According to this framework, historical intelligibility deals not only with a 'de facto' grasp of intelligibility, but also with the reality of the surd arising from sin as well as the reality of the mystery of redemption. "For spontaneously every collapse is followed by a reconstruction, every disaster by a new beginning, every revolution by a new era."[35] Ignoring or not considering deeply the reality of collapse, the possibility of regression instead of progress, the surd of sin and evil and its effects on the human person's contribution to societal development could adversely affect social ethics.[36] For example, Charles E. Curran suggests that the Catholic social teaching's emphasis upon the fundamental goodness of creation could result in the neglect of the reality of evil and hence create a possible discomfort among

---

29. Pope Paul VI, *Octogesima Adveniens*.
30. Lonergan, *Early Works on Theological Method 1*, 242.
31. Lonergan, "Analytic Concept of History," 14.
32. Ibid., 28.
33. See Chapter 2 of *Method in Theology*, pp. 52–55 on Progress and Decline.
34. See Lonergan, "Natural Right and Historical Consciousness," 169–76. Here Lonergan asserts that "it is in the dialectic of history that one finds the link between natural right and historical mindedness." He describes the various plateaus (six in number) of human development from human collaboration to dialogue.
35. *Insight*, 240–41. Lonergan's position above is not much different from the position of Christian ethicists who see history as involving the triad of progress, decline brought about by sin, and renewal or reconstruction or redemption made possible by the grace of God.
36. *Insight*, 260.

some scholars about historical consciousness as its theological methodology. He writes: "A danger in the Catholic emphasis on the basic goodness of all that God has made has been a failure to give enough recognition to the presence of sin . . ."[37] But Curran's fear is already overcome as Catholic social teaching already emphasizes the reality of historical consciousness as we saw in our examples above.

Lonergan's contribution is the strengthening of this historical consciousness by emphasis on progress, decline and redemption, on the reality of evil and the redemption from evil through the love of God.

Integral Development

Both Catholic social teachings and Lonergan's philosophical anthropology emphasize integral human development. However, they diverge in the ways they express it. In Catholic social teachings integral human development means that development must cater to the human person as a whole—personal, social, cultural, religious, economic and political. Such development is described in the words of Paul VI in *Populorum Progressio* as "the development of each man and of the whole man."[38] Nothing about human life is to be neglected. And there should not be an overemphasis of any dimension, so that development may be integral. As Paul VI asserts, "We cannot allow economics to be separated from human realities, nor development from the civilization in which it takes place. What counts for us is man—each individual man, each human group, and humanity as a whole."[39]

This position of Catholic social teaching converges with Lonergan's scale of values: vital, social, cultural, personal and religious. Vital values ensure that we eat, are healthy and care for the basic needs of life—food, clothing, shelter. Social values refer to the social order arising from the already accepted modes of human cooperation. It includes such social institutions as "family and mores, community and education, state and law, economics and technology."[40] Cultural values give meaning to social values. It includes

---

37. Curran, *Catholic Social Teaching 1891-Present*, 22.

38. *Populorum Progressio* [*On the Development of Peoples*], 14, Cf. http://www.vatican.va/holy_father/paul_vi/encyclicals/documents/hf_p-vi_enc_26031967_populorum_en.html; Gremillion, *The Gospel of Peace and Justice*, 387–415. See also Benedict XVI's encyclical *Caritas in Veritate*, 29.

39 *Populorum Progressio* [*On the Development of Peoples*], 14; *Caritas in Veritate*, 32.

40. Lonergan, "Philosophy and the Religious Phenomenon," 138.

such areas as art, religion, science, philosophy, history etc.[41] Personal value is the human person in his gradual process of self-transcendence, in the various processes of transformations and conversions that heal blocks in development. The person is the originator of values and meanings that inform the culture, the common meaning of a community. Religious value is the ultimate reality upon which the human person exists, grows, and gives meaning to the social order etc.

Catholic social teaching emphasizes adherence to 'the hierarchy of values' as a means of attaining integral development. For instance, the Pastoral Constitution of the Second Vatican Council observes with regret that "the great advantages of human progress are fraught with grave temptations: *the hierarchy of values* has been disordered, good and evil intermingle, and every man and every group is interested only in its own affairs, not in those of others."[42] While *Gaudium et Spes* did not elaborate on "the hierarchy of values" it mentions as disordered the modern idea of infinite progress. Paul VI's encyclical *Populorum Progressio* mentions a "scale of values" in hierarchical order as a prerequisite for the progress of peoples. It states: "Man's personal and collective fulfillment could be jeopardized if the proper scale of values were not maintained."[43] Unless this scale of values is placed in proper perspective people will lack "authentic development."[44]

In the scale of values recognized by Catholic social teaching, an important place is reserved for religious, moral and cultural values. For instance, in *Populorum Progressio* Paul VI elaborates on the scale of values by bemoaning the deplorable condition of those who lack the vital values of life as well as the poverty of those deluded by self-interest and greed, those who lack moral value.[45] He equally recognizes the place of cultural values in development as being open to the human spirit. He suggests that the cultural traditions of a people that preserves human dignity should not be preferred to one which destroys it no matter how civilized it may appear or where it may come from.[46]

---

41. Ibid. Cf. "Dimensions of Meaning," CWL 4, 234; "Natural Right and Historical Mindedness," 170.

42. "Pastoral Constitution on the Church in the Modern World" (*Gaudium et Spes*), #37, in Flannery, ed., *Vatican Council II*, 822. Emphasis mine.

43. *Populorum Progressio*, 18.

44. Ibid., 20.

45. Ibid., 21.

46. Ibid., 40.

Catholic social teaching also emphasizes religious value as the measure of true humanism. Paul VI calls humanism with religious value "full-bodied humanism"[47] In the same vein, John Paul II's encyclical on social concern (*Solicitudo Rei Socialis*) identifies the problems of development with a misplacement of the values that guide human life. He emphasizes that whatever goods are available must be subordinate to the transcendent reality of the human being.[48] Similarly, Benedict XVI asserts that at the apex, and underlying every other value for integral human development, is religious value—the eschatological truth of belief in eternal life. He writes:

> Without the perspective of eternal life, human progress in this world is denied breathing-space. Enclosed within history, it runs the risk of being reduced to the mere accumulation of wealth; humanity thus loses the courage to be at the service of higher goods, at the service of the great and disinterested initiatives called forth by universal charity. Man does not develop through his own powers, nor can development simply be handed to him…. Only through an encounter with God are we able to see in the other something more than just another creature, to recognize the divine image in the other, thus truly coming to discover him or her and to mature in a love that "becomes concern and care for the other."[49]

The religious value of belief in God determines the nature and goal of development, of the personal life of human beings and of society. It determines the nature of social institutions and what they are to achieve. Development can be said to start from 'above downwards' [as Lonergan would say] and is meaningful and beneficial to human beings only from this vantage point. Thus Catholic social teaching admits of a hierarchy of values, religious, moral and cultural, by which every development is assessed either as authentic (integral) or not.

The difference in emphasis between Catholic social teaching and Lonergan's anthropological insight on integral human development is that Lonergan lays out the scale of values in a much more explicit and comprehensive form than is implicit in the various documents of Catholic social teaching. Specifying the scale of values is therefore one of Lonergan's contributions to Catholic social teaching. Lonergan's scale of values can help the church explicate the intellectual framework for an integral notion of

---

47. Ibid., 42.
48. *Solicitudo Rei Socialis*, 33.
49. *Caritas in Veritate*, 11.

development. Its emphasis on, and distinction of, the vital, social, cultural, personal and religious values provides a framework for a more systematic treatment of Catholic social teaching in order to dialogue with the various theories of development. Without such an intellectual framework, prima facie Catholic social teaching's insistence on religious values without clearly distinguishing the scale of values often begs the question. But borrowing from Lonergan's scale of values and Doran's appropriation of the scale as integral promises to clarify and ground Catholic social teaching intellectually. For instance, the human ability to move from the various levels of consciousness—common sense, theory, interiority and religiously differentiated consciousness—can clarify the sense of integration emphasized in Catholic social teaching's notion of integral human development. Correlatively one understands integral human development as development that brings together all the dimensions of development: satisfying the basic needs of human beings and creation, establishing a good social order, attending to the cultural and personal development of human beings and respecting ultimate reality underlying sustainable human development.

Limitations of Lonergan's Philosophical Anthropology

Although Lonergan's philosophical anthropology could make some contributions to contemporary theories of development and to a systematic understanding of Catholic social teaching, his anthropological insights have some limitations. Two of these include: an ambiguity or lack of clarity concerning the language of 'cosmopolis' and the limited prognosis on the scope of globalization. In this section we are concerned with how his work can be complemented by the work of developmental theorists and Catholic social principles.

Vagueness on the Language of "Cosmpolis"

In Chapter 7 of *Insight*, Lonergan posits the notion of cosmopolis as a higher viewpoint that can integrate the distorted dialectic of community. As we saw earlier, the integral dialectic of community, abiding in the creative tension of the constitutive elements of community, spontaneous intersubjectivity and practical intelligence, is very important in Lonergan's theory of social order. Distortion of the dialectic of community is serious because it upsets conditions for societal development and transformation. Neglect of theory and preference for shortsighted practicality results in the longer cycles of decline. In the event of such distortion, restoration of the integral dialectic of community is vital for the process of history. Consequently, the higher viewpoint responsible for reintegrating the distorted dialectic of community is an important element in Lonergan's philosophical anthropology. In view of this, one expects Lonergan to have expounded on this higher viewpoint with greater clarity.

However, what Lonergan means by 'cosmopolis' is not immediately clear when he introduces it in *Insight*. In Chapter 7 of *Insight* Lonergan introduced the word 'cosmopolis' noting that "what is necessary is a cosmopolis that is neither class nor state, that stands above all their claims, that cuts them down to size, that is founded on the native detachment and disinterestedness of every intelligence . . ."[50] As Frederick E. Crowe and Robert M. Doran observe, "his type-script for *Insight* (Archives) shows him changing the original capital to lower case—as if to say that 'cosmopolis' should become a common noun in our language."[51] Perhaps Lonergan presumed that cosmopolis, as a higher viewpoint, is self-explanatory and that the reader who has followed his argument thus far would understand what it means. As a higher viewpoint cosmopolis is expected to free intelligence, allowing it to operate in accordance with its own immanent norms which, of course, give free rein to the unrestricted desire to know. It is to allow the dynamic structure of human knowing to operate fully in order to generate insights for progress by acknowledging the fact of decline and working towards redemption through God's help, freeing intelligence from bias, especially from general bias. Lonergan writes:

> The basic service of the higher viewpoint will be a liberation from confusion through clear distinctions. Progress is not to be confused with decline; the corrective mechanism of the minor principle of decline is not to be thought capable of meeting the issues set by the major principle.[52]

The difficulty is that in explaining what cosmopolis means, Lonergan defines it by distinguishing what it is not. Cosmopolis is not a body charged with enforcing the rules of a state or compliance to any directive from any authority. It is neither a police force nor an administrative body. It does not seek to promote the ideology of any group or dominance of any state

50. *Insight*, 263.
51. Frederick E. Crowe and Robert M. Doran, "Editorial Notes," in *Collection 4*, 277.
52. *Insight*, 260.

over another. It is not part of either of the linked but opposed principles of spontaneous intersubjectivity or of practical intelligence. Instead it criticizes the overemphasis of these constituents of community. Furthermore, cosmopolis is not easy to achieve.[53]

In a subsection of Chapter 7 of *Insight* on Common Sense as Object, Lonergan suspends judgment on the exact nature of the higher principle that integrates the distorted dialectic of community until "other notions as truth and error, right and wrong, human science and philosophy, culture and religion"[54] have been discussed. In Chapter 18 of *Insight*, having treated these other notions, Lonergan thought of a higher integration besides the higher viewpoint; a higher integration that "leaves underlying manifolds with their autonomy and yet succeeds in introducing a higher systematization into their non-systematic coincidences."[55] Whether this higher integration is different from the higher viewpoint, above the higher viewpoint, an integrator of the higher viewpoint or the operator of the higher viewpoint is not so clear. The problem is not solved by Lonergan's use of the phrase "than any that has so far been considered" in reference to the higher integration, nor is it by the fact that he thought of the need for "a further manifestation of finality" in his writing about the higher integration.[56] He muddied the waters further by relating the still higher integration to cosmopolis:

> Earlier, in the chapter on common sense as object, it was concluded that a viewpoint higher than the viewpoint of common sense was needed; moreover, that X was given the name 'cosmopolis,' and some of its aspects and functions were indicated. But the subsequent argument has revealed that, *besides the higher viewpoints in the mind, there are higher integrations in the realm of being*; and both the initial and subsequent argument have left it abundantly clear that the needed higher viewpoint is a concrete possibility only as a consequence of an actual higher integration.[57]

However, the very first time Lonergan used the term 'cosmopolis,' in a 1951 article entitled "The Role of a Catholic University in the Modern World," he referred to it as "cultural community."[58]

53. Ibid., 263–65.
54. Ibid., 259.
55. Ibid., 655.
56. Ibid., 655–56.
57. Ibid. Emphasis mine.
58. Lonergan, "Role of a Catholic University in the Modern World," 111. It first

By using cosmopolis only sparingly and not stating clearly what it actually means, Lonergan leaves the notion of cosmopolis and his idea of a critical culture ambiguous, resulting in commentaries which, at best, only guess at his meaning.[59] As the editors of *Collection* comment: "Lonergan did not create this term, but he gave it a meaning that has not been sufficiently studied."[60] To this, I will add that he did not distinguish his notion of cosmopolis clearly enough to help those who care to study it understand what he means. Lonergan writes that "the basic service of the higher viewpoint will be a liberation from confusion through clear distinctions."[61] But, unfortunately, when his very use of the word cosmopolis confuses, one wonders how it will be able to liberate from confusion. Lonergan does tell us, though, that "it [cosmopolis] is a dimension of consciousness, a heightened grasp of historical origins, a discovery of historical responsibilities."[62] In Chapter 18 of *Insight*, he identifies it as a "higher viewpoints in the mind"[63] meaning, perhaps, that it is a dimension of consciousness. Yet this attempt at explaining what he means by cosmopolis is not clear enough. We do not know whether it is an attitude and, if it is, what type of attitude it is. As interiorly differentiated consciousness, we do not know to which level it belongs. In "The Role of a Catholic University in the Modern World" Lonergan places it in the third level of consciousness correlated to judgment.[64]

Also in the midst of the vagueness in expressing what it means, or perhaps on account of it, Lonergan burdens cosmopolis with too many responsibilities or perhaps his account is too schematic and general. Because it is the higher viewpoint to reverse the longer cycle of decline generated by the general bias, cosmopolis "is to break the vicious cycle of an illusion."[65] It is to make operative ideas that would ordinarily be inoperative because

---

appeared as a leading article in the Montreal Jesuit magazine, *Relations*.

59. Some of the attempts at understanding or at clarifying Lonergan's notion of "cosmopolis" include the following: Robert M. Doran, "Cosmopolis and the Situation: A Preface to Systematics and Communications," in Doran, *Theological Foundations II*, 331–61; Fallon, ed., "Lonergan and Cosmopolis"; Matusik, "Democratic Multicultures and Cosmopolis: Beyond the Aporias of the Politics and Identity and Difference"; Nordquest, "Cosmopolis: Bourget's and Lonergan's"; M. Smith, "Lonergan's Cosmopolis." See also Tekippe, *Bernard Lonergan's Insight*, 115–16.

60. Crowe and Doran, "Editorial Notes" *Collection 4*, 277.

61. Lonergan, *Insight*, 260.

62. Ibid., 266.

63. Ibid., 656.

64. "Role of a Catholic University in the Modern World," 109.

65. Lonergan, *Insight*, 264.

ruled out of court by general bias. It is "concerned with the fundamental issue of the historical process."⁶⁶ Its role is also political—to reveal the myths and rationalizations those thirsting for political positions deceitfully use to justify their grab of power. He writes:

> It is the business of cosmopolis to prevent the formation of the screening memories by which an ascent to power hides its nastiness; it is its business to prevent the falsification of history with which the new group overstates its case; it is its business to satirize the catchwords and the claptrap and thereby to prevent the notions they express from coalescing with passions and resentments to engender obsessive nonsense for future generations; it is its business to encourage and support those that would speak the simple truth though simple truth has gone out of fashion.⁶⁷

Cosmopolis appears relevant for any situation to be addressed, to solve every problem of society–from morality to politics, from history to philosophy, from culture and the human sciences to theology–cosmopolis will restore the integral dialectic of community. In fact it is understood as authentic cultural values.⁶⁸ It runs the risk of espousing an utopian ideal. Such inclusiveness and broadness of the function, role and responsibility of cosmopolis as critical culture is ambiguous.

Robert Doran tries to clear up this vagueness by seeing the praxis of theology as fulfilling the indispensable responsibilities of cosmopolis. Doran in fact, suggests theology as cosmopolis with the hope that such theology will "display the stereological significance of the divinely originated solution to the mystery of evil with respect to both cosmological fatalism and the mechnomorphic distortion of anthropological insight and truth."⁶⁹ His effort at constructing a systematic theology is an attempt in this direction. Such a theology, he says, must embody "not only the empirical but also the critical, dialectical and normative capacities of human intelligence."⁷⁰ Doran explains:

> It is the function of the dimension of consciousness that Lonergan calls cosmopolis to inform an intellectual collaboration at the

---

66. Ibid., 263.

67. Ibid., 265.

68. Lonergan writes that "if men are to meet the challenge set by major decline and its longer cycle, it will be through their culture that they do so." Cf. *Insight*, 261.

69. Doran, *Theological Foundations II*, 358–59.

70. Ibid., 336.

superstructural level of culture that would assume responsibility for the dialectic of community, by attending to the cultural meanings and values that are operative at *both* the infrastructural and the superstructural level of culture. Authentic cultural values, truly operative and *correct* assumptions about the right way to live, constitute the higher synthesis upon which the integrity of the dialectic of community depends, whereas the breakdown of the dialectic of community is due to the breakdown of culture, either because culture has been 'forced into an ivory tower of ineffectualness by the social surd' or because it has 'capitulate[d] to its absurdity' by becoming narrowly practical or exclusively instrumental.[71]

Doran's appropriation in the light of the integral scale of values is concerned with a religiously and theologically transformed cosmopolis, that is, "with the new and higher collaboration of intellects through faith in God."[72] Such cosmopolitan intelligence assumes as its function the integrity of culture through a reorientation, especially of the human sciences and of commonsense practicality, to promote in society and history an integral dialectic of community. This is so because, as Doran notes, culture is the link between spontaneous intersubjectivity and practical intelligence. As Darrell J. Fasching explains, "Doran refines Lonergan's proposed scale of values by observing that 'the differentiation of their ascending order is a matter of emergent probability; but the actual functioning of the levels depends upon the fact that the lower order values are conditioned by the successful functioning in a social order of the intention of the higher values.'"[73] Doran's appropriation in the light of the scale of values as an orientation at the superstructural level "that would take responsibility for the dialectic of community by attending to the integrity of the cultural values at both the superstructural and the infrastructural levels,"[74] successfully explicates Lonergan's notion of cosmopolis. However, a clear cut unambiguous statement from Lonergan on the meaning of what he means by cosmopolis would have helped Lonergan in clarifying his theory of society that prioritizes the dignity of the human subject.

It has to be noted though that in spite of the vagueness in expressing its meaning, Lonergan's notion of cosmopolis, his emphasis on culture as the integrator of distorted dialectic of community remains valid. This is

71. Ibid., 353.
72. Ibid., 370
73. Fasching, "Theology and Public Policy," 67.
74. Doran, *What is Systematic Theology?* 190.

because the disembedding of practical intelligence from social relations can only be counterbalanced by reinventing the culture, the common meaning upon which the infrastructure of society is founded. Lonergan is right in proposing that:

> ... If men are to meet the challenge set by major decline and its longer cycle, it will be through their culture that they do so. Were man a pure intelligence, the products of philosophy and human science would be enough to sway him. But as the dialectic in the individual and in society reveals, man is a compound-in-tension of intelligence and intersubjectivity, and it is only through the parallel compound of a culture that his tendencies to aberration can be offset proximately and effectively. The difficulty is, of course, that human aberration makes an uncritical culture its captive.[75]

Thus Lonergan emphasizes not just culture but critical culture as uncritical culture serves practical intelligence instead of guiding it. The vagueness I am pointing out is that Lonergan should have been much more explicit than he was on his language of cosmopolis.

From Doran's appropriation cited above however, it will be helpful to see cosmopolis as an upper blade and the various theories of development as the lower blade of exactly how cosmopolis would work out. In various places in *Insight*[76] Lonergan describes intellectual development using the image of the action of a pair of scissor with upper and lower blade. For instance, describing reflective understanding Lonergan thinks that "not only is there a lower blade that rises from data through measurements and curve fitting to formulae, but also there is an upper blade that moves downward from differential and operator equations and from postulates of invariance and equivalence."[77] This scissor-like action applies more so to genetic method which we mentioned in Chapter 2, determines a development "from generic indeterminacy towards specific perfection." As Doran explains, "the upper blade is the set of heuristic notions needed to arrive at the desired conclusion, while the lower blade provides the data that will be clarified by the meeting of the two blades."[78] In the present case, cosmopolis as an orientation at the supernatural level "that would take responsi-

---

75. Lonergan, *Insight*, 261–262.
76. See ibid., 87, 114–15, 337–38, 486, 546, 554, 600–601, 603, 609; See also Lonergan, *Method in Theology*, 293.
77. Lonergan, *Insight*, 337. See also ibid., 486, 546.
78. Doran, "Non-violent Cross."

bility for the dialectic of community by attending to the integrity of the cultural values at both the superstructural and the infrastructural levels"[79] is an upper blade while the theories of development and the principles of Catholic social teaching that respectively prioritizes the human good and sets principles for its realization by upholding integral human development is a lower blade. The orientation that will bring about changes in society towards improving the well-being of people is realizable in the concrete by implementing the various theories of development reoriented towards striving for human well-being and adhering to such principles as enunciated by the catholic social teachings. Implementing these will not be easy and would demand psychic, intellectual, moral and religious conversion. Because of this, it lies not in the everyday culture but as Doran asserts, in the superstructural level of culture:

> The theoretical developments required to institute alternative technologies, economies, polities, and communities are a function of the superstructure of culture, where refinement of the dialectic of culture can be elaborated, and where particular communities can communicate and collaborate in the institution of social schemes that promote a just social order . . . The breakdown of everyday cultural values can often be reversed only by prolonged and difficult artistic, theoretical, scientific, philosophic, and theological work.[80]

In other words, seen in the light of an upper and lower blade, Lonergan's notion of cosmopolis is complementary to the theories of development and to the principles of Catholic social teaching. It attempts at the superstructural level to ensure the provision of the human good for the well-being of the human person. In this way, as the catholic social teaching proposes, it strives for integral human development. Also, the principles of development, and those of Catholic social teaching could be seen as upper blade heuristic notions while the human situation itself forms the lower blade. What Lonergan and Catholic social teaching are trying to do is reorient and correct development discourse precisely as an upper blade.

---

79. Doran, *What is Systematic Theology?* 190.
80. Ibid., 192–93.

Limited Prognosis of the Scope of Globalization

Lonergan grasps the dynamics of globalization, but his scope is limited by the context of his time. His initial interest predisposed him to a broader range of issues and topics which he studied and tried to master. As the editors of Lonergan's *Verbum* discovered, Lonergan's "interest in the 1930s were economic, political, sociological, cultural, historical, religious, rather than gnoseological and metaphysical . . . . The human good proved to be more of a magnet than was cognitional theory. It was in the social order that the restoration would take place and the human good realized, so there was a crying need for a *summa sociologica*."[81] The Great Depression of the 1930s prompted Lonergan to ask moral questions of the social order of his student days. For instance, in *Panton Anakephalaiosis* (1935), he asked: "Why were there economic forces making it impossible for industrialists to pay workmen a wage and for workmen to raise a family? Why are there political forces holding the world in the unstable equilibrium of a balance of power secured by *Realpolitik*?"[82]

Lonergan's call for a '*summa sociologica*' is linked to Pope Pius XI's call in "*Quadragesimo Anno*" for the creation of an alternative social order between liberal capitalism and Marxism, the two competing theories of history and political economy in 1930s Europe. Rising to the occasion is central to Lonergan's intellectual quest expressed in his philosophical anthropology. The editors of his *Verbum* articles acknowledge this and write, ". . . in 1927 he [Lonergan] had expressed an initial interest, which he never lost, in cognitional theory—but their context was found in thinkers like Hegel and Marx and Spengler, and somewhat later Toynbee, rather than in Aristotle and Thomas. The restoration of all things in Christ (Ephesians 1:10) was closer to a motto for him than 'thoroughly understand what it is to understand.'"[83] By 1976, Lonergan's interest remained the same, as evident in his testimony:

> The modern world has been dominated then by one and now by another theory of history. From the eighteenth century came the liberal doctrine of progress. From the nineteenth came the Marxian doctrine of dialectical materialism. It has long been my conviction that if Catholics . . . are to live and operate on the level of

---

81. Crowe, "Editor's Preface," vii.
82. Lonergan, "Panton Anakephalaiosis (The Restoration of All Things)," 150.
83. Crowe, "Editor's Preface," vii.

the times, they must not only know about theories of history but also must work out their own.[84]

Lonergan repudiates both the idea of infinite progress inherent in liberal capitalism and the Marxist ideal that human history is internally oriented towards progress. On the contrary, he, like other Christian ethicists, holds that history always remains open, open to sin, to destructiveness and to redemption. Thus he fashions an analysis of history with three categories, progress, decline and redemption.[85] He substantiates this with examples drawn from the liberal theory of progress and the Marxian theory of dialectical materialism thus:

> To ignore the fact of decline was the error of the old liberal views of automatic progress. The far more confusing error of Marx was to lump together both progress and the two principles of decline under the impressive name of dialectical materialism, to grasp that the minor principle of decline would correct itself more rapidly through class war, and then to leap gaily to the sweeping conclusion that class war would accelerate progress.[86]

As Doran explains for Lonergan, the problem with Marx is that he elevates economics and politics to cultural value. Marxist analysis thus promotes general bias in these ways:

> (1) it elevates facts into norms or laws and seeks a solution at the level of these facts rather than at a genuinely normative level; (2) it ignores the dialectical counterpart of practicality that is spontaneous intersubjectivity, and thus turns praxis without remainder into instrumentalized technique; and (3) it neglects cultural integrity as the condition of the possibility of an integral social dialectic, and so adopts a viewpoint that would understand social reality exclusively 'from below'.[87]

This neglect of the corresponding movement 'from above' brought ideological influence into the constituents of community, leading to the exaltation of an aspect of practical intelligence over other aspects, and thus distorting the integral dialectic of community. In a paper titled "Moral Theology

---

84. "Questionnaire on Philosophy," cited in Shute, "Economic Analysis with Redemptive Praxis," 248.
85. Lonergan, "Analytic Concept of History," 14.
86. Lonergan, *Insight*, 260.
87. Doran, *Theology and the Dialectics of History*, 410.

and the Human Sciences" (1974), Lonergan calls for a radical criticism of economics as human science in its three principal variants—the traditional market economy, the Marxist-inspired socialist economy and the new transactional economy constituted by the giant corporations which are neither socialist nor controlled by the market. The radical criticism Lonergan offers is 'a pure economics analysis of the exchange process' untainted by any ideology in order to rid economics of ideological influences.[88]

Lonergan thus shows mastery of the literature on globalization as practiced by the trans-national corporations of his time. In "Healing and Creating in History" (1975), he analyzes Richard Barnet and Ronald Muller's *Global Reach: The Power of the Multinational Corporations* (1974). He observes that globalization is characterized by global governance, use of large capital, quests for cheap raw materials, a global market network and stiff competition. He notes that the multinational corporation has adverse effects on developing countries and to developed countries as well. He observes that the activities of these corporations are in continuity with the aim of economic enterprise—to maximize profit. He alludes to the danger they pose as well as their inadequacies and their potential for disaster.[89] In order to avoid this danger, he recommends healthy interaction of economics and ethics:

> If we are to escape a similar fate, we must demand that two requirements are met. The first regards economic theorists; the second regards moral theorists. From economic theorists we have to demand, along with as many other types of analysis as they please, a new and specific type that reveals how moral precepts have both a basis in economic process and so an effective application to it. From moral theorists we have to demand, along with their other various forms of wisdom and prudence, specifically economic precepts that arise out of economic process itself and promote its proper functioning.[90]

As Frederick E. Crowe notes, in Lonergan's essay in circulation analysis,[91] "there is a lengthy section on [the] chief element of liberation theology, the multinational corporations."[92] There Lonergan "discusses the factors

88. Lonergan, "Moral Theology and the Human Sciences," 311.
89. Lonergan, "Healing and Creating in History," 111–32.
90. Lonergan, "Moral Theology and the Human Sciences," 108.
91. See Lonergan, *Macroeconomic Dynamics*, 75–103.
92. Crowe, "Lonergan and Liberation Theology," 123.

leading to recession, depression, and crash in the economy; he deals with the colonial economy, armaments, unemployment, unions, inflation; . . . undeveloped and developed countries," etc.[93]

Although Lonergan's analysis above indicates a grasp of the inner workings of multinational corporations and their possible adverse effects on both the developing and on the developed countries, his prognostication of globalization falls short of the further dynamics of the role of the international financial institutions and of the role of the World Trade Organization in furthering economic globalization. Lonergan mentions correctly that the multinational corporation "is built on the very principles that slowly but surely have been moulding our technology and our economics, our society and our culture, our ideals and our practice for centuries. It remains that the long-accepted principles are inadequate."[94] He is right in suggesting a harmonious interaction of economics and ethics. As we argued above, his philosophical anthropology does indeed go a long way toward providing the conceptual clarity needed to understand the features of globalization. However, besides his emphasis of the dialectic of transcendence and limitation and the need to maintain creative tension of the dialectic in the integral dialectic of community, Lonergan did not dwell further on the dynamics of globalization—it was a notion that did not really come into play until after his death.

Therefore, his analysis has limited value for engaging the complexity of globalization and contemporary development discourse in the current climate. Lonergan did not consider the many visions of development, alternative paths, the ethics and politics of change. He did not pay sufficient attention to the diverse and conflicting discourses of development debates like the emergence of post-colonial and de-colonial discourses. The new critical traditions—feminist and/or ecological economics—that emerged in the latter years of his writing did not feature in Lonergan's purview. Furthermore, and most surprising, Lonergan did not mention the traditions of Catholic social teaching on development or on globalization. He did not refer specifically to such a momentous document as *Populorum Progressio*, the encyclical which appeared five years before *Method in Theology*, a book that marked a significant shift in his notion of the good. He may however, have been influenced by it as reflected in Chapter 2 of *Method in Theology* titled 'The Human Good' which treats, among other themes, the structure

93. Ibid.
94. Lonergan, "Healing and Creating in History," 103.

of the human good, progress and decline, but there is no way to determine this.

Thus Lonergan studies stand to benefit from secular contemporary development discourse in its grasp of globalization. For instance, in spite of its limitations, Lonergan studies can benefit from liberal capitalism a better understanding of the internal dynamics of free market economy and the operations of the international financial institutions. Such knowledge will sharpen the critical tools of Lonergan studies in its analysis of the dynamics of the market. This is important as Lonergan economics pertained to the industrial labour economy and not the free market economy today or to the information/service age we are in. Furthermore, Lonergan studies stands to learn a lot from the concept of sustainable development. On a very fundamental level, without sustainability, human development is not true human development. Sustainable development will broaden Lonergan's genetic method to emphasise sustainability of development that "if human development is about enabling people to lead long, healthy, educated and fulfilling lives, then sustainable human development is about making sure that future generations can do the same."[95]

Areas for Further Development/Emphasis

We have outlined some areas of convergence and limitations [divergence] of Lonergan's philosophical anthropology with contemporary development discourse in both secular literature and in the principles of Catholic social teaching. While doing this, we emphasised their complementarity especially with Lonergan's thought providing the general categories of what the Catholic social teaching specifies in special categories. We also thought of possible ways Lonergan's anthropology could contribute to contemporary development discourse. In this section, we wish to consider areas of Lonergan's philosophical anthropology that could benefit from Catholic social teaching's principle of solidarity as a virtue.

Appropriation of the Principle of Solidarity

Lonergan felt that general bias was more serious because it is a bias for commonsense against theory. This could be attributed to Lonergan's belief that individual and group biases reverse themselves. But the tenacity of

---

95. Neumayer, *Human Development and Sustainability*, 1.

ethnic tensions and the age-old perpetuation of self-interest that resulted from Adam Smith's economics indicate that these group and individual biases are more tenacious than is apparent from Lonergan's treatment. The endemic problem of ethnicity and the often violent clashes in Africa, especially in the sub-Saharan region, remind us of the seriousness of, and prevalence of, these biases of the subject that affect the whole of human knowing. In light of this, it is important for Lonergan studies not only to emphasize the general bias, but also to complement Lonergan's solution with an equal emphasis on the problems of social relations with a view to finding solutions to dramatic, individual and group bias. This position is equally informed by the close relationship to, and the complementary role in, the pursuit of the human good of human intelligence and the mutual interdependence of human beings. Ideally, the unrestricted desire to know seeks the good, not only of oneself, but for the good of order, the common good of all. This common good demands, not only a recognition of the mutual interdependence of human beings, but also an implementation, a living out of this mutual interdependence in order to set in motion a recurrence of schemes for the constant provision of the human good for all members of one's community. In this regard, I believe that an appropriation of Catholic social teaching's principle of solidarity will complement Lonergan's efforts at integrating the distorted dialectics of community.

The principle of solidarity is linked with the dignity of the human person arising from the fact that human beings are created by God. Consequently Christians believe all human beings belong together to one family of God and bound together in solidarity and deserve mutual respect. Although human persons are individuals, they are also social beings. In the words of Gregory Baum, "a society is characterized by cooperation and co-responsibility that recognizes the personal dignity and equality of its citizens."[96] According to *Encyclopaedia of Catholic Social Thought, Social Sciences and Social Policy*, "in its general meaning, solidarity refers to union arising from community of interests and responsibilities."[97] As we saw in Chapter 1, John Paul II sees solidarity as "undoubtedly a Christian virtue"[98] and explains the interdependent relationship of economic, cultural, political and religious elements in the contemporary world as a moral category based on the principle of solidarity. Thus, as a concept and virtue, solidarity,

---

96. Baum, *Karl Polanyi on Economics and Ethics*, 33.
97. Ederer, "Solidarity," 1010.
98. Pope John Paul II, *Solicitudo Rei Socialis*, 38.

'fills-in' the more generic, philosophical language of 'authenticity' and 'scale of values' with particular content drawn from socio-political and theological sources.

The principle of solidarity is a moral response to the interdependence of peoples this time brought about by increasing globalization. In contrast to the economics of self-interest, solidarity presents development as involving not only the total good of a person but the good of all people. It underscores the implications of interdependence as an increased concern for one another and a greater readiness to be involved with one another for the common good. As a virtue, solidarity is not just a warm feeling, but "a firm and persevering determination to commit oneself to the common good."[99] Thus, the principle of solidarity is linked to social relations. According to Donal Dorr, "within any particular country, the virtue of solidarity transforms the *interpersonal relationships* of individuals with the persons around them."[100] It solidifies the bond people have with one another and could possibly create relationships where such bonding is lacking. For instance, in heterogeneous societies like sub-Saharan Africa which are bedevilled by ethnic tension and conflict, resulting in what Lonergan calls "cumulative decline," the principle of solidarity could create a relationship of acceptance and tolerance if the fact of mutual interdependence of peoples, irrespective of differences in ethnic affiliations, diversity of languages, rites, rituals and cultures, is accepted by those communities. The virtue of solidarity could thus promote tolerance and co-existence in society. Pope John Paul II writes:

> Solidarity helps us to see the "other"—whether a person, people, or nation—not just as some kind of instrument with a work capacity and physical strength to be exploited at low cost and then discarded when no longer useful, but as our "neighbor," a "helper" to be made a sharer, on a par with ourselves, in the banquet of life to which all are equally invited by God.[101]

The virtue of solidarity enables us to treat people as persons, not as things. In community, it promotes mutual trust and collaboration. When relationship sours, solidarity is the path to reconciliation, justice and peace.

---

99. Ibid.

100. Dorr, "Solidarity and Integral Human Development," 149. Emphasis is in the original.

101. Pope John Paul II, *Solicitudo Rei Socialis*, 39, cited in Dorr, "Solidarity and Integral Human Development," 152.

The principle of solidarity through its emphasis of interdependence is thus complementary to Lonergan's philosophical anthropology. Because interdependence of peoples presupposes cordial social relations, the virtue of solidarity complements Lonergan's emphasis on practical intelligence in the distorted dialectic of community. This will help in understanding what Lonergan meant by the distortion of the dialectic of community as not favoring practical intelligence to the eclipse of spontaneous intersubjectivity. Integral dialectic of community will thus consist in a creative tension of spontaneous intersubjectivity and practical intelligence. The higher viewpoint for integral dialectic of community will not only restore intelligence, but will also emphasize human mutuality, the interdependence of peoples who, as social beings, are bound to live cordially in community. This will validate the importance Lonergan places on recurrence of schemes for the provision of the human good and that Doran spells out as the implementation of the integral scale of values.

At the heart of Lonergan's structure of the human good is the importance of working for the common good. The products of practical intelligence, technology, economy and the polity, arise from human creativity, from the unrestricted desire to know aimed at strengthening human relations with the aim of enhancing human well-being. The human good is provided by members of community interdependently working together. Where this interdependence is lacking the good of order is disorganized; the community is distorted and gradually heads towards decline. At issue in distorted dialectic of community is the loss of cultural values and the common meaning under which people live. Restoring the integrity of community entails strengthening once again social relations in the community so that people feel that they belong to a community and are not merely utilitarians seeking only what they will gain from the community. Therefore, the virtue of solidarity complements Lonergan's emphasis of restoration of intelligence towards the integral dialectic of community.

The virtue of solidarity will transform globalization by freeing it from the limits of liberal capitalism and dialectical materialism. Thus instead of merely bemoaning globalization, proponents of the virtue of solidarity will humanize it by emphasizing the needs and values of persons and peoples. Recognition of the mutual interdependence of peoples could bring about an appreciation of globalization as necessary for the promotion of human good. In contrast to the mutual suspicion engendered by protection of self-interest, the virtue of solidarity could promote the cordiality in human relations necessary for social transformation and sustainable human development.

In doing this the virtue of solidarity will draw from the religious value of God's love which crowns the scale of values and is at the heart of integral dialectic of community. The religious value of God's love not only justifies the fact of interdependence by grounding the common humanity of human beings in God, but on account of this common humanity gives the raison d'être for the pursuit of the common good of all peoples, who were created equal by God and, having been so, equally deserve dignified living conditions. The religious value of God's love thus extends the meaning of solidarity as comprising, not only the interdependence between and among human beings, but also the interdependence of humanity and the rest of creation. Sustainable development is thus a development that, while continuously providing the human good for the present generation, is conscious of the good of the next generation. In this way religion is potentially transformative of society in two ways: (1) by creating conditions for the constant provision of the human good for all peoples through altruistic love and (2) by fostering social relations that promotes human authenticity at all levels. Lonergan writes:

> As human authenticity promotes progress, and human unauthenticity generates decline, so Christian authenticity—which is a love of others that does not shrink from self-sacrifice and suffering—is the sovereign means for overcoming evil. Christians bring about the kingdom of God in the world not only by doing good but also by overcoming evil with good (Rom. 12, 21).[102]

As a holistic virtue, solidarity opens up precisely the genuine human development we are advocating in this book. It would help more adequately to attend to the issues of justice and peace.

The dialogue of Lonergan's philosophical anthropology with contemporary development discourse shows how mutually beneficial they are. Lonergan's anthropology has much to contribute to the various theories of development. At the same time, these theories are beneficial to Lonergan's endeavor. As we just argued, some aspects of Lonergan's philosophical anthropology could be clarified by such principles of Catholic social teaching as the principle of solidarity, a principle which emphasizes interdependence and hence the importance of spontaneous intersubjectivity for societal development and transformation.

102. Lonergan, *Method in Theology*, 291.

Secular contemporary development discourse like the theories of development we examined in Chapter 1 generally aim at the human good understood as improving human well-being, increasing income per capita and growing the gross national product of a country so as to enable her people to live an improved human life free from all forms of servitude. That this is a noble goal cannot be disputed. The problem is that the method and the values offered by these theories are limiting for they concentrate on material improvement without sufficiently accounting for the spiritual, moral and cultural dimensions and the implications for human self-constitution. Even worse, it gives rise to various forms of inequality and the marginalization of both the poor and such peoples who are as yet to attain the mature stage of development. This limits the breadth and scope of such theories as liberal capitalism, as we illustrated with reference to W.W. Rostow's stages of growth theory and some sustainable development theories. In the words of the post-developmentalist theorist A. Escobar, "Development was—and continues to be for the most part—a top-down ethnocentric and technocratic approach, which treated people and cultures as abstract concepts, statistical figures to be moved up and down in the charts of progress."[103] For instance, as we saw in Chapter 1, by the institution of globalization, the 'developed world' exercises power not only by controlling the flow of money, but also by creating the dominant ideas, representations and discourses through such large organizations, as the World Bank, the IMF, and the U.S. Agency for International Development (USAID).

Consequently, development has been "successful" to the extent that it managed and controlled populations and that it has created a type of manageable underdevelopment in a more subtle form than colonialism.[104] Thus one can say that underdevelopment is only a cultural form of domination whereas development as merely economic growth is unsustainable.[105] An instance of the cultural and economic-political form of domination is reflected in the famous clash between two reports on African development—the *Lagos Plan of Action* of 1980 by the African heads of State of OAU (Organization of African Unity, present day African Union) and the *Accelerated Development in Sub-Saharan Africa: An Agenda for Action* commissioned by the World Bank. While the World Bank report attributed

---

103. Escobar, *Encountering Development*, 44.

104. Cited from Peet and Hartwick, *Theories of Development*, 148.

105. *The Development Dictionary* passes similar judgment on development seen in terms of economic growth. See Sachs, ed., *Development Dictionary*, 1.

Lonergan and Development: Points for Dialogue

Africa's woes to insufficient attention on primary production, particularly agricultural production, urging therefore free marketing economy, *The Lagos Plan of Action* argued that Africa's economic problems were partly caused by Africa's concentration on agricultural production in a hostile market. This perpetuates Africa's dependence and openness to exploitation; hence the necessity for self-reliance:

> Africa is susceptible to the disastrous effects of natural and endemic diseases of the cruelest type and is a victim of settler exploitation arising from colonialism, racism and apartheid. Indeed, Africa was directly exploited during the colonial period and for the past two decades; this exploitation has been carried out through neo-colonialist external forces which seek to influence the economic policies and directions of African states.[106]

When African leaders insisted that the *Lagos Plan of Action* offered authentic and authoritative goals and objectives for Africa, Claude Ake reports that "the Bretton Woods institutions and the West would not accept the approach of the Lagos Plan . . . They expressed their rejection of the plan by ignoring it and refusing to reorient their economic relations so as to connect with and address the programs and policies of the plan. That was enough to render the plan inoperable. In the end African leaders found that they were too dependent and too weak to have their way, and they started to retreat."[107]

Furthermore, the neglect of the religious dimension of humankind has equally made development projects unsustainable. This point is not lost on scholars and institutions interested in articulating the crisis in the global set up. For example, referring to the inadequacies of the development project, Lee Cormie observes that "ultimately they call into question taken-for-granted values and the very meaning of life itself. Thus, not only economic and political issues are at stake, but also religious issues concerning human meaning and value."[108] Even Michael Novak, who is sympathetic to 'democratic capitalism', acknowledges the undermining of culture as its basic flaw thus: "the ironic flaw . . . in democratic capitalism is this: that its *successes* in

---

106. Organization of African Unity, "Lagos Plan of Action for the Economic Development of Africa 1980–2000," cited in Ake, *Democracy and Development in Africa*, 23.

107. Ibid., 26.

108. Cormie, "Sociology of National Development and Salvation History," 56–85.

the political order and in the economic order *undermine* it in the cultural order. The more it succeeds, the more it fails."[109]

Catholic social teaching's emphasis on the dignity of the human person, the proper beneficiary of development, takes a middle position between liberal capitalism and Marxist communism. With the end of the Cold War, the collapse of Russian communism in 1989 and the attendant triumph of Western capitalism, Catholic social teachings caution against the tendency to reduce human beings and value to profit in a free-market economy. Their emphasis of the cultural, moral and spiritual dimensions of development correct the extremes of democratic capitalism. Authentic and integral development is the development of each and every person.

Lonergan's philosophical anthropology brings to contemporary development discourse both an appreciation of the human person as one who experiences, understands, judges and decides and the integral scale of values that is intimately related to these operations. Development must take into consideration the process of history. There cannot be an automatic progress as if it is not dependent on the human person obeying the transcendental precepts: be attentive, be intelligent, be reasonable, be responsible and be in love. Development must then take into consideration the realities of sin and decline and be open to transformation arising from the religious value of God's love. This is achieved by taking note of the integral scale of values, vital, social, cultural, personal and religious, mutually conditioning one another from above downwards and from below upwards. While theories of development emphasize vital and social values, Lonergan's philosophical anthropology's emphasis on the scale of values Doran develops as the *integral* scale of values opts for the integral development which Catholic social teaching understands as the development of each man and of the whole man.[110] Development founded on an integral scale of values is considered comprehensive because it denotes development, not only as economic growth, but as including cultural, personal and religious values which give meaning to human life as a whole. Societal development and transformation can only be considered sustainable, not only to the extent it respects the fact that natural resources are not inexhaustible, but also to the extent that it respects the cultural, personal and religious values that are important in humankind's search for meaning.

109. Novak, *Spirit of Democratic Capitalism*, 31. Emphasis in the original.

110. Paul VI, *Populorum Progressio* [*On the Development of Peoples*], 14. See also Pope Benedict XVI, *Caritas in Veritate*, #30.

5

Conclusion

In the Forward to the *UN Report on the Millennium Development Goals* (2010), Ban Ki-moon, Secretary-General to the United Nations, emphasizes the goal of development as the promotion of human well-being. The indices of human well-being as articulated by the Millennium Development Goals (MDGs) include freedom from extreme poverty and hunger, quality education and decent employment; good health and shelter, a sustainable environment and the equality of men and women the world over.[1] The various themes in contemporary development discourse both secular and religious seek to promote human freedom by the provision of the human good to enhance the quality of human life. However, secular theories of development often neglect other important aspects of human life like the cultural, personal and religious values constitutive of life in society. Even the MDGs in all their expanded concepts of human well-being fail to account for these.

Development, as Richard Jolly et al. observe, "concerns not only man's material needs but also the improvement of the social conditions of his life and his broad aspirations, [to which must be added cultural and religious aspiration]."[2] Thus, according to World Faiths Development Dialogue (WFDD, 1998),[3] development processes will only be successful—even in

---

1. United Nations, *Millennium Development Goals Report 2010*. Millenium Development Goals aims not at eliminating poverty or even changing the structures that perpetuates it but as Gilbert Rist notes "just to halve it by 2015." See, Rist, "Is 'Development' a Panacea?" 348.

2. Jolly et al., *UN Ideas That Changed the World*, 187.

3. See Tyndale, "Religions and the Millennium Development Goals," 216; Cf. "World Faiths Development Dialogue," http://www.compasnet.org/afbeeldingen/Magazines/

material terms—if they take into consideration, not only the economic, but also the cultural, social, environmental and spiritual aspects of life.[4] The harsh living conditions of most developing countries such as those in Africa witness to this truth. The one dimensional approach of economic developmental theories has failed to provide effective reconstruction, leaving these countries badly and bitterly underdeveloped. This narrow approach is inimical to these peoples' anthropological concepts of life as ontologically integral and relational. Their policies create a split between the human community and its environment, its culture and ecology. They weaken the very bonds that hold the people together, their source of resistance to injustice and thus leave them helpless. For this reason, such bodies as the International Development Research Center are dissatisfied with the various theories that describe development as economic growth. These theories, they claim, "dealing in money and the economically quantifiable inputs, ignore or dismiss the *cultural, moral, spiritual* dimensions of human well-being as either irrelevant to development or so intractably subjective as to be amenable to a 'practical paradigm.'"[5]

This work, through a dialogue of Lonergan's philosophical anthropology with contemporary development discourse, argues for an integral human development that consists in adherence to the integral scale of values, vital, social, cultural, personal and religious, interdependently working together for sustainable societal development and transformation. It critically analyzed contemporary theories of development by introducing select themes from the secular theories of development and correlating these with principles of development in Catholic social teachings, such as the principles of the common good, the universal destination of earth's goods, integral human development, the principles of solidarity and subsidiarity, etc. Through an exposition and analysis of Lonergan's philosophical anthropology, it introduces a hermeneutic tool for an interpretation and evaluation of development discourse as consisting, not merely of economic growth, but of a concern for the human good, that is, with human well-being that includes cultural, personal and religious values constitutive of the human beings individually and collectively.

CM4/cm4_08.PDF. Cf. also http://berkleycenter.georgetown.edu/wfdd/about for an expanded history of the World Faiths Development Dialogue.

4. Tyndale, "World Faiths Development Dialogue."

5. Ryan, *Culture, Spirituality, and Economic Development*, vi, 14–15.

While the various forms of development as economic growth emphasize the importance of financial capital, this work included in its emphasis the necessity of human capital including wisdom and such virtues that promote human relationship as compassion, kindness and charity which, though unquantifiable, enhances cooperation in society. It argued that social progress and development result from the actions of authentic human subjects obeying the transcendental precepts: be attentive, be intelligent, be reasonable, be responsible and be in love. Because sustainable development results from the actions of human beings under the direction of God's grace, this book argues that societal progress and transformation demand the conversion—religious, moral, intellectual and psychic—of the human person from irreligious, amoral, unintelligent and less meaningful existence lost in self-interest, resulting in a life guided by God's love, characterized by the unrestricted desire for knowledge and truth, fully integrated and whole.

The dialogue initiated here is beneficial to the theories of development, to the principles of Catholic social teaching and to Lonergan studies. For example, Lonergan studies' appropriation of the principle of solidarity can help fill out what he means by the integral dialectic of community. The mutual interdependence of peoples emphasized by the principle of solidarity could promote social relations and responsibility, enhance the importance of spontaneous intersubjectivity and support the collaborative enterprise of critical culture towards the restoration of intelligence both practically and theoretically. Catholic social teaching can draw from Lonergan's philosophical anthropology both the categories relevant to convey its teaching to the modern secular minds and its historical consciousness, and this will lead to a development of its methodology. It can find in Lonergan's scale of values and Doran's integral scale of values an intellectual framework to critically assess theories of development and the whole range of values upon which human beings anchor their lives. From Lonergan's philosophical anthropology the theories of development could learn to emphasize both the distortions of the particular good of self-interest and the good of order for others. In this way, theories of development could measure the impact of development, not only by the quantity of consumer goods produced, but also by the consequences of developmental process on the common meaning of community, on the human person and on relations with some ultimate reality.

In light of the integral scale of value that implements and promotes the whole range of values, this work has taken the position that development discourse should not be divorced from promoting human well-being and happiness. Preference should not be given to the economic means of development to the neglect of the end of development which ought to be improving the living condition of human beings. It is the human subject's intentional consciousness raising and answering questions for understanding, questions for reflection and questions for deliberation in the human search for meaning that brings about progress and development. Furthermore, it is the human subject's openness to insight that sets up the social order that makes the provision of vital values recurrently possible. Social progress and development cannot therefore neglect human welfare and well-being, flourishing and happiness. It is by taking seriously this other and often neglected aspect of human well-being that even the economic dimension of development may be guaranteed.

Above all, the consistent religious voice of Lonergan's philosophical anthropology maintained in this dialogue, namely, that these transformations, societal and human, are made possible by the assistance of the religious value of God's grace, is very significant. It strengthens the religious voice in development discourse and exposes the hypocrisy and ideological priorities of the present economic dominated paradigm. It lays the foundation for this critical assessment of the role of religious value towards a sustainable and integral development of Africa. In its calls for religious, moral, intellectual and psychic conversion, it places all stakeholders in international development–the recipients, international organizations and agencies–in a better position to respond to obstacles of sustainable and integral development. Most importantly, in situations where ethnicity and religion often lead to bad administration of economy and politics, as in Africa, where people have been grappling with the vicious circles of poverty, socio-political conflict and underdevelopment, this call for conversion should be gladly answered.

Bibliography

Primary Literature:

Lonergan, Bernard. "The Analogy of Meaning." In *Philosophical and Theological Papers 1958-1964*, edited by Robert C. Croken, Frederick C. Crowe, and Robert M. Doran, CWL 6:183-313. Toronto: University of Toronto Press, 1996.

———. "Analytic Concept of History." *Method: Journal of Lonergan Studies* 11:1 (1993) 1-29.

———. "Aquinas Today: Tradition and Innovation." In *A Third Collection: Papers by Bernard J. F. Lonergan, S.J.*, edited by Frederick E. Crowe, 35-54. New York: Paulist, 1985.

———. "Belief: Today's Issue." In *A Second Collection: Papers by Bernard Lonergan*, edited by William F. J. Ryan and Bernard J. Tyrrell, 87-99. Toronto: University of Toronto, Press, 1996.

———. "Christology Today: Methodological Reflections." In *A Third Collection: Papers by Bernard J. F. Lonergan, S.J.*, edited by Frederick E. Crowe, 74-99. New York: Paulist, 1985.

———. "Dialectic of Authority." In *A Third Collection: Papers by Bernard J. F. Lonergan, S.J.*, edited by Frederick E. Crowe, 5-12. New York: Paulist, 1985.

———. *Early Works on Theological Method*. Vol. 1. Edited by Robert M. Doran and Robert C. Croken. CWL 22. Toronto: University of Toronto Press, 2010.

———. "Existenz and Aggiornamento." In *Collection*, edited by Frederick E. Crowe and Robert D. Doran, CWL 4:222-31. Toronto: University of Toronto Press, 1988. *Collection*.

———. "Healing and Creating in History." In *A Third Collection: Papers by Bernard J. F. Lonergan, S.J.*, edited by Frederick E. Crowe, 100-112. New York: Paulist, 1985.

———. "History." In *Topics in Education*. edited by Robert M. Doran and Frederick E. Crowe, CWL 10: 233-57. Toronto: University of Toronto Press, 2000.

———. "Horizon, History, Philosophy." In *Phenomenology and Logic: The Boston College Lectures on Mathematical Logic and Existentialism*, edited by Philip J. McShane, CWL 18:298-317. Toronto: University of Toronto Press, 2001.

———. *Insight: A Study of Human Understanding*. Edited by Frederick E. Crowe and Robert D. Doran. CWL 3. Toronto: University of Toronto Press. 1992.

———. "Insight Revisited." In *A Second Collection: Papers by Bernard Lonergan*, edited by William F. J. Ryan and Bernard J. Tyrrell, 263-79. Toronto: University of Toronto, Press, 1996.

Bibliography

———. *Macroeconomic Dynamics: An Essay in Circulation Analysis*. Edited by Frederick G. Lawrence, Patrick H. Byrne, and Charles C. Hefling. CWL 15. Toronto: University of Toronto Press, 1999.

———. *Method in Theology*. Toronto: University of Toronto Press, 1990.

———. "Mission and the Spirit." In *A Third Collection: Papers by Bernard J. F. Lonergan, S.J.*, edited by Frederick E. Crowe, 23–34. New York: Paulist, 1985.

———. "Moral Theology and the Human Sciences," In *Philosophical and Theological Papers 1965–1980*, edited by Robert C. Croken and Robert M. Doran, CWL 17: 301–12. Toronto: University of Toronto Press, 1999.

———. "Natural Right and Historical Mindedness." In *A Third Collection: Papers by Bernard J. F. Lonergan, S.J.*, edited by Frederick E. Crowe, 169–83. New York: Paulist, 1985.

———. "Natural Right and Historical Mindedness." In *The Lonergan Reader*, edited by Mark D. Morelli and Elizabeth, 580–95. Toronto: University of Toronto Press, 1997.

———."The Notion of Structure." *Method: Journal of Lonergan Studies* 14:2 (1996) 117–31.

———. "On Being Oneself." In *Phenomenology and Logic: The Boston College Lectures on Mathematical Logic and Existentialism*, edited by Philip J. McShane, CWL 18: 234–46. Toronto: University of Toronto Press, 2001.

———. "The Ongoing Genesis of Methods." In *A Third Collection: Papers by Bernard J. F. Lonergan, S.J.*, edited by Frederick E. Crowe, 146–68. New York: Paulist, 1985.

———. "Panton Anakephalaiosis [The Restoration of All Things]." *Method: Journal of Lonergan Studies* 9:2 (1991) 134–71.

———. "Philosophical Positions with Regard to Knowing." In *Philosophical and Theological Papers 1958–1964*, edited by Robert C. Croken, Frederick C. Crowe, and Robert M. Doran, CWL 6:214–243. Toronto: University of Toronto Press, 1996.

———. "Philosophy and the Religious Phenomenon." *Method: Journal of Lonergan Studies* 12:2 (1994) 125–46.

———. "Pope John's Intention." In *A Third Collection: Papers by Bernard J. F. Lonergan, S.J.*, edited by Frederick E. Crowe, 224–38. New York: Paulist, 1985.

———. "A Post-Hegelian Philosophy of Religion." In *A Third Collection: Papers by Bernard J. F. Lonergan, S.J.*, edited by Frederick E. Crowe, 202–23. New York: Paulist, 1985.—

———. "Religious Experience." In *A Third Collection: Papers by Bernard J. F. Lonergan, S.J.*, edited by Frederick E. Crowe, 113–28. New York: Paulist, 1985.

———. "Prolegomena to the Study of the Emerging Religious Consciousness of Our Time." *A Third Collection: Papers by Bernard J. F. Lonergan, S.J.*, edited by Frederick E. Crowe, 55–99. New York: Paulist, 1985.

———. "Respect for Human Dignity." In *Shorter Papers*, edited by Robert C. Croken, Robert M. Doran, and H. Daniel Monsour, CWL 20:121–27. Toronto: University of Toronto Press, 2007.

———. "The Response of the Jesuit as Priest and Apostle in the Modern World." In *A Second Collection: Papers by Bernard Lonergan*, edited by William F. J. Ryan and Bernard J. Tyrrell, 168–69. Toronto: University of Toronto, Press, 1996.

———. "The Role of a Catholic University in the Modern World." In *Collection*, edited by Frederick E. Crowe and Robert D. Doran, CWL 4:108–13. Toronto: University of Toronto Press, 1988.

---. "Self-transcendence: Intellectual, Moral, Religious." In *Philosophical and Theological Papers 1965-1980*, edited by Robert C. Croken and Robert M. Doran, CWL 17:313-31. Toronto: University of Toronto Press, 2004.

---. "The Subject." *A Second Collection: Papers by Bernard Lonergan*, edited by William F. J. Ryan and Bernard J. Tyrrell, 69-86. Toronto: University of Toronto, Press, 1996.

---. "Theology in its New Context." In *A Second Collection: Papers by Bernard Lonergan*, edited by William F. J. Ryan and Bernard J. Tyrrell, 55-67. Toronto: University of Toronto, Press, 1996.

---. "Time and Meaning." In *Philosophical and Theological Papers, 1958-64*, edited by Robert C. Croken, Frederick E. Crowe, and Robert M. Doran. CWL 6: 94-121. Toronto: University of Toronto Press, 1996.

---. "The Transition From a Classicist World-View to Historical-Mindedness." In *A Second Collection: Papers by Bernard Lonergan*, edited by William F. J. Ryan and Bernard J. Tyrrell, 1-10. Toronto: University of Toronto, Press, 1996.

---. "The World Mediated by Meaning." In *Philosophical and Theological Papers, 1965-80*, edited by Robert C. Croken and Robert M. Doran, CWL 17:107-18. . Toronto: University of Toronto Press, 2004.

---. *Understanding and Being: The Halifax Lectures on Insight*. Edited by Elizabeth A. Morelli, Mark D. Morelli, and Frederick E. Crowe. CWL 5. Toronto: University of Toronto Press, 1990.

---. "Unity and Plurality: The Coherence of Christian Truth." In *A Third Collection: Papers by Bernard J. F. Lonergan, S.J.*, edited by Frederick E. Crowe, 239-50. New York: Paulist, 1985.

Secondary Literature

Ake, Claude. *Democracy and Development in Africa*. Washington, DC: The Brookings Institution, 1996.

Archibugi, Daniele, and Immarino Simona. "The Globalization of Technological Innovation: Definition and Evidence." *Review of International Political Economy* 9:1 (2002) 98-122.

Arrighi, Giovanni. "The African Crisis." *New Left Review* 15 (2002) 5-36.

Bangura, Abdul Karim. "A Time Series Analysis of the African Growth and Opportunity Act: Testing the Efficacy of Transnationalism." *Journal of Third World Studies* 26:2 (2009) 31-50.

Baum, Gregory. *Karl Polanyi on Ethics & Economics*. Quebec: McGill-Queen's University Press, 1996.

---. "Liberal Capitalism." In *The Logic of Solidarity*, edited by Gregory Baum and Robert Ellsberg, 75-89. Maryknoll, NY: Orbis, 1989.

---. *Religion and Alienation*. Toronto: Paulist, 1975.

Bellah, Robert N., et al. *Habits of the Heart: Individualism and Commitment in American Life*. Berkeley: University of California Press, 2008.

Berry, Wendell. "Inverting the Economic Order." *Communio: International Catholic Review* 36:3 (2009) 475-86.

Boafo-Arthur, Kwame. "Tackling Africa's Developmental Dilemmas: Is Globalization the Answer?" *Journal of Third World Studies*. 20:1 (2003) 27-54.

Bibliography

Braedley Susan, and Meg Luxton. "Competing Philosophies: Neoliberalism and Challenges of Everyday Life." In *Neoliberalism and Everyday Life*, edited by Braedley Susan and Meg Luxton, 3–21. Montreal and Kingston: McGill-Queen University Press, 2010.

Brooks, Rodney Allen. *Flesh and Machines: How Robots Will Change Us*. New York: Pantheon, 2002.

Caldecott, Stratford. "Caritas in Veritate and 'Integral Human Development.'" *Communio: International Catholic Review* 36:2 (2009) 182–85.

Canel, Eduardo, et al. "Rethinking Extractive Industry: Regulation, Dispossession, and Emerging Claims." *Canadian Journal of Development Studies* 30:1–2 (2010) 5–25.

Cavanagh, John, and Jerry Mander, editors. *Alternatives to Economic Globalization: A Better World is Possible*. San Francisco, CA: Berret-Koehler. 2004.

Cavanaugh, William T. *Being Consumed: Economics and Christian Desire*. Grand Rapids, MI: Eerdmans, 2008.

Chew, Sing C., and Robert A. Denemark, editors. *The Underdevelopment of Development: Essays in Honor of Andre Gunder Frank*. California: Sage, 1996.

Coleman, John A. and William F. Ryan, editors. *Globalization and Catholic Social Thought: Present Crisis, Future Hope*. Maryknoll, NY: Orbis, 2005.

Coleman, John, editor. *One Hundred Years of Catholic Social Thought: Celebration and Challenge*. Maryknoll, NY: Orbis, 1991.

Commission for Africa. *Our Common Interest: Report of the Commission for Africa*. March 2005.

Conn, Walter E. "The Desire for Authenticity: Conscience and Moral Conversion." In *The Desires of the Human Heart*, edited by Vernon Gregson, 36–56. New Jersey: Paulist, 1988.

Cormie, Lee. "Genesis of a New World: Globalization from Above vs. Globalization from Below." In *The Twentieth Century: A Theological Overview*, edited by Gregory Baum, 118–31. Maryknoll, NY: Orbis, 1999.

———. "The Sociology of National Development and Salvation History." *Sociology and Human Destiny*, edited by Gregory Baum, 56–85. New York: Seabury, 1980.

Cottingham, John. "Descartes: Metaphysics and the Philosophy of Mind." In *The Renaissance and 17th Century Rationalism, Routledge History of Philosophy*, edited by G. H. R. Parkinson, 4:201–34. London: Routledge, 1993.

Cronin, Brian. *Value Ethics: A Lonergan Perspective*. Nairobi: Consolata Institute of Philosophy Press, 2006.

Crowe, Frederick E. "Editor's Preface." In *Verbum: Word and Idea in Aquinas*, edited by Frederick E. Crowe and Robert D. Doran, CWL 2: vii–xxiv. Toronto: University of Toronto Press, 1997.

———. "An Expansion of Lonergan's Notion of Value." In *Appropriating the Lonergan Idea*, edited by Michael Vertin, 344–59. Washington, DC: The Catholic University of America Press, 1989.

———. "An Exploration of Lonergan's New Notion of Value." In *Appropriating the Lonergan Idea*, edited by Michael Vertin, 51–70. Washington, DC: The Catholic University of America Press, 1989.

———. "Lonergan and Liberation Theology." In *Appropriating the Lonergan Idea*, edited by Michael Vertin, 116–26. Washington, DC: The Catholic University of America Press, 1989.

———. "Lonergan at the Edges of Understanding." *Method: Journal of Lonergan Studies*. 20:2 (2002) 175–98.

———. *Old Things and New: A Strategy for Education*. Atlanta, GA: Scholars, 1985.
Crysdale, Cynthia. "Lonergan's 'Philosophy and the Religious Phenomenon': A Commentary." *Method: Journal of Lonergan Studies* 12:2 (1994) 181–204.
Curran, Charles E. *Catholic Social Teaching 1891–Present: A Historical Theological and Ethical Analysis*. Washington, DC: Georgetown University Press, 2002.
Dadosky, John. "Healing the Psychological Subject: Towards a Fourfold Notion of Conversion?" *Theoforum* 35:1 (2004) 73–91.
———. *Meaning and History in Systematic Theology: Essays in honor of Robert M. Doran*. Milwaukee: Marquette University Press, 2009.
———. "Methodological Presuppositions for Engaging the Other in a Post-Vatican II Context: Insights from Ignatius and Lonergan." *The Journal of Inter-Religious Dialogue* 3 (2010). Online: http://irdialogue.org/journal/issue03/methodological-presuppositions-for-engaging-the-other-in-the-post-vatican-ii-context-insights-from-ignatius-and-lonergan-by-john-d-dadosky/.
———. "Sacralization, Secularization and Religious Fundamentalism." *Studies in Religion/Sciences Religieuses*. 36 (2007) 513–29.
———. *The Structure of Religious Knowing*. Albany: State University of New York Press, 2004.
Deck, Allan Figueroa. "Commentary on *Populorum Progressio* (*On the Development of Peoples*)." In *Modern Catholic Social Teaching: Commentaries and Interpretations*, edited by Kenneth R. Himes, 292–314. Washington, DC: Georgetown University Press, 2005.
Di Marco, Luis Eugenio, editor. *International Economics and Development: Essays in Honor of Raul Prebisch*. New York: Academic, 1972.
Donadio, Rachel, and Laurie Goodstein. "Pope Urges Forming New World Economic Order to Work for the 'Common Good.'" *The New York Times*, July 7, 2009. Online: http://www.nytimes.com/2009/07/08/world/europe/08pope.html?_r=1.
Doorley, Mark J. "Nonviolence, Creation, Healing." *Method: Journal of Lonergan Studies* 17:2 (1999) 97–108.
Doran, Robert M. "Consciousness and Grace." *Method: Journal of Lonergan Studies* 11:1 (1993) 51–75.
———. "Duality and Dialectic." *Lonergan Workshop* 7 (1988) 59–84.
———. "Education for Cosmopolis." *Method: Journal of Lonergan Studies* 1:2 (1983) 134–57.
———. "From Psychic Conversion to the Dialectic of Community." *Lonergan Workshop* 6 (1986) 85–108.
———. "The Non-violent Cross." *Theological Studies* (2010). Online: http://www.faqs.org/periodicals/201003/1979521521.html.
———. *Subject and Psyche*. Milwaukee, WI: Marquette University Press, 1994.
———. *Theological Foundations I Intentionality and Psyche*. Marquette, WI: Marquette University Press, 1995.
———. *Theological Foundations II Theology and Culture*. Marquette, WI: Marquette University Studies, 1995.
———. *Theology and the Dialectics of History*. Toronto: University of Toronto Press, 1990.
———. *What is Systematic Theology?* Toronto: University of Toronto Press, 2005.
Dorr, Donal. "Solidarity and Integral Human Development." In *The Logic Solidarity: Commentaries on Pope John Paul II's Encyclical "On Social Concern,"* edited by Gregory Baum and Robert Ellsberg, 143–54. Maryknoll, NY: Orbis, 1989.

Bibliography

Dunne, Tad. "Being in Love." *Method: Journal of Lonergan Studies*. 13:2 (1995) 161–76.

———. *Lonergan and Spirituality: Towards a Spiritual Integration*. Chicago: Loyola University Press, 1985.

Ederer, Rupert J. "Solidarity." In *Encyclopaedia of Catholic Social Thought, Social Sciences and Social Policy*, edited by Michael L. Coulter et al., 1010–1011. Lanham, MD: Scarecrow, 2007.

Escobar, Arturo. *Encountering Development: The Making and Unmaking of the Third World*. Princeton, NJ: Princeton University Press, 1995.

Fallon, Timothy P., editor. "Lonergan and Cosmopolis." Papers and discussions at the 12th Eleanor Guiffre Memorial Lonergan Conference, Santa Clara University, March 18–20, 1994.

Fasching, Darrell J. "Theology and Public Policy: Method in the Work of Juan Luis Segundo, Jacques Ellul and Robert Doran." *Method: Journal of Lonergan Studies* 5:1 (1987) 41–91.

Flanagan, Joseph. "Insight: Chapters 1–5." *Lonergan Workshop 8*. (1990) 85–107.

———. *Quest for Self-Knowledge: An Essay in Lonergan's Philosophy*. Toronto: University of Toronto Press, 2002.

Flannery, Austin, edtior. *Vatican Council II: The Conciliar and Post-Conciliar Documents*. New Delhi: St Pauls, 2001.

Gaukroger, Stephen. "Descartes: Methodology." In *The Renaissance and 17th Century Rationalism, Routledge History of Philosophy*, edited by G. H. R. Parkinson, 4:167–200.

George, Susan, and Fabrizio Sabelli. *Faith and Culture: The World Bank's Secular Empire*. Boulder, Colorado: Westview, 1994.

Goulet, Dennis. *The Cruel Choice: A New Concept in the Theory of Development*. New York: Atheneum, 1972.

———. "Search for Authentic Development." In *The Logic Solidarity: Commentaries on Pope John Paul II's Encyclical "On Social Concern,"* edited by Gregory Baum and Robert Ellsberg, 127–42. Maryknoll, NY: Orbis, 1989.

Gremillion, Joseph. *The Gospel of Peace and Justice: Catholic Social Teaching Since Pope John*. Maryknoll, NY: Orbis, 1976.

Henriot, J. *Catholic Social Teaching: Our Best Kept Secret*. Maryknoll, NY: Orbis, 2003.

Himes, Kenneth R., editor. *Modern Catholic Social Teaching: Commentaries and Interpretation*. Washington, DC: Georgetown University Press, 2005.

———. *Responses to 101 Questions on Catholic Social Teaching*. New York: Paulist, 2001.

Hinze, Christine Firer. "Commentary on Quadragesimo Anno (After Forty Years)." In *Modern Catholic Social Teaching: Commentaries and Interpretation*, 151–74.

Hirschberger, Johannes. *The History of Philosophy, Vol. II*. Translated by Anthony N. Fuerst. Milwaukee: Bruce, 1959.

Hite, Timmons, J., and Amy Bellone, edtitors. *The Globalization and Development Reader*. Malden, MA: Blackwell, 2007.

Hobbes, Thomas. *Leviathan*. Oxford: Basil Blackwell, 1957.

Holland, Joe, and Peter Henriot. *Social Analysis: Linking Faith and Justice*. Maryknoll, NY: Orbis, 1983.

Hoyt-O'Connor, Paul. "Macroeconomic Dynamics and the Work of Nations: Lonergan and Reich on the Global Economy." *Method: Journal of Lonergan Studies* 17:2 (1999) 111–32.

Huq, Mahbub ul. *Reflections on Human Development*. New York: Oxford University Press, 1999.

Idemudia, Uwafiokun. "Corporate Social Responsibility and the Rentier Nigerian State: Rethinking the Role of Government and the Possibility of Corporate Social Development in the Niger Delta." *Canadian Journal of Development Studies* 30:1–2 (2010) 131–51.

Ilesami, Simeon. "Leave No Poor Behind: Globalization and the Imperative of Socio-Economic and Development Rights from an African Perspective." *Journal of Religious Ethics* 32:1 (2004) 71–92.

Jolly, Richard, et al. *UN Ideas That Changed the World*. Bloomington and Indianapolis: Indiana University Press, 2009.

Keynes, John Maynard. *The General Theory of Employment, Interest and Money*. La Vergne, TN: BN, 2008.

Komonchak, Joseph A. *Foundations in Ecclesiology*. Edited by Frederick Lawrence. Supplementary Issue of the Lonergan Workshop Journal 2 (1995).

Lamb, Matthew. *Solidarity with Victims: Toward a Theology of Social Transformation*. New York: Crossroad, 1982.

Lambert, Pierrot, et al., editors. *Caring About Meaning: Patterns in the Life of Bernard Lonergan*. Montreal: Thomas More Institute, 1982.

Landes, David. *The Wealth and Poverty of Nations: Why Some are Rich and Some are Poor*. New York: Norton, 1999.

Lawrence, Frederick. "The Human Good and Christian Conversation." In *Searching for Cultural Foundations*, edited by Philip McShane, 86–112. Lanham, MC: University Press of America, 1984.

Lebret, L. J., O.P. *Dynamique concrète du développement*. Paris: Economie et Humanisme, Les editions ouvrières, 1961.

Letiche, John M. "Forward to Amartya Sen On Ethics and Economics." In Amartya Sen, *On Ethics & Economics*, ix–xiii. MA: Blackwell, 1987.

Luxton, Meg. "Doing Liberalism: Perverse Individualism in Personal Life." In *Neoliberalism and Everyday Life*, edited by Susan Braedley and Meg Luxton, 162–83. Montreal and Kingston: McGill-Queen's University Press, 2010.

MacIver, R. M. "Forward to Karl Polanyi." *The Great Transformation*, ix–xii. Boston: Beacon, 1957.

Maritain, Jacques. *Reflections on America*. New York: Scribners, 1958.

Martin, Stephen L. *Healing and Creating in Economic Ethics: The Contribution of Bernard Lonergan's Economic Thought to Catholic Social Teaching*. Lanham, MD: University Press of America, 2008.

Matusik, Martin J. "Democratic Multicultures and Cosmopolis: Beyond the Aporias of the Politics of Identity and Difference." *Method* 12:1 (1994) 63–89.

Mazrui, Ali Al'Amin. *The African Condition: A Political Diagnosis*. London: Heinemann Educational, 1980.

———. *The Africans: A Triple Heritage*. Boston: Little, Brown, 1986.

McCarthy, Michael. "Liberty, History, and the Common Good: An Exercise in Critical Retrieval." *Lonergan Workshop* 12 (1996) 111–46.

McMichael, Philip. *Development and Social Change: A Global Perspective*. Los Angeles: Pine Forge, 2008.

Melchin, Kenneth M. "History, Ethics, and Emergent Probability." *Lonergan Workshop* 7. (1988) 269–94.

Bibliography

———. *History, Ethics and Emergent Probability: Ethics, Society and History in the Work of Bernard Lonergan*. Lanham: University Press of America, 1987.
Morelli, Mark D., and Morelli Elizabeth A., editors. *The Lonergan Reader*. Toronto: University of Toronto Press, 1997.
Neumayer, E. *Human Development and Sustainability*. Human Development Reports, Research Paper Series. New York: United Nations Development Programme, 2010.
Niebuhr, Reinhold. "The Children of Light and the Children of Darkness." In *Social Ethics: Issues in Ethics and Society*, edited by Gibson Winter, 143–64. New York: Harper & Row, 1968.
Nordquest, David A. "Cosmopolis: Bourget's and Lonergan's," *Method* 11:1 (1993) 37–50.
Novak, Michael. *The Spirit of Democratic Capitalism*. New York: Simon & Schuster, 1982.
O'Brien, David J. "A Century of Catholic Social Teaching." In *One Hundred Years of Catholic Social Thought: Celebration and Challenge*, edited by John A. Coleman, 13–24. Maryknoll, NY: Orbis, 1991.
Onyango, Charles. *Lonergan's Notion of Cosmopolis: A Study of a Higher Viewpoint and a Creative Framework for Engaging Individual and Social 'Biases' with Special Reference to Socio-Political Challenges of Kenya and the Continent of Africa*. PhD thesis, Boston College, 2005.
Orji, Cyril. *Ethnic and Religious Conflict in Africa: An Analysis of Bias, Decline and Conversion based on the Works of Bernard Lonergan*. Milwaukee, WI: Marquette University Press, 2008.
Ormerod, Neil. "Theology, History and Globalization." *Gregorianum* 88:1 (2007) 23–48.
Peet, Richard, and Elaine Hartwick. *Theories of Development: Contentions, Arguments, Alternatives*. New York: Guilford, 2009.
Philips, John L. *The Origins of Intellect in Piaget's Theory*. San Francisco: Freeman, 1969.
Polanyi, Karl. *The Great Transformation*. Boston: Beacon, 1957.
Pontifical Council for Justice and Peace. *Compendium of the Social Doctrine of the Church*. Ottawa: CCCB, 2005.
Pogge, Thomas, and Keith Horton. *Global Ethics: Seminal Essays II*. St Paul, MN: Paragon House, 2008.
Pope Benedict XVI. "Apostolic Journey to the United States of America and Visit to the United Nations Organization Headquarters: Meeting with the Members of the General Assembly of the United Nations Organization." Online: http://www.vatican.va/holy_father/benedict_xvi/speeches/2008/april/documents/hf_ben-xvi_spe_20080418_un-visit_en.html.
———. *Caritas in Veritate: On Integral Human Development in Charity and Truth*. Washington, DC: United States Conference of Catholic Bishops, 2009.
Pope John Paul II. *Centesimus Annus*. Sherbrooke, Quebec: Pauline Edition, 1991.
———. *Familiaris Consortio*. Online: http://www.vatican.va/holy_father/john_paul_ii/apost_exhortations/documents/hf_jp-ii_exh_19811122_familiaris-consortio_en.html.
———. *Laborem Exercens*. Online: http://www.vatican.va/holy_father/john_paul_ii/encyclicals/documents/hf_jp-ii_enc_14091981_laborem-exercens_en.html.
———. *Solicitudo Rei Socialis*. Sherbrooke, Quebec: Pauline Edition, 1988.
Pope Leo XIII. *Rerum Novarum*. Online: http://www.vatican.va/holy_father/leo_xiii/encyclicals/documents/hf_l-xiii_enc_15051891_rerum-novarum_en.html, 4.
Pope Paul VI. *Octogesima Adveniens*. Online: http://www.vatican.va/holy_father/paul_vi/apost_letters/documents/hf_p-vi_apl_19710514_octogesima-adveniens_en.html.

———. *Populorum Progressio* [*On the Development of Peoples*]. In Joseph Gremillion, *The Gospel of Peace and Justice: Catholic Social Teaching Since Pope John*. Maryknoll, NY: Orbis, 1976.

Pope Pius XI. *Quadragesimo Anno, Forty Years After: On Reconstructing the Social Order and Perfecting It Comformably to the Precepts of the Gospel*. Online: http://www.vatican.va/holy_father/pius_xi/encyclicals/documents/hf_p-xi_enc_19310515_quadragesimo-anno_en.html.

Ravallion, Martin. "The Debate on Globalization, Poverty and Inequality: Why Measurement Matters." *International Affairs* 79:4 (2003) 739–53.

Ruggiero, Renato. "Reflections from Seattle." In *The WTO after Seattle*, edited by Jeffrey J. Schott, xiii–xviii. Washington, DC: Institute for International Economics, 2000.

Rist, Gilbert. *The History of Development: From Western Origins to Global Faith*. Translated by Patrick Camiller. London & New York: Zen, 1997.

———. "Is 'Development' a Panacea? How to Think Beyond Obsolete Categories." *Canadian Journal of Development Studies* 30:3–4 (2010) 345–54.

Rostow, W. W. *The Stages of Economic Growth: A Non-Communist Manifesto*. 3rd ed. New York: Cambridge University Press, 1990.

Ryan, William F. *Culture, Spirituality, and Economic Development*. Ottawa: International Development Center, 1995.

Sachs, Wolfgang, editor. *The Development Dictionary: A Guide to Knowledge as Power*. London: Zed, 1992.

Smith, Adam. *The Theory of Moral Sentiments*. Edited by A. L. Macfie and D. D. Raphael Oxford: Oxford University Press, 1976.

———. *The Wealth of Nations: An Inquiry into the Nature and Causes of the Wealth of Nations*. Edited by Edwin Cannan. New York: Random House, 1937.

Smith, Marc. "Lonergan's Cosmopolis." In *Violence and Human Coexistence*, 197–202. Montreal: Montmorency, 1994.

Sen, Amartya. *Development as Freedom*. New York: Anchor, 2000.

———. "Globalization, Inequality and Global Protest." *Development* 45:2 (2002) 11–16.

———. *On Ethics & Economics*. MA: Blackwell, 1987.

Shute, Michael. "Economic Analysis within Redemptive Praxis: An Achievement of Lonergan's Third Decade." *Lonergan Workshop 14* (1998) 243–64.

———. "'Let us be Practical!' The Beginnings of the Long Process to Functional Specialization in the Essay in Fundamental Sociology." In *Meaning and history in Systematic Theology: Essays in Honor of Robert M. Doran*, edited by John D. Dadosky, 465–85. Milwaukee: Marquette University Press, 2009.

Somerville, Margaret. *The Ethical Imagination*. Toronto: Anansi, 2006.

Taylor, Charles. *A Secular Age*. Cambridge, MA: Belknap, 2007.

———. *The Malaise of Modernity*. Toronto: Anansi, 1991.

———. *Sources of Self*. Cambridge, Massachusetts: Harvard University Press, 1989.

Tekippe, Terry J. *Bernard Lonergan's Insight: A Comprehensive Commentary*. New York: University Press of America, 2003.

The Challenge to the South: The Report of the South Commission. Oxford: Oxford University Press, 1990.

Toulmin, Stephen. *Cosmopolis: The Hidden Agenda of Modernity*. Chicago: The University of Chicago Press, 1992.

Bibliography

Tyndale, Wendy. "Religions and the Millennium Development Goals: Whose Agenda." In *Religion and Development: Ways of Transforming the World*, edited by Gerrie ter Haar, 207-29. New York: Columbia University Press, 2011.

Tyrell, Bernard J. "Affectional Conversion: A Distinct Conversion or Potential Differentiation in the Spheres of Sensitive Psychic and/or Affective Conversion?" *Method: Journal of Lonergan Studies* 14:1 (1996) 1-36.

United Nations. *The Millennium Development Goals Report 2010*. Online: http://mdgs.un.org/unsd/mdg/Resources/Static/Products/Progress2010/MDG_Report_2010_En.pdf.

Vatican Information Service. "Pope Benedict XVI: Build the Common Good." *Catholic Online International News*, 5/6/2008. Online: http://www.catholic.org/international/international_story.php?id=27844.

Vertin, Michael. "The Finality of Human Spirit: From Marechal to Lonergan." *Lonergan Workshop* 19 (2006) 267-86.

———. "Lonergan on Consciousness: Is There a Fifth Level?" *Method: Journal of Lonergan Studies* 12:1 (1994) 1-36.

———. "'Three Basic Questions' and a Philosophy of Philosophies." *Lonergan Workshop* 8 (1990) 213-48.

Voegelin, Eric. *Order and History vol. 1, Israel and Revelation*. Baton Rouge: Louisiana State University Press, 1956, 1994.

Weber, Max. *The Protestant Ethic and the Spirit of Capitalism*. Trans. Talcott Parsons. New York: Dover, 2003.

Wogaman, J. Philip. *Economics and Ethics: A Christian Inquiry*. Philadelphia: Fortress, 1986.

World Commission on Environment and Development. *Our Common Future*. London: Books, 1988.

Worsely, Peter. *The Three Worlds: Culture and World Development*. Chicago: University of Chicago Press, 1984.

Zoellick, Robert B. "The End of the Third World? Modernizing Multilateralism for a Multipolar World." *Woodrow Wilson Center for International Scholars*, April 10, 2010. Online: http://web.worldbank.org/WBSITE/EXTERNAL/NEWS/0.

Zolo, Danilo. *Cosmopolis: Prospects for World Government*. Cambridge: Polity, 1997.

www.ingramcontent.com/pod-product-compliance
Lightning Source LLC
Chambersburg PA
CBHW062040220426
43662CB00010B/1581